Praise for *Here for It*

"If you're yearning for that laugh-out-loud on the subway, 'damn-I-left-my-book-at-home' kind of read, look no further than R. Eric Thomas's *Here for It*."

—*InStyle*

"With humor, candor, and some self-deprecation, Thomas, a playwright and *Elle* columnist, delivers a debut essay collection that explores his search for self, love, and stable employment. . . . Whether dealing with love, breakups, or other setbacks, Thomas is an affable narrator with a penchant for pop culture, funny quips, and charming humility."

—*Publishers Weekly*

"Alternately hilarious, touching, reflective, and insightful, this memoir will delight readers, who may find themselves reading sections of the book aloud to anyone within earshot. . . . A laugh-out-loud memoir that is strongly recommended for everyone."

—*Library Journal* (starred review)

"A quirky, funny, and deep meditation on being black and queer in America."

—*Interview*

"*Here for It* is Thomas at his finest: funny, clever, thoughtful, and compelling. I'm glad more of the world will not only get to experience more of Thomas's talent, but another much-needed story from another gay Black man in America."

—Michael Arceneaux, *New York Times* bestselling author of *I Can't Date Jesus*

"Every book says on the jacket that it is a 'razor-sharp tour de force,' but this one actually is a razor-sharp tour de force, with an enormous heart to boot. Please give yourself the gift of reading this book."

—Alexandra Petri, *Washington Post* columnist

"By turns laugh-out-loud funny and deeply moving, intensely personal and impeccably of-the-moment, *Here for It* is exactly what we need in 2020. No one writes quite like R. Eric Thomas, and his memoir proves it."

—David Litt, *New York Times* bestselling author of *Thanks, Obama: My Hopey, Changey White House Years*

"This book was a lovely gift of hope and hysterical wit that kept me warm during the apocalypse. I laughed. I cried. I wish I would have written it myself."

—Jenny Lawson, *New York Times* bestselling author of *You Are Here* and *Furiously Happy*

"*Here for It* is a blockbuster and R. Eric Thomas is a visionary. This collection moved me from laughter to tears and back to laughter again in the span of a single page. This is a book readers will happily devour in a single sitting. Thomas is a bright, shining light and the world is so lucky to have him and his work."

—Kristen Arnett, *New York Times* bestselling author of *Mostly Dead Things*

"Hilarious, revelatory, hopeful, incisive—*Here for It* feels like splitting dessert with your funniest friend, if that friend was also your smartest professor and a devastatingly sharp pop culture historian."

—Casey McQuiston, *New York Times* bestselling author of *Red, White & Royal Blue*

"If I were stocking a time capsule to show future generations how it felt to be alive at this exact moment in American culture, this is the book I'd toss in first. Readers of all stripes will relate to Thomas's hilarious, touching observations on love, success, and identity. I adore this book."

—Mary Laura Philpott, author of *I Miss You When I Blink*

"If you've read Eric's column you already know that he's ten times funnier than your funniest friend. With *Here for It,* he proves that he's so much more than that: observant, wise, and a singular, necessary voice. I dare you to read this book and not quote entire paragraphs to strangers on the street."

—Grant Ginder, author of *The People We Hate at the Wedding* and *Honestly, We Meant Well*

Here for It

Here for It

Or, How to Save Your Soul in America

ESSAYS

R. Eric Thomas

BALLANTINE BOOKS
NEW YORK

Here for It is a work of nonfiction. Some names and identifying details have been changed.

2021 Ballantine Books Trade Paperback Edition

Published in the United States by Ballantine Books,
an imprint of Random House, a division of Penguin Random House LLC,
New York.

BALLANTINE and the HOUSE colophon are registered trademarks
of Penguin Random House LLC.

Originally published in hardcover in the United States by Ballantine Books, an imprint of Random House, a division of Penguin Random House LLC, in 2020.

RANDOM HOUSE BOOK CLUB and colophon are trademarks of Penguin Random House LLC.

LIBRARY OF CONGRESS CATALOGING-IN-PUBLICATION DATA
Names: Thomas, R. Eric, author.
Title: Here for it: or, how to save your soul in America; essays / R. Eric Thomas.
Other titles: How to save your soul in America
Description: New York: Ballantine Books, 2020. |
Identifiers: LCCN 2019037442 (print) | LCCN 2019037443 (ebook) | ISBN 9780525621058 (trade paperback) | ISBN 9780525621041 (ebook)
Subjects: LCSH: Thomas, R. Eric. | Authors, American—Biography. | Journalists—United States—Biography. | African American gay men—United States—Biography. | Christian gay men—United States—Biography. | Men—Identity. | United States—Social conditions—21st century.
Classification: LCC PS3620.H6375 H44 2020 (print) | LCC PS3620.H6375 (ebook) | DDC 818/.603 [B]—dc23
LC record available at https://lccn.loc.gov/2019037442
LC ebook record available at https://lccn.loc.gov/2019037443

Printed in the United States of America on acid-free paper

randomhousebooks.com
randomhousebookclub.com

9 8 7 6 5 4 3 2 1

Book design by Diane Hobbing

For my parents, Bob and Judi Thomas,

and their parents, Clara and Adelita and
Walter and Columbus.

For everyone further on down the line and
everyone yet to come.

If you suddenly and unexpectedly feel joy,
don't hesitate. Give in to it.

—MARY OLIVER, "DON'T HESITATE"

CONTENTS

INTRODUCTION

The Monster at the End of This Book

For a number of years, I was under the impression that my birth was the result of an immaculate conception. Not *the* Immaculate Conception; a regular immaculate conception of an ordinary variety. I didn't think I was particularly special or meant to die so that the world might be saved from their sins. (I struggle to get through a CrossFit class, so actual crucifixion might be a bit of a heavy lift.) I understood that some people got pregnant to have babies; I simply thought I'd been opted out of that particular program. It made just as much sense to me that the universe had given a baby to my parents because they were nice people who photographed well.

When my mother would tell me about life before me, she would always say the same thing: "We wanted a child so badly.

My arms used to ache for the weight of a baby. We prayed and we prayed and we prayed, and finally, God gave you to us."

How would you interpret that story? Immaculately, that's how.

I thought some people just got babies handed to them like party favors at a quinceañera by a creator-type figure. Bob and Judi asked very nicely; cue my entrance, *avec* jazz hands.

This all checks out. At least as much as the *other* Immaculate Conception, aka the birth of Jesus. On that I was an expert, having gotten straight A's in Sunday school for years (there were no grades, but I scored myself). Plus, I was a very good child—obedient, pleasant, an avid reader, an unrepentant snitch—so of course I knew the story backwards and forwards—the angel and the three kings and the sheep and Mariah Carey singing "All I Want for Christmas Is You," etc. My own sudden appearance on the scene—regular yet also extraordinary, sans animals, no royalty RSVPs—was totally within my conceptual wheelhouse. What I couldn't figure out, however, was *why*.

As a child I liked certainty, and order, and clear explanations, even if they tended to involve miracles. But life, of course, can quickly get complicated and human and not at all miraculous. I'd sometimes find myself so lost in a question or a problem that the only solution I could think of was for an older version of myself to walk through a rift in the space-time continuum and let me know what happens. Immaculately. As my concept of self expanded and evolved beyond my extraordinary beginnings, different parts of who I was began to prompt queries that I thought only the future could answer. I had this idea that the challenges I suddenly encountered—my Blackness or my gayness or my Christianness or my Americanness and their intersections—would somehow get uncomplicated through the magic of time, like a movie montage.

Spoiler alert: they did not.

But I would think about the supposed perfection of the future constantly. I'd be sitting in my childhood bedroom or my college dorm or my first apartment, just staring at the door like "Any minute now in the future they're going to invent time travel and some well-dressed old Black man with no wrinkles is going to come bursting through and give me the answers to this take-home quiz or whatever." (Sometimes my questions were existential; sometimes they were AP Statistical.) The basic concern was always the same: am I really here for this?

The big idea, as I saw it, was this: You don't exist for a long time. Before you arrive, there are ages, eons—an eternity—without you. (Can you imagine? How boring!) And suddenly there you are. Alive. How you doing? How's it feel? Immaculate? What if it feels bad? Don't worry; it gets better, right? But what if it doesn't get better, it just gets. It just keeps getting. What then? You still interested? You still trying to be good, still moisturizing your T-zone, still working through your stack of *New Yorkers,* still fighting systemic oppression, still speaking truth to power, still attempting to exist? Still? What if I told you, at another point—fixed, supposedly, but totally unknown—you suddenly, mysteriously, immaculately won't *be* anymore? Again.

Does that sound like something you want to do?

I'm a spoiler kween. My favorite part of reading mystery novels is flipping ahead to the last chapter. Of course at that point I'm always like, "Who are all of *these* people? How did this happen? When did they go to *Nova Scotia*?" So I have to go back to reread and find out. Ugh, it's a whole process. My relationship with mystery is *fraught*. It was the same with Choose Your Own Adventures. I certainly wasn't about to go flipping through a book willy-nilly letting fate take me on a ride like Chitty Chitty Bang Bang. I always turned to an option, read it, kept my finger in it, and then flipped back and read the other option. Like a normal American. Some books tried to get slick and give you four or five choices. The joke was on them, though: I had five fingers.

Ten actually, now that I think about it.

This book is not a Choose Your Own Adventure, much as I would have liked the option in real life. It's the opposite of that, actually, if such a thing is possible. It might be a mystery, though. At the end I gather all the suspects in a room and there are some very bold accusations made. It involves a luxury ocean liner. There's a caftan. Things escalate!

More than anything, this book is a version of the book where I, as a child, found all my answers and all my questions. You guessed it: the most sacred of tomes, *The Monster at the End of This Book*, starring Grover (the Muppet, not the U.S. president). Lovable, furry old Grover. Blue. Fuchsia nose. Scatterbrained. Sometimes Super. Here's the plot: Grover shows up, reads the title, realizes there's a monster at the end of the book, and then asks you, the reader, not to continue reading, so as not to bring him face-to-face with the thing that he fears.

"Listen, I have an idea," he says to us on page two, breaking the fourth wall like he's in a midnight screening of *Rocky Horror*. "If you do not turn any pages, we will never get to the end of this book. And that is good, because there is a Monster at the end of this book. So please do not turn the page."

flip

"YOU TURNED THE PAGE!" he screams. So much is already happening.

Grover's horror escalates with every page turn, eventually getting to the point where he is futilely building a wall, putting up caution tape, pleading with you. Pitilessly, you persist. By the end of the book, Grover is in full hysterics.

But then we turn the last page, and Grover realizes that the monster at the end of the book is himself.

Stunning. He is the Keyser Söze of Muppets. And that's the book.

This book is meta as *hell*. It's like Borges for toddlers. Who does this? Also, this book is terrifying. It's psychological torture. *Gone Girl* for Muppets.

When I read it as a child, I didn't *want* to turn the page. I didn't want to torture Grover. I wonder if there's ever been a child who, when asked not to continue, simply closed the book and went on with their life. I want to know that obedient child. But the book's success is predicated on the assumption that we will not heed his simple request.

That is terrible. And I think that's why I like this book so much. I am Grover. I walk with him every step of the way on his journey. *The Monster at the End of This Book* is a lighthearted book about anxiety—anxiety about being confronted with the kind of person you really are (LOL!), anxiety about the inevitable passage of time (LOL), anxiety about being trapped by forces beyond your control (lol), anxiety about a deep, dreadful uncertainty (. . . meep). Even when I read it for the first time at age three, I got that.

I was an anxious, though immaculately conceived, child. And an anxious, square, pious preteen. And an anxious half-zealot/half-gay teen. And an anxious, aimless young adult careening toward this moment. I'm anxious right now, actually, come to think of it. I'll definitely be an anxious dad. I'm sure I'll be an anxious old man, and I'll probably end up lying in my grave going, "Ugh, I feel like there's something I should be doing right now. I wonder if everyone is angry at me. Oh my God, how long is this going to take? And what happens next?"

Grover, too, is struggling. He is using every tool at his disposal to keep the thing that he fears the most at bay, and that thing is himself. He is almost crippled by his own fear. But he is still trying. Grover is the Willy Loman of Sesame Street.

On the internet, I play more of an Elmo than a Grover: I write funny columns, most visibly for ELLE.com; I make jokes about the news on Twitter; sometimes I write plays about social justice that have the audacity to end happily. I try to take what's dark about the world and shake out the satirical and the silly.

Everybody loves Elmo, right? Elmo is a closer. Elmo gets all the Glengarry leads. Elmo stares into the abyss and the abyss whispers, "Tickle me." But in real life, I'm a Grover. I have always been Black in a white environment, not Black enough in a Black environment, working-class in an upper-class environment, Christian in a secular environment, questioning in a devout environment, gay in a straight environment. Never quite right.

I grew up a little ball of potential (but oblivious) gay energy in a Baptist family from a Black Baltimore neighborhood where there were more abandoned houses than lived-in ones. My parents sent me to school in a rich suburb where most of my classmates were white. Every moment from then on, I was an Other. The thing is, I felt it, but I didn't realize it.

Other felt like a funhouse narrative; it felt like doing something wrong. Or worse, being something wrong. So I ignored it for as long as I could, creating certainty where I could. And when that didn't work, I anxiously awaited a spoiler to burst through time and let me know if this whole thing was going to end badly.

That, for a while, seemed like life. And if I was really being honest with myself, I wasn't into it. The only option was to sit in the pews every Sunday at church and casually wonder if I was going to go to hell because of who I was? No, thank you. Or to understand that the structures on which the country was built were engineered against me? Hard pass. What choice did I have besides constantly code-switching between identities as a means of hiding in plain sight? And wasn't it just normal to feel like such a mistake as an adult that every time I walked over a bridge or stood on a subway platform, I had to talk myself out of stepping over the edge? I came to believe I was a monster and that I deserved to feel the way I felt. And I didn't want to turn the page.

But through it all there was a constant tethering me to the idea of a future: the library. The library is the place where I could borrow first Grover's philosophical tome, then a couple of Choose Your Own Adventures I could cheat at, and later a stack of mysteries I could spoil for myself, all attempts to look for some other way of understanding who I was.

In the book stacks, I found *The Bluest Eye* and *The Color Purple* and *Giovanni's Room* and David Rakoff's *Fraud* and more. I saw a new vision of Otherness in those books, and the pages kept turning. At the end of every one was a wall waiting to be broken down—a lurch toward becoming—a new paragraph in a story with an ending far different from what I'd ever dared imagine. Every story, whether truth or fiction, is an invitation to imagination, but even more so, it's an invitation to empathy. The storyteller says, "I am here. Does it matter?" The words that I found in these books were a person calling out from a page, "I am worthy of being heard and you are worthy of hearing my story." It seems simple but it's a bold declaration. How many times in life do we receive the message, implicit or explicit, that what we've experienced or what we feel isn't noteworthy or remarkable? The books that I found in the library, ones that I deeply understood and ones that seemed so outside of my experience they might as well have been written in Klingon, all carried the same hopes: to be seen, to be heard, to exist.

Hope is tricky, however, when what's waiting at the conclusion is monstrous, literally or figuratively. You can declare your own worthiness to the world, but that doesn't always mean you believe it yourself. There's a Nayyirah Waheed quote: "If someone does not want me, it is not the end of the world. But if I do not want me, the world is nothing but endings." That is the problem that troubles this book. "Listen, I have an idea," Grover says. "If you do not turn any pages, we will never get to the end of this book." And yet . . .

I'm a spoiler kween; I'll see you at the end.

Here
for
It

The Audacity

I am awake because everything is hilarious. And also terrifying. And also embarrassing.

Don't pick up the phone, I tell myself as I lie in bed on the first night of the Democratic National Convention, 2016. *Go to sleep,* my brain hisses, as I slip my hand out from beneath the sheet and unlock my phone. I open the Notes app and my bedroom is suddenly illuminated by garish, gray-blue light, like I'm in a reboot of *Poltergeist. Well,* I think to myself, *it's not like I have a choice now.* I hitch myself up in bed and start to type. There is a joke emergency.

I don't realize it at the time, but I am entering a season of sleepless nights. It's the middle of July and I am three weeks into my new job as a person who contributes to this great democracy by making fun of politics online for money. It's immensely enjoyable but it does have the strange side effect of forcing me to know more about what's happening in the world, particularly in the political world, and as I said, that's hilarious and terrifying and deeply embarrassing. So, perfect for the internet. I've never been a particularly internet-y person. I like a good meme like the rest of the youths, but I'm never on the cutting edge of internet culture. Though I've had a couple of lackluster blogs, I've never been a blogger. I read television recaps on the legendary site Television Without Pity for years but never commented or engaged in any meaningful way beyond wishing that they'd miraculously email me and ask me to join the team. I must admit I know what Tumblr is but every time I think I know how to search for something on it I am proven wrong. I am a consumer on the internet, a regular, a normal. And, suddenly, recently, a viral creator. Clearly, the internet is broken.

Four weeks earlier, I'd come across a photo of President Obama, Canadian prime minister Justin Trudeau, and Mexican president Enrique Peña Nieto grinning as they strode down a red-carpeted walkway in bespoke suits. I was immediately deeply shewk. So I told the internet about it. I fired up my aging computer, posted the shot on Facebook, and wrote, "Whoever took this photo deserves a GD Pulitzer Prize. We may be two minutes from doomsday but thank the Lord we still live in a universe where three world leaders can strut into a room like they're the new interracial male cast of *Sex and the City*. Like I have ALREADY pre-purchased tickets to this film. Out here in these streets looking like Career Day Ken. Looking like Destiny's DILF. Looking like the Alternate Universe version of our Current Political Universe. Looking like Tom Ford presents *The Avengers*." It went on like that for a while. As I said, I was deeply shewk.

At this time, I had about 1,500 Facebook friends, almost exclusively people I'd actually met. I had, on occasion, posted something funny online that friends shared with their friends who shared with their friends, eventually giving whatever I'd written a temporary social lift. That's how the internet works, and the first time it happened on Facebook—when my blog post about how expensive Beyoncé concert tickets were got 100,000 page views—I thought I was famous. The internet will quickly remind you that you are not famous; you just did this one thing this one time and that was yesterday so why are we still talking about it?

The world leaders photo was different, though. My crazed-thirst rant about the president and his hot friends zigzagged across the internet with a speed that shocked me. It was liked 77,000 times, generated almost 6,000 comments (some of them not terrible!), and was shared 17,000 times. The great aggregation machine of the internet whirred to life and articles started popping up with headlines like "Internet User Has Hilarious Reaction to Obama Photo." I was an Internet User! People started friending me on Facebook by the hundreds—strangers! And, a few days after the post, Leah Chernikoff, the site director of ELLE.com, sent me a Facebook message. "I saw your post shared by so many acquaintances. Would you consider doing more of this kind of writing?" she wrote.

That message, to which I responded with a level of overzealous exuberance that still sends shivers of embarrassment down my spine, would lead to a daily freelance humor column, called Eric Reads the News, and, later, a full-time, salaried position at ELLE.com. It would also eventually bring me to the attention of editors at *The New York Times,* provoke theater makers to express interest in reading my plays, and pave the way for this book. Publicly thirsting after a sitting president would, it turns out, change my life.

"My husband was called to his profession by God," I would later tell people at parties or mumble to my houseplants. "I was called to my profession by a very accomplished woman in Manhattan."

I should be asleep. It is the responsible thing to do. Although I am writing the daily column—for three weeks now!—on ELLE.com, I am also holding down a day job as a program director at an LGBTQ community center. Every day, I wake a few hours early, chat with Leah on Facebook Messenger about what's happening in the news, decide on something to write about, and attempt to fire it off before running to the center. Sometimes that actually works. Other times, I am squeezing writing into my lunch breaks or carving out a quiet half hour in which I can type madly into my phone before jumping back into my day. I have never freelanced at this level before—I've written a couple of hyperbole-filled concert reviews for *Philadelphia Magazine* ("Ms. Ross's third costume change was into a king-size periwinkle duvet cover"), but those were the kinds of things I could dash off on a Saturday morning at a coffee shop, or spend an evening after work on.

This column is a whole different animal. It feels like the already lightning-fast news cycle is speeding up. The presidential campaign is kicking into high gear now that, improbably, C-list grifter Donald Trump has made an ascent in the Republican Party and it seems clear that Hillary Clinton will not face any obstruction to her nomination in a few days from Bernie Sanders. We are in a moment where the news is, blessedly, fairly predictable, which makes it easier to make fun of. But I find that you have to be quick about it. If something happened last night, you have until maybe midday to write about it. Otherwise, the world—and the internet—will have moved on. As a spectator on the internet, someone who lives in Philadelphia and whose only understanding of the New York fashion media world of which the column is tangentially a part comes from *The Devil Wears Prada,* I understand the speed and the drive but I don't really know what to do with it yet.

I am still trying to figure out what this column is, and if it will continue past, say, tomorrow. I am convinced that everyone will realize they have made a mistake in giving me money to make jokes. I am writing summaries of happenings or "reads" of newsworthy photos that, I hope, have the tone of a late night comedy monologue screamed through a bullhorn by a very excited gay Black person. There are moments when I wonder if this is problematic—the audience I'm writing for is largely straight-identified, so my use of my communities' vernaculars might read as a performance rather than a genuine expression. But this is how I was writing before—Diana's duvet ain't gonna describe itself, honey—and that writing was for my friends. Even the Obama thirst was, ostensibly, for people who knew me, a little note dashed off to a small community that also happens to be the entire internet. So when I wonder about the column and the hyperbole I find works well for it, I have to ask if everything about myself is minstrelsy and whether there is any part of me that actually exists in reality, and I don't have time to sort through that. I am an Internet User and I am trying my best!

I have to get this column up and get to work. Which is why I should be asleep. I can't be burning the midnight oil when I need to wake up in three hours, figure out what to say about the Democratic National Convention or Jeff Goldblum's hair or Idris Elba's absolutely everything, and then hop on the subway to my job where I am trying to make community for LGBTQ people. In reality.

I scan the darkened bedroom—the window with a view of the South Philly stadium where the convention is currently being held, the two copies of *The Life-Changing Magic of Tidying Up* that I keep meaning to read, the armchair that I bought from a thrift store because it was on sale but that I will never sit in because I am afraid it is haunted, and my phone, now in my hand, waiting.

Don't do it, I tell myself. *Close your eyes, go to sleep, wake up, show up to work on time for once in your life, do a good job, answer all of your unread emails, donate to charity, vote, care about the world, raise a good kid or a dog (tbd), yell at fewer strangers on Facebook, smile more (unless someone on the street tells you to, in which case don't smile), have hope (shoutout to Barack!) but also be realistic about what you can expect out of this life (shoutout to systemic oppression!), figure out what a realistic expectation for hope in this life is, be a better person, die eventually.*

You know, the usual.

I have a joke that I want to jot down for the next day's column, but I am resisting (or should I say, I am #Resisting. A few months early). If I start writing, I'll have to admit I'm awake, and then I'll want to keep writing and probably tweeting, and then I'll check the news, and then I will never get to sleep and I will be either grumpy or late to work (survey says: both!), which will lead to me not responding to emails or being a better person or building a community or figuring out what I'm supposed to be doing in this life.

And what is the benefit if I do write it down? The best thing that can happen: Everyone laughs. That's the point, right? It's a humor column on the internet in the days before nothing was ever funny again. When the jokes work, people like them and share them and it feels for a moment like all of the internet laughs. Positive internet attention is the best thing that can happen in this scenario.

The worst thing: No one laughs. Public scorn. Being canceled. And also lateness, not being a better person, eventual death, etc. The over-under isn't great.

I am aware that this is not the way anything is supposed to work. The job, the opportunity, the positive attention. It feels unearned, even though I am in my mid-thirties and it's not like I haven't been unsuccessfully writing things—some of them funny—for years. But the thing about success is that it doesn't seem like a natural result of unsuccessfulness. It feels like success comes despite a lack of success. Or, if you achieve some level of success, your lack of success in the past should be retrofitted as stepping-stones along the path of your rise. And that's true and not true. Did I have a plan? No. Did it work out? Seems like it. It's easy for me to see the blind luck at play and hard for me to see the parts of me that put in the work. On top of that, writing the column is fun, and as someone who has started many games of Monopoly and finished zero, I know that capitalism is not supposed to be fun.

Though I do have a constant hum of low-level anxiety about organizing my time, and producing a punchline, and keeping this gig, I still feel like I should be struggling more. Remember how Carrie Bradshaw got drunk at lunch every day and stayed out till four in the morning on dates, and wrote just one weekly column but was still on the side of a bus? I'm not on a bus and I write every day, but I couldn't help but wonder if I've put enough effort in to deserve this.

Deserving anything related to money is a fraught concept for me, particularly when it comes to art. If you're pursuing some kind of artistic product—and I think of writing as art—then you're doing what you love, and your labor is one of love. So, money is good, and money is necessary, and money is that thing that tells you that what you're doing is not a fool's errand. But the money is also an albatross, changing your relationship to the art. It's like writing a random joke for a couple hundred people you've met throughout your life and then suddenly having thousands of people you don't know respond. It is not bad, but it is hard to navigate. Who am I doing this for and do they want what I want?

The Notes app is a blank slate that celebrities use to apologize publicly and which I use to shape the random asides in my brain into textual non sequiturs I hope to understand in the morning. On the night of the 2016 DNC, I write, "Michelle Obama is Usain Bolt–ing her way out of that White House," referencing the intended effect of the First Lady's powerful speech at the DNC hours earlier. You know the one. "I wake up every morning in a house built by slaves." The one that I can't even think about without automatically giving praise hands and letting out a low hum, church-style. The Declaration of Independence, remixed. That one.

I am lying awake filled with inspiration and a little bit of heartsickness and that good ole American low-level rage as I replay Mrs. Obama's words, which convey both a fervent love for this country and a soul-shaking desire for it to be less terrible. And I am doing the thing that I do with things that I love, or am frustrated by, or don't understand, or am infuriated by: I am making jokes.

Mrs. Obama is, rightfully I think, totally over the ugly presidential campaign and probably the presidency in general, but has been doing everything in her power to ensure that the next president is someone who will carry on her husband's legacy of, at best, hope, and at worst, less terribleness. She has lip-synced for the country's life and, hours later, I am still thinking about it. I will probably think about it forever. It feels, to me, consequential. Life-changing. Even though it is, ultimately, a campaign speech at a political pageant. It's theater. The only way it could preach to the choir more is if there were an actual choir (suggestion for next time). And of course, it doesn't end up winning her chosen candidate the election. So, what is the consequence, really? Or rather, who was she doing it for? I guess I believe she was doing it for me. For her. For the future.

In the moment, that's enough. I don't know if anyone is actually tracking the movement of the moral universe, but I'd wager that bend is a lot longer than any of us can bear. This is not to suggest that Dr. King's famous quote is wrong. Rather, justice may be a lot farther than we think. I'm a Bend Truther.

And yet, we get out of bed, sometimes we give speeches, we have kids and/or dogs, we take those kid-dogs to Washington, D.C., and we show them that place in stone where it says the arc of the moral universe is long but it bends toward justice as if that's something they'll see in their lifetime. Why? Hope. That's the only thing I can come up with. We must all, even in some small way, be angling toward hope. And who am I to joke about that? Michelle Obama is trying to change the course of history and I'm making quips online. Who is this for? And what does it add?

The comedic surprise I'm always trying to get to in the column is hope. A joke is built on a surprise. You might anticipate a punchline, you might see it coming from a mile away, but if you laugh it's because there is some part of you that is surprised. I find that interesting because comedy is also made up of formulas. Jokes have structure and those structures have been in place for years. They're probably hardwired into our brains or the way language is organized. The structures evolve and shift, of course, but the basic arithmetic of what makes us laugh remains the same. That's the reason "Who's On First?" still works and that's the reason the latest meme works. That's, really, the reason memes exist at all. Memes are open-source joke structure. A meme shows you how the joke works and then invites you to fill in your own details. Comedy on the internet, like everything else on the internet, can be democratic. But, because it's comedy and because it's the internet, it can also be a fucking trash fire.

My goal is not to add trash to the fire. I know it's not a given, but I realized early on in the writing that the thing that interested me most was not punching down on the world that seemed to be sinking ever faster, but rather punching up to an idea of what we *could* be. I'm aware I'm not writing a motivational column for *O, the Oprah Magazine* (hello, Oprah, I am available whenever you need me), but it seems to me if I'm going to try to make people laugh on the internet, maybe it should also make them happy. Like the original viral Facebook post said, "We may be two minutes from doomsday *but* . . ."

Okay. Back to bed. No time to search the darkness for the bend in the moral universe tonight. I turn my phone off. I pause. And then pick my phone up again. Another thought about Mrs. Obama:

"You ever seen someone work this hard to leave a job?"

Now I'm done. Phone off, head on pillow, deep breathing, better life, etc.

My eyes spring open again as if my eyelids are like "Child, who you think you foolin'?" I grab the phone. "On her way to the convention, Michelle stopped by Independence Hall and snatched all of the Founding Fathers bald. And then she rang the Liberty Bell, just because."

I turn on the bedside lamp and get comfortable. If I'm doing this, I might as well be able to see. Plus, the light keeps that haunted-ass chair in its place. At work the next day, I will explain my sleepiness by muttering, "Sorry. I was up late. Got called into a jokes emergency online. Michelle Obama is Shawshanking through the walls of the Oval Office."

I don't exactly know what I'm doing. Or why. (Put that on my tombstone: *Here lies R. Eric; he didn't exactly know what he was doing.*)

Nevertheless, I'm trying it.

(Correction: please put that on my tombstone. *Here lies R. Eric. He tried it.*)

There's Never Any Trouble Here in Bubbleland

When I was a kid, maybe six, Maryland Public Television (MPT) took *Lassie* rebroadcasts off the air. My younger brother Stephen and I were incensed. Our youngest brother Jeffrey hadn't been born yet, but I'm sure he was furious in utero. The Saturday morning following, Stephen and I came marching downstairs and went right to the set of desks our parents had set up for us in the living room. My mom asked what we were doing. Stephen told my mother, in no uncertain terms, that he'd decided I was going to write a letter to MPT and make them turn *Lassie* back on. Stephen was the spokesman and idea man, even at three, so I deferred to him.

We fumed about *Lassie*'s removal. We were shaking with anger. It was outrageous. I excused myself and went to scream in another room for a moment. Who did these people think they were?! I was determined to let them have it.*

Even from an early age, my parents imbued in us the knowledge that although life wasn't just, we could always do something about it. We lived, the soon-to-be five of us, in a big house in the middle of a broken-down neighborhood in West Balti-

* We were unaware that we were watching a television show that had gone off the air thirty years before our births. But even if we had known that, it wouldn't have mattered. Are we serious about getting Timmy out of that well or not, dammit?

more, lassoed by red-lining and crippled by the drug trade. My parents' pleas to elected officials and city agencies, about everything from broken streetlights to increased police presence near open-air drug markets, were constant. Sometimes they got a response, sometimes they didn't. But they were relentless because they were trying to create the world that they wanted their children to live in. At six, I saw the discontinuation of *Lassie* as a perhaps less urgent injustice but an injustice nonetheless. I assumed my parents' mantle and set about to make the world I wanted: a world containing a highly communicative collie with an impressive sense of urgency. At Stephen's prompting, I wrote a strongly worded letter to MPT on that beige paper with the big blue lines that they give you in first grade. My mother mailed it and we waited. I remember going to the television the next day, turning it on, and being thunderstruck that they were still playing whatever trash they'd replaced *Lassie* with. "Haven't you received my letter?!" I bellowed, as I threw a plastic plate filled with plastic food against the wall of our playhouse. "What is this world coming to?"

Eventually, MPT sent us a couple of tchotchkes for our trouble, among them a mug with Disney characters on it. I unwrapped it and poured myself a juice, shaking with indignation. If this was a parable, I guess the lesson would be that life isn't fair but if you complain sometimes you get free things. Useful.

For much of my childhood, the only television channel we were allowed to watch was MPT, so *Lassie* (RIP), *Mr. Rogers,* and *Sesame Street* were in heavy rotation. This was fine with me, especially considering *Mr. Rogers* was home to the original dramatic queen Lady Elaine Fairchilde, the fearsome, overly rouged, cardigan-wearing antagonist of the Neighborhood of Make-Believe. I was obsessed with her, with her feckless but fangless villainy, with her catchphrase "Toots!", with her all-business dirty-blond bob. (Lady Elaine would *always* like to speak with the manager.) And, although I was a very nice child, I absolutely loved the contempt with which Lady Elaine Fairchilde viewed literally everyone else. Her misanthropy was electrifying. To this day I am amazed that someone as chill and Presbyterian as Fred Rogers created someone as over-the-top fabulous as Lady Elaine. She has a royal title and she is constantly in feuds with her brother; she's essentially a reality star. And like the most successful reality stars, Lady Elaine Fairchilde is the gay icon we need and want. She has all the hallmarks of gay iconography, eighties edition: an old-timey name, frequent appearances in musicals despite a lack of apparent singing ability, *eyebrows,* no time to date because she is too busy plotting drama, hates people. Why is there not a Lady Elaine float at every Pride? Why can't I buy a bedazzled tank top that says "TOOTS!" to wear to the beach? Where is the justice in this world?!

I didn't have as complex a read of Lady Elaine as a child. I just knew that this queen was extra as hell and I was living for every terse line reading. I would frequently turn from a television playing *Mr. Rogers* and say to an empty room, "I can't wait until Patricia Clarkson and Sarah Paulson play her at different stages in her life in a biopic that I am currently writing."

One of my favorite Lady Elaine moments also spawned one of our household's favorite catchphrases. It came from the episode titled "Mr. Rogers Makes an Opera." Oh, by the way, because he was relentless in his pursuit of eccentricity, Mr. Rogers cast all of the puppets in the Neighborhood of Make-Believe as characters in an opera that would form the basis of many future homosexual personalities. I *really* want to tell you, from memory, the in-depth plot of the opera *Windstorm in Bubbleland,* because, honey, it will blow your wig back. But it would take too long because every single detail is essential. Put this book down right now and google it and then come back. Wait, first grab a snack, then come back. You gotta eat, Toots.

Suffice it to say, Lady Elaine played Hildegarde Hummingbird, a resident of a burg called Bubbleland who sensed that there was trouble on the horizon that would threaten the primary feature of the landscape—bubbles. No one believed her. In fact, they sang a whole song called "There's Never Any Trouble Here in Bubbleland," which is the kind of petty, extra shit I live for.

There's a whole lot that happens—an evil executive who hates the environment reveals himself to be a wind monster! The dramatic reveal is accompanied by a costume change into a silver caftan! It's EVERYTHING!—but the thing that I was most affected by was the idea that Lady Elaine, despite her eccentric, sometimes antisocial ways, was not the villain. She was the only resident of Bubbleland who saw its weaknesses and therefore the only resident who could save it from destruction.

The rest of my household picked up a different takeaway. "There's never any trouble here in Bubbleland" became my mother's frequent ironic refrain, a sardonic way of expressing frustration at a situation that was set up for my parents to fail. Our neglected neighborhood was crumbling around us; my parents worked tirelessly but still struggled financially; their parents were ailing. When the weight of it all threatened to overtake her, my mother, with a lightness, would sigh, "There's never any trouble here in Bubbleland." It became a relief valve, a code word, a cry for help. It also served as a guiding metaphor. The world outside was troublesome, but the house and the world my parents built for us within it was a bubble. A delicate, permeable utopia.

Utopia came at a figurative and literal price. I was aware as a child that the economics of making a life were hard. I knew it in simple ways, like "We don't have money to add every available cereal to the grocery cart just because Eric would like to taste one spoonful and then decide he doesn't like it." I wasn't sure if a cereal smorgasbord was something that happened at other people's houses, but I knew that it didn't happen at ours and I presumed it was because every time we asked to add something to the cart, we were informed that it wasn't on The List. The List was a buzzkill. I did not like The List. I also knew that money was an issue for my parents, because I'd sometimes walk in on them in the middle of tense conversations, and even though I had yet to watch a Lifetime movie about hardscrabble people trying to make ends meet, I had a sense of what the air in that particular room felt like. I didn't think that we were poor, per se. But after nearly four decades on this planet and a long, nightmarish conversation about "economic anxiety" and the "forgotten working class," I am willing to entertain the idea that there are many kinds of poverty, that your mortgage can be paid on time and your children can be fed and you can still live in Poor America.

As an adult, I have an even clearer, more terrifying understanding of what the stakes must have been for my parents. As a child, I had no way of contextualizing how much things cost or how difficult it can be to stay on top of everything, even without kids. Now I know and I look back at the feat my parents pulled off with awe and a shiver, as I shovel one spoonful of every kind of cereal into my mouth. I also know that I'll never fully get it. I'll never be in their exact context: I'll never know *exactly* how much the frequent ER visits for their children's asthma set them back, *exactly* how many times car repairs or school uniforms or a layoff or the cost of heating a four-story house in the middle of a dilapidated neighborhood knocked them off course.

One thing I didn't know then but now can't forget is that my mother didn't purchase an item of clothing for herself for over a decade during my childhood. As she explains it now, "There simply wasn't money. My clothes didn't make The List." In the present, my parents will drop details about how things used to be for them with a casualness that belies how stunning those facts are. They shared a car for many years, so my father sometimes walked for miles to get home; he worked three jobs to afford school for me and my brothers, including a paper route in the wee small hours of the morning. My mother worked tirelessly to build a nurturing and educationally vigorous home for a decade and then went back to teaching elementary school, while putting herself through grad school and taking care of her ailing parents. And, for a ten-year stretch, they didn't buy themselves clothing.

When I ask my parents about that decade, they demur. "It's what we had to do," they say, which, as an adult, I both recognize and refuse to accept. I tinker with my budget constantly. I download apps and spreadsheets and read blog posts and complain to friends about money all the time. I know that every money decision comes with a choice. Even a choice that is compelled is still a choice. So when they say it's what they had to do, I know that the choice implicit in that sentence is me and my brothers. They chose us. And in so doing they created a world motivated by that choice. That's the goal. You work hard so that your children are able to live a life somewhat free from the burdens that plagued you. That's the gift my parents gave us, free of charge. Or, at least, I assume that's a parent's goal. I don't have any kids but I want those things for my houseplants.

Much of my family's financial difficulty came from trying to put me and my brothers through private school, a decision that made everything in my life possible. My brothers went to a private Episcopalian school and I went to Park, a progressive K-12 school with a campus comprised of one hundred acres of woodland. It's a remarkable place that functions more like a small liberal arts college than a traditional private school. A pond sits in the middle of campus; a stream winds between athletic fields. The students are empowered to be part of decision-making about the school but not in a ridiculous way where you end up having every kind of cereal for lunch every day. At Park, they recognize that students are people and worthy of being listened to, but they're also a school and, as such, recognize that children are lunatics.

This lunatic thought he had died and gone to heaven when he enrolled at Park in fourth grade. It is hard to put into words how perfect an environment it was for me. The faculty saw me. That's the whole thing. They saw my creative spirit and my curiosity and my tactile learning habits and my aversion to being outside and they affirmed all of it. Prior to Park, I'd gone to a very tiny arts conservatory that may have been a Ponzi scheme, to a Baptist elementary school, and, for three months, to public school. At the public school, one of my classmates bit me on the hand in protest for having to share computer time with me, and my mother rolled up on that place like a flash flood to whisk me and my lightly bleeding hand out of there.

The people at the school had the temerity to try to keep the computer lab fee my parents had paid at the beginning of the year. Guess how well that went over? My mother arrived at school to collect me, most of my hand, and our computer fee, wearing a black wool pantsuit with chalk stripes that I knew as "Betty Grey's suit." Betty Grey, a woman at our church, had befriended my mom and offered her some of her professional attire at some point. When my mother talks about it, her voice gets soft; it catches a bit. "She didn't have to do it," she will say. "She could have thrown them out or kept them. But she knew I needed clothes to wear to work, and that generosity has always stayed with me."

Betty Grey's winter-weight blazer and skirt were the most serious of the items in my mother's closet. She wore this outfit to funerals and to meetings in which she had to set someone straight. She called it her death suit because if she was wearing it, "either someone is already dead or someone's going to die."

We didn't have money in Bubbleland, but we were rich in bon mots.

The world outside Bubbleland was unjust and frightening and sometimes violent, but inside was different. Inside, our futures were brimming with possibilities and our backs were straight and we had as many choices available to us as any of our contemporaries. And that bubble extended seventeen minutes up I-83 to Park, where I was classmates with the daughters and sons of some of Baltimore's wealthiest families. We rode horses as an after-school activity and I went to bar and bat mitzvahs in every fancy building in the city. I knew I was not the same as my classmates, but I was compelled to believe that my options were just as promising. Demographically, I, a Black male growing up in West Baltimore, didn't have great odds. But inside the bubble, even statistics seemed to work differently.

Not everything at Park was foreign and new to me. Though we couldn't necessarily afford the resources that some of my classmates' families could, my parents used everything at their disposal to expand the walls of our bubble. They filled our home with new experiences and ideas; they took every opportunity to expose us to the worlds outside of our neighborhood; they told us about the things they couldn't yet show us. They crafted new spaces inside our minds and our imaginations just waiting to be filled up with details and experiences. And I brought all of that to Park with me. I didn't always feel different. I think that's the point. Most of the time, I actually felt like I belonged there.

These days we tend to talk about bubbles like they're bad things. A bubble connotes a lack of awareness of what's *really* happening, a disconnect from the real world. But bubbles have transparent walls and gossamer skin that allows sound to permeate. Bubbles, like the kind you blow from a wand dipped in soapy liquid, don't keep anyone out or anyone in. They're just different environments.

I also like to think of bubbles as transportation systems, the bubble as flotation device, as oxygen, as a sign of life. In Bubbleland, we were separated from forces that sought to harm us and given resources that could expand our worlds. This mobility is the best kind of intention to set for your child, I think. And not only that, it's what every child should have. It's what they deserve. And if the world were just, they could have it. And so, if you're my parents, you do everything in your ability to make that world appear, even if it is partly an illusion, even if the effort is breaking you. You do it, because perhaps if your child can live in this more just world for long enough, it will become their reality.

As is probably the case with nearly all independent private schools in the nation, Park is mostly white. (I have done no research on what other independent private schools are like, but I have a hunch based on literally everything I know about America.) I was one of three Black students in my grade when I started, and by the time I graduated I believe there were eight of us. The majority of my classmates were Jewish, which provided an exciting secondary education for me. Much of the first couple of years I spent at Park were comprised of learning by doing, learning by reading, and learning by asking things like "What is Rosh Hashanah and why is no one in school today and does this mean we can watch a movie?"

The exposure to a different culture was invigorating for me. I felt like every day I stumbled into new terrain. I wasn't a pioneer, of course. I knew that. That was part of the appeal of Judaism—I was not discovering it; it was being revealed to me. And just as I peppered people with queries about Judaism, my classmates were curious about Blackness and Christianity. I guess we learned from each other. Sometimes it was awkward—Baltimore has a long history of difficult relations between Black and Jewish communities, although that rarely carried over into school—but it was seldom ugly. I think it's a testament to the school's ability to create a safe environment that microaggressions didn't turn into macroaggressions and that students treated one another with respect. Another bubble.

Which is why it was such a surprise when one of my classmates called me a nigger in fifth grade.

It happened, as I suppose these things can, for no reason. The class was briefly unattended, working on a project and talking. One girl was needling a boy. Let's call the girl Dora and let's call the boy Prentice because those names are quaint and if we're going to use pseudonyms, they ought to bring joy. So Dora says, "You know, another word for 'Prentice' is 'nerd,'" or something equally toothless. I don't really remember the quote so much as I remember thinking, *This utopia is terrible at shade.* Somehow, Prentice thought it might be fun to get me involved in this, which is odd because although we were friends I was definitely not volleying back and forth with the bush-league put-downs. He replied to Dora, "Another word for 'Eric' is 'nigger.'"

Everyone fell silent and then I burst into tears. Someone ran out of the room and got a teacher. My thoughts and prayers are with a teacher at a mostly white, very liberal bastion of progressive education who has a ten-year-old run up screaming, "Someone called Eric a nigger." It sounds like a lot of paperwork at the very least.

Prentice and I got whisked off to the principal's office and asked to explain. I, understandably, had no explanation. Prentice said he hadn't meant it. Our parents were called. Betty Grey's suit came out of the closet.

My first "nigger" was what I think of as a *casual* "nigger." (*Casual Nigger* was the first title of this book but literally everyone started screaming the minute I said it, so I came up with some alternatives.) Even as a child, I understood that Prentice was pushing a button he knew was a button but was unsure of what the result would be. It was an experiment, I think. Testing out language. The way Prentice said it was not at all loaded, unlike the other times in my life I would be called that word.

The point is, this wasn't a battle between him and me. We remained friends, and I wonder if he even remembers it, or if the people in the classroom that day remember it. I'm not sure it matters to me either way. I was in my utopian bubble and what I learned was that even in a bubble someone can casually toss off a racial slur and go about their day.

There's no response to being called a nigger. I've been called a nigger a fair number of times. (How many times is acceptable? That's the question of our age. I think it varies by region of the country, but that may be my Mid-Atlantic prejudice showing. Also, does it count if it's online versus in person? What are the rules?) Every time it happens, I'm like, "I'm not sure what you want me to do with this information." We're not engaged in a dialogue; we never have been. And we weren't engaged in the room in fifth grade. So, the why of the "nigger" is on that guy. I'm not part of it. And the why of the moment is of less concern to me. It's like Baldwin says, "What white people have to do is try to find out in their hearts why it was necessary for them to have a nigger in the first place. Because I am not a nigger. I'm a man. If I'm not the nigger here, and if you invented him, you the white people invented him, then you have to find out why." If it hadn't been him calling me a nigger for the first time, it would have been someone else someplace else. But in the middle will always be me. I am the one I seek to understand.

To that end, I get stuck, in the retelling, on my own casualness. I've never forgotten the mortification of the moment, the shock, the sensation of all the blood running out of my face. Yet, here I'm sanguine. "It's just a thing that happens," I'll say with the sort of horrific matter-of-factness that my parents have adopted when talking about their lives in segregated Baltimore. Is the point that some part of the past will always sound horrific as a price for living in a presumably better future?

Because of the incident at school, the principal decided she wanted to put me and Prentice in racial sensitivity training. *Both of us?* Honey! The two of us, together, learning about difference. My mother, perspiring in Betty Grey's suit in the humid late spring, was having absolutely none of it. She walked into the principal's office in that black suit with white stripes, spoke to her *at length*, and then walked out and took me home. I don't know what Betty Grey's suit told them, but you should already know I didn't take anybody's racial sensitivity training. Obviously. I mean, hello, I am *problématique*! And besides, my parents didn't sacrifice themselves, their time, their prospects, the clothes on their backs, for me to go to school, get called a nigger, and then take a class about it.

My mother showed up to fight for the world my parents so desperately wanted for us, a world that must have seemed ephemeral and fleeting in that moment. I'm sure they never thought that the world they were trying to craft would be perfect for me; why would they? But this particular controversy—a mix of nineties bureaucracy and age-old prejudice—must have seemed a strange kind of trouble.

In the bubble, however, the trouble didn't last. Things went back to normal relatively quickly. And, to be frank, I was glad. I was a fifth grader and I thought the moment was an anomaly, completely divorced from me or who I might be able to be. It was all just so weird and random and nobody really *disliked* Blacks, so what was one really to do? Besides, we were studying the Middle Ages that year, so there were, truly, larger concerns like flying buttresses and the plague. I never forgot the incident, though, never figured out where to put it.

Prentice and I didn't stop being friends. In retrospect, maybe this reflects badly on me. I can feel your judgment. And I would like to remind you that you are judging a ten-year-old. And I am judging you for that. So. We're all just trying here, okay? Maybe it doesn't reflect badly. Maybe it's like one of those "heartwarming" race movies where a white person with suspect ideas and a Black person become friends and they both learn a lesson about difference except nothing that's learned is new to the Black person, who was just going about their Black business when this whole thing started. If you see it that way, please feel free to option this story for an Oscar-winning Hollywood movie. (I am not above this, honey.) But that's not why I'm telling this to you. Oh God! Can you imagine? All those trees chopped down and made into books so I could tell you about how we all bleed red, white, and blue? How embarrassing for everyone involved. How embarrassing for those trees! No. I'm telling you this because it was a moment that felt both strange and familiar, and I tucked it away inside myself, to fidget with and worry at until its rough parts disappeared and it shone. I'm telling you this because the more I think about that incident, that moment in a bubble, the more it tells me about the delicate, permeable utopia my parents were striving to create. And it suggests to me that they succeeded.

I know that my parents wanted me to live in a better world than they had, but they must have also desperately hoped I'd be prepared to live in the *real* world. Why else would they teach me to raise my voice against injustice, to write letters, to make hard choices? And so that painful moment in the classroom was as much an answer to their prayers as the moments of triumph and discovery and freedom, of which there were far more. As they prepared me for the world, they prepared the world for me, one difficult decision at a time. And it's a world that's complex and misshapen and poised for discovery and ripe with promise. I look back and I can see the dreams they had, glimmering and evanescent and steely and diffuse, forming a trail from the place where we started to the place where we are, and the place we hope to be. And I know what it means when they sigh, "There's never any trouble here."

Molly, Urine Danger Girl

Technically, I grew up in a dangerous area. Sometimes people got killed nearby. I never saw any dead bodies, although once the movie *Homicide* needed a kid to play a corpse at a crime scene set a couple of doors up. They approached my mother and asked her if one of her sons wanted to earn money lying in the street. I was very excited about this; I thought that this would be my big break. She was like, "Rosa Parks didn't sit in the front of that bus so that you could lie in a gutter and collect Equity points." (I'm paraphrasing.) (Probably.) Anyway, despite the fact that I grew up in a dangerous area, that's my only experience with murdered bodies. It's possible my neighborhood was just dangerous on film.

Nonetheless, I avoided telling my classmates about where I lived, and I only invited one person over one time. I guess I was embarrassed. The things we saw out of our windows were so dramatically different from the things they saw. My classmates, by and large, lived in suburban neighborhoods—some with mega-mansions, some with the regular homes of your standard middle-class white family—none the setting for a television show about murders and the detectives who investigate said murders. My parents wanted more for us than what our surroundings could provide, so it's probably no surprise that my mother was less than keen about me lying in a gutter outside our front door drenched in fake blood. I see that now; I didn't then. Truth be told, I always thought the pastoral neighborhoods where my classmates lived were scarier. Yeah, it was a common occurrence to hear gunshots ringing out somewhere in our neighborhood, but in the suburbs, my friends had floor-to-ceiling windows that looked out on acres of woodland. And you know what lives in the woods? Horrors limited only by your own imagination (and, I guess, your knowledge of woods and the creatures therein).

Are there bears in the city? No, there are not. Are there hockey-mask-wearing killers in the city? Who in the city has a hockey mask? Are there Babadooks and Mothmen in the city? Honey, the rent is too high for all that. True, there is the threat of mugging and an air-conditioning unit falling out of a window and crushing you and buses driving by and splashing your tutu. But that's about it, at least as far as physical threats go. The danger in a city is systemic and endemic; it's built into the walls and the street corners and written in invisible ink on the mortgages and in the local newspaper headlines; it powers the public transportation and funds the political campaigns. The danger in the city is all around you, but has clearly delineated borders. The suburbs, on the other hand, are places of literally endless physical peril for everyone everywhere. The worst of the worst are those super suburbs for people so rich they can't stand the sight of other people, where you have so much land that you basically live in a house hidden in a national park. You might as well be Sigourney Weaver in *Alien* going into some of the places with a mile-long private drive. Like, you are *forsaken* out there. If you call the police, they let you know their anticipated arrival time in *days*. And who wants to live that far from a Costco? You're so rich you've started to inconvenience yourself. Look at your life.

I actively distrust the suburbs. I especially distrust the sprawling ones, the ones built on top of old rock quarries, the ones where everything is alike in sameness and remoteness and perfection. I have trouble understanding the melting pot when by order of the neighborhood association every ingredient looks identical or you have to squint to see your neighbors. That said, the suburban house, the patch of land in a ticky-tacky Hooverville, is the pinnacle of the American dream, so who am I to judge it? If it's good enough for Audrey in *Little Shop of Horrors,* shouldn't it be good enough for me?

The fact is, when it comes to living space and *Little Shop,* I've always preferred "Downtown" to "Somewhere That's Green," both musically and symbolically. I decided early on that you would *never* catch me out in some cul-de-sac with minimum light pollution. I'd rather take my chances on Skid Row with a person-eating plant than try to navigate the foreboding open space of a suburb. This is especially true if there are woods involved. It's too quiet. It's too dark. There are too many crevices and corners and crags and scritches and crackles and shrieks. If there's a copse, there's a corpse, I always say. (I am a *delight* at parties.) The woods, as I'm sure you're aware, are where roughly 65 percent of all terrible things happen in horror movies. The other 35 percent happen in beautiful suburban houses where no one (except me, apparently) would ever imagine such a thing taking place. This rule isn't even restricted to horror movies, actually. I love a good *Dateline* investigation or British mystery novel or *Gone Girl,* and all of them are basically infomercials about the inherent danger of living anywhere with a lawn. *Dateline* investigations are never in crack houses.

They are always in split-level homes owned by a dentist who snapped. You never see Jane Pauley or whomever walking through a neighborhood like mine, pockmarked with abandoned buildings and soundtracked by sirens, asking neighbors if they ever expected a thing like this to happen here. It's assumed that it will happen here. And something has taught us that when it does happen, we shouldn't be surprised. I don't happen to agree with that understanding of the differences between city life and suburban life. But I will definitely take it to heart. I'm not trying to spend years saving up all my coins and pouring all of my worth into a three-bedroom, two-and-a-half-bathroom rancher in some neighborhood where there are stringent rules for what color your mailbox is just to be *surprised* by my own *murder*.

If you're going to kill me, I want to expect it. That's the real American dream.

The fact is, white people did this to themselves. Red-lining and white flight are basically like when someone in a horror movie hears a noise in the basement and everybody (Black) in the movie theater is yelling "Don't go in there!" and they go in there anyway. The city, as a concept, is not objectively dangerous. (Unless you're Batman's parents.) But literally everyone is in danger in the suburbs. You may not know this, but *A Raisin in the Sun* is actually a thriller about a Black family almost escaping the sinister pull of backyards and barbecue. *A Raisin in the Sun* should have been called *Get Out*, because that's what I shout every time I see it. And everyone in the theater is like, "I don't think you understand the American dream." And I'm like, "I'm an *expert* on the American Dream *actually*. I've seen

Little Shop of Horrors many times." And I am escorted from the theater. Which is fine with me; the ending of *A Raisin* is a real bummer. Spoiler alert: they get the house in the white neighborhood.

It is both a total coincidence and a very intentional, brilliant bit of dramatic synergy that I first read *A Raisin in the Sun* in tenth grade, the same year I started babysitting for people who lived in the suburbs. I was hired, mainly, by two families, both of whom had children who went to my school. I worked at the after-school daycare program, so I had begun to develop a reputation as a semi-reliable, friendly person who could keep children alive. Even though I had literally no qualifications other than "willing to play many games of Chutes and Ladders" and "can dial a phone," I became very popular in the babysitting scene. One of the kids I babysat once told me, "You're different—you play with us!" which seemed like a natural thing to do, but was apparently a rarity. Frankly, I liked playing with the kids I babysat. I enjoyed pulling out board games, making up magic kingdoms, losing at videogames, and reading them stories. And their houses, with their romper rooms and toy closets and wall-to-wall carpet, did, I must admit, make for the perfect play space. But I wasn't so easily beguiled. Outside every playroom, just past the floor-to-ceiling windows that so stunningly captured the sunset, was a world of darkness masquerading as the quiet comforts of a suburban neighborhood. Sometimes the kids would be running around, shrieking with glee as they pretended to be warrior knights or superheroes or people who love to clean up very quickly before their parents get home (a very fun game for children), and I would space out and stare into the abyss. Past my own reflection in the glass, through the trees that lined the property, into the unknown. *No,* I would remind myself, quickly drawing the curtain like a novel's circumspect housewife who has a terrible secret that she telegraphs through small modifications of her decorative accoutrements, *this is not the dream. You are inside a nightmare. It has central air and a gas fireplace. It's super cute but also terrifying.*

Every time I look out of a black window in a suburban house, I expect to see the face of a killer on the other side of the glass. Every single time. Nowadays, my brothers live in suburbs; I refuse to visit them. Every Christmas, I RSVP "Can't make it cuz of psychos." Why am I RSVP'ing to family Christmas? Because I like formality. I'm a classic fifties housespouse with a fine sense of decorum and a terrible secret and the creeping suspicion that there is a person on the loose in the woods back there. I'll never get used to it, I think. I don't trust the perfection and the wide open expanses. Basically, all of the selling points are a source of deep anxiety for me. But that's just me; maybe you like it. I'm not judging you. (Oh, I should have said this before: I'm not judging you.) But I'm just saying no one has ever peered into the streetlamp-illuminated window of my third-floor urban apartment with a sinister glint in their eye, so draw your own conclusions.

And you know what's worse than the face of your doom in the black mirror of a double-insulated window? The sound of your encroaching demise played out in creaks of floorboards, the rustle of animals outside (preparing themselves for the blood sacrifice, of course), and the unidentified noises that you hear when your house is surrounded by nothingness. Have you ever slept in a house that was so quiet you could hear a clock ticking in another room? WHY? If I wanted a soundtrack for my existential dread, I'd download a bunch of Ben Folds songs on iTunes like a normal person.

I didn't get into Ben Folds until midway through college, so I had to come up with other ways to drown out the darkness in tenth grade. So, like every other babysitter in the history of the world, I watched TV after the kids went to bed. If I had ever seen a horror movie, I would have known that killings of babysitters spike in the hour after the kids go to bed, especially if the babysitter has secretly invited a boyfriend over and/or if the babysitter has just put a bag of popcorn in the microwave. I had never even *heard* the word "gay," so a boyfriend was out of the question at this point, and I had late-in-life braces, so popcorn was a no-go. Instead, I entertained myself and kept my fear at bay by watching whatever Disney movies the kids had lying around. I was the picture of innocence, wandering around a sprawling McMansion with all the lights turned on, waiting to be slaughtered.

One night, I found the newly released videotape of *Hercules,* the retelling of the Greek myth with a chorus of gospel-singing muses and music by Alan Menken, who also wrote the music for *Little Shop of Horrors*. Clearly I, not the kids I was babysitting, was the target demographic for this movie. I took it downstairs and set myself up on a couch. The family I was babysitting for had one of those houses out of a Nancy Meyers film: the gleaming kitchen with a marble-top kitchen island next to a plush TV room and breakfast nook with three walls of windows; the doorbell that played a full concerto; the rooms that weren't decorated, but *curated*. I understand the allure of this kind of space. Everything was new in this place, even the things that weren't new. The antiques were polished to a shine; the books in the library were like set decorations from a box labeled "Intelligent, Wealthy Person." When I was growing up, my mother used to joke that our interior design style was "Deceased," meaning someone has died and left us their furniture, whether we wanted it or not. So the pristine order of a suburban house was like an alien spaceship to me: attractive but deeply foreign; potentially home to something sinister.

I didn't understand how a house came to be like this. I didn't understand the lack of mess, the pile on the counter with exactly three pieces of mail and one catalog, the dust-free floors, the litter-free street, the noise-free air. It was clear that people lived here, but I didn't know how.

Their house was so big that I didn't even wander around it for fear of getting lost. They didn't have a pantry; they had a dry-goods room. I spent twenty minutes standing inside it, smelling spices. There were so many rooms on the ground floor, I worried that I would stumble into a secret passageway and never return.

Midway through the movie, I paused and went to the Sub-Zero fridge to help myself to one of the thirteen juices they had inside. I'm exaggerating the number of juices, but you believed me and that's the point. Coming back, glass in hand, I stepped in a puddle next to the kitchen island. I assumed that I had somehow spilled the juice that I was pretty sure I was allowed to have but not so sure that I would ever actually admit to having drunk the juice.

It was true that I had just poured the juice and therefore couldn't have spilled it on the other side of the room, but I assumed that the suburbs had different rules and they extended to include space and time. I got a paper towel and knelt down to wipe up the juice that I was convincing myself I'd preemptively spilled. As I got close I noticed its aroma. It didn't have the same smell as what was in my glass—fresh-squeezed money—in fact, it smelled like pee. I drew back and scanned the room. Who was peeing on the floor? Had I peed on the floor? Maybe one of the kids was sleepwalking? Or maybe this was a passive-aggressive act of defiance. What had I done to deserve this? Hadn't I thrown enough games of Chutes and Ladders to avoid this?

I crept upstairs and checked on the kids; they were both sleeping peacefully as far as I could tell. I whispered, "Is this some sort of class-based hazing?" but they didn't respond. I finished cleaning up and went back to the movie. The dark glass behind the screen seemed more ominous now; the empty perfect rooms were more forbidding.

The movie ended. I got up to change the video and heard a scratching sound behind me. *It's just the constant terrifying symphony of innocuous sounds,* I assured myself. *It's the plink of gold doubloons shifting in their safe or the rustle of eight-hundred-thread-count Egyptian cotton in the guest bedroom. It's nothing.* I turned my head with all the measured drama of a silent film star and saw, to my relief, nothing. Just the bluish glow of the light on the backsplash, the shine of the marble countertop on the kitchen island, and . . . on the gleaming hardwood floor, another puddle in the spot I had just cleaned up. I raced to the island and stuck my nose in the puddle. Urine! Again! "What does it mean?" I screamed very quietly so as not to wake the children who, I half suspected, were standing behind me, pee-soaked and wielding knives. But no, I was alone. Just me, a strange house, and about five ounces of fresh urine.

As I wiped up the second puddle, it suddenly occurred to me that there was another potential answer beyond "This is a bed-wetter's way of telling you to take your ass back to the city." It was possible that the children and I weren't alone in the house.

What if they had a pet? To paraphrase a great suspense film that I was, at that point, too scared to see: The pee was coming from inside the dog.

The thing was, the kids had never mentioned a dog, the parents had never mentioned a dog, and I had never seen a dog. On top of that, I am allergic to dogs. Even if the parents had the canine version of the first Mrs. Rochester from *Jane Eyre* that they kept locked away, my nose would still have alerted me to the danger unseen. My watering eyes and persistent sneezes are the modern equivalent of Jane's ripped wedding veil.

So, if the parents don't say there's a dog and my histamine doesn't say there's a dog, what's the most logical conclusion? You guessed it: I decided that there was a dog and that said dog was most likely a ghost and/or a demon of some sort. Suburban houses aren't usually haunted, because they are of relatively new construction, so the logic goes that no one has had time to die in them. That logic omits, however, the large number of babysitters who are killed in suburban homes by deranged Woods People. I assumed this incontinent Hound of the Bladdervilles had been the unintended victim of said Woods People and was stalking me, the beautiful young babysitter, as revenge. Or perhaps it was warning me, a helpful hellhound! The puddle of pee was its way of alerting me that my fears were correct: the picturesque suburban tranquility was but a mask for the violent underbelly that swallowed up unsuspecting interlopers. Whether a friendly warning or a wet threat, the message of the mess was clear. To paraphrase Oda Mae Brown in *Ghost:* "Molly: urine! Danger, girl."

It was clear that I was going to have to fight the spirit world for my life until the parents of the kids came home. I turned on all the lights, grabbed an Evian bottle, said a little prayer over it, and searched the dry-goods room for a leftover box of Hi-C

Ecto Cooler, the official beverage of Ghostbusters. And then I waited. For death or deliverance, I knew not which.

I am happy to announce that I did not die in a suburban home in 1997. (OMG, what if this book was written by a *ghost*?! Can you imagine?) The parents of the kids came home within an hour and were kind enough to not ask why I'd lit all their decorative candles and arranged them to spell out "Not today, Satan." I called my father to come pick me up and discovered he was already waiting outside. My father is exceedingly prompt and also a very holy person, so although he explained his presence by saying he'd asked the parents when they'd be returning, I knew the truth was he had sensed the unholy disturbance of suburban tranquility and hurried out to help me fight the darkness.

I walked down the driveway toward my dad's car, illuminated by a floodlight. I turned back to the house; the parents stood framed by the doorway and the bluish glow of the light inside. They waved. I waved back and kept walking. I reached the outer border of the floodlight's glow. I stepped into the darkness and turned back once more. The car was running beside me, waiting to ferry me back to the city, with its noise and its streetlights and its puddles of urine that were not passive-aggressive messages. "Um," I called out, "this is going to sound weird but I'm just wondering: do you have a dog?"

The parents leaned forward into the light, their faces porcelain masks of horror. "A dog?!" they exclaimed. "Why, we haven't heard that word in years . . ." They threw their heads back and cackled sinisterly. I heard the snarl of a hellhound growing closer in the darkness; it seemed to come from all directions at once. I jumped in the car and screamed, "Drive! Just drive!" as we tore off into the night.

She's Got Herself a Universe

Is there anything as fat with possibility as a crush? Before I knew that I was gay, before I knew that sexuality exists on a spectrum and attraction is no respecter of gender, before I knew what possibilities awaited me in the wide world of adult emotions and relationships, I had crushes. Crushes on celebrities, crushes on classmates of all genders, crushes on books. I had a lot of crushing to do. And sometimes it was disconcerting, like the moments in high school when I'd let myself wonder, *Do I just think this guy is really cool or do I have a crush on him?* I would never answer, though, because that seemed too frightening a prospect. I was resolutely good, very Christian, and deeply focused on excelling in school and extracurriculars so that my parents' sacrifice would be worth it. Discovering a crush on a boy would have thrown all of that into disarray, I thought. Besides, this was the mid-nineties, so it was illegal to even say the word "gay" in a positive way in most municipalities. Plus, I also had crushes on girls, on friends, on life. Better not to look too hard.

My graduating class was small, ninety-two people, so by the time we entered high school we all knew each other backwards and forwards. Or as well as a group of people who are just starting to know themselves can know each other. I knew how my classmates ticked, I collected trivia and gossip like a magpie, and had considered having a crush on everyone. While there was uncertainty about what, exactly, the future held, there was a concomitant reliability in the patterns that we'd established and the lives that we were being set up to live. Most of us would end up going to college and after that, we presumed, get jobs, get married, have kids, donate a portion of our substantial earnings back to the school (they hoped!), and gracefully proceed to old age. While our individuality and creativity were encouraged, part of the promise of a school like Park was that it would help set you up for success in life. Of course, you had to get into college and do well on exams and decide if you were going to take AP History and all the other usual high school stuff. It wasn't a leisurely idyll. But in retrospect the anxiety sheers off and most of what remains is the predictability and the possibility.

At the center of those two poles, in my memory, stands Electra. She was new to Park in high school, a year older than me, and a curious anomaly. While other new students seemed quick to try to find their footing, she was quiet, reticent. All I knew, to start with, was that she had moved from New York and she was Black. Frankly, this was all I really needed to know to pique my interest in finding out what her deal was. I was obsessed with New York, so her mere presence suggested a cosmopolitan finesse and an understanding of the world that was more expansive and sophisticated than anything I'd ever heard of.

Plus, her entrance raised the number of Black students in the Upper School by like 25 percent. I was, at this time, trying to make sense of what it meant to be Black in the larger world, having realized that the experience of being a minority in as progressive and unique an environment as Park was far from typical. I didn't really know how to go about it. I read *Roots*. That seemed like a good idea. It was very long. *Do I feel Blacker?* I wondered. I couldn't say yes, but I couldn't say no. I read it again.

I also joined the Black Awareness Club, an extracurricular in the Upper School that was part affinity group and part educational group. Once a year, we'd host a Black Awareness Day for the Upper School, which, from the title, sounds like someone marching up and down the halls banging together pots and pans and yelling, "Slavery! Have you heard of it?!" It wasn't that, but I do suggest that for all your diversity needs. We'd put together workshops on various aspects of Black life in America, invite speakers, and host discussions. The rest of the year, when we weren't planning the event, we would meet in a French classroom to have discussions about our experiences and conceptions of ourselves. And sometimes have snacks.

Electra never came to the Black Awareness Club meetings. I found that fascinating. We would sometimes send various emissaries from the club to invite her. Perhaps she was not aware of the Awareness Club? She still never came. I found that even more fascinating.

I was not an emissary. I think by the time I met her we'd gotten the hint. We were introduced formally in the middle of her tenth-grade year. Up to that point, she'd been an enigma, the new Black girl who kept to herself. Passing her in the hall or seeing her in the cafeteria, I'd sometimes stare, trying to intuit what her deal was. I ticked off the details in my mind with all the precision and remoteness of a police sketch artist. She had light skin and huge, alert eyes. Her voice was high-pitched but gravelly. When she spoke, it was a sort of chirp and a croak. She was tall and thin and moved spryly but perhaps cautiously. She never wore makeup, and though she relaxed her hair, she didn't usually style it beyond brushing it back, away from her face. She wore black jeans seemingly every day, and they were always just a little short.

One day, in the library, we said hello to each other like a couple of normal people and not one normal person and one dude who is constantly gaping and filling in the other person's details from his imagination. I was using the microfiche catalog to do research on birth order, as was my ritual. I did this literally once a week, retrieving and printing the same articles that said maybe the reason I was the way I was came from my position as the oldest child or maybe it didn't. Who can say? I was obsessed with finding a root cause for my being, and more broadly, I was obsessed with figuring out who I was.

I asked her the origin of her name, assuming that she had a connection to Greek mythology. No, she said, that would be weird. Her mother had heard the name on a New York City bus and liked it. She said it matter-of-factly and I nodded as if it wasn't blowing my mind. To be fair, this is the least weird New York City transit story anyone has ever told. And the name does have a certain ring to it.

She'd grown up in New York City, I soon learned, raised by her mom. Then her mother had gotten sick and passed away the year before she came to Park, forcing her to move to Baltimore, with an uncle and an aunt and their new baby. Though we were essentially strangers, she spoke with an open wistfulness about her life in New York and her mother. And she spoke with a glum wariness about her new life now. I was surprised by how forthcoming she was. It didn't feel like she was oversharing; instead, it seemed to me that she had a level of self-awareness and vulnerability that is rare for anyone, let alone a teenager. She knew that grief was the thing that had forced her out of her old life, waving from the train platform as she left. And it was the malevolent mystery sending her postcards from the past with the words "Wish you were here" scribbled across the back. Grief had been her first friend in this new world. It made itself known, an apparition, at points throughout her history and her present and, she presumed, her future, too.

Though she had mapped the path of the sadness that glowed within her, it was clear that grief wasn't all there was to her story. She was funny, too, that day in the library and in the days and weeks following when we'd run into each other. Her sense of humor was dry and weird and casual, and just a hair shy of nerdy. Contrary to the early observations of the Black Awareness Club, she was social. She was trying to be, anyway; quietly sometimes, other times tinged with grief, but trying nonetheless. I asked her, finally, after months of after-school chats and run-ins in the hall, why she never joined the Black Awareness Club. It had become obvious that she wasn't antagonistic toward the club, and I'd really started to like her, so I just needed an answer to make sense of this one thing. Maybe it was some deep personal grievance. Maybe she wasn't Black and this had all been a wild mix-up? Really, anything was possible. I was willing to suspend any and every belief. She answered with the same matter-of-factness that she used when telling me about her name. "I don't go because I don't want to," she replied. I stared at her slack-jawed. It had never occurred to me that that was an option. She just wasn't into it and it didn't belie some sort of inner racial turmoil. A whole world of affable ambivalence opened up to me. It was possible to be authentic and Black and aware and not part of a club, much like it was possible to be constantly hounded by grief, yet funny and charming.

We saw more and more of each other, working together in the after-school daycare program and congregating in the school library with a crew of erudite girls from both of our grades, the kind of slightly-too-smart group that talked about *Rent* and gossip and foreign languages with equal passion, that dated only occasionally—as teenage boys are, by and large, a disappointment—and earned kind but clear reprimands from librarians for laughing too loud on a regular basis. We spent so much time in the library that the summer between her junior and senior years, she was hired as a library assistant for a reshelving project. She encouraged me to snatch up the other position, which I did because I love libraries, and I love money, and I really liked her.

This job was the bee's knees, the perfect summer activity for a couple of nonathletes who liked books more than sunshine. We spent eight hours a day on either side of a book cart, slowly making our way up and down each aisle, scanning the books for inventory and replacing misfiled items. We were supposed to work separately to maximize our time, but when we tried it on the first day, we found that it was too hard to shout things to each other through the stacks. We decided that the working-separately thing was just a suggestion. Did they really want us to be focused on the task at hand all summer? How boring! The library was the center of our social lives and we assumed that an unspoken but crucial part of the job description was "hang out in the air-conditioning with one of your favorite people." Why else would anyone want to come to work?

Park's school library, like many libraries, uses the Dewey decimal system for categorizing and filing books. As a lifelong library-goer, I'd always been captivated by the numbers on the spine of every book. I loved that every possible thing, every story, every fact, everything in the universe of knowledge, could be classified. I loved that by understanding the Dewey decimal system, even at a rudimentary level, I gained access to an ever-deepening world of information. Knowing what the ten divisions in the system were and what many of the divisions' subcategories were made what was often overwhelming and mysterious suddenly comprehensible. A library looks like endless possibility in this way, rather than rows of closed covers. A library is a universe of smaller universes contained within pages, and to me the Dewey decimal system was the key.

One of the most fascinating things about the Dewey decimal system is that while there are distinct categories for every subject imaginable, it also allows for internal referencing, acknowledging that while a book may be about one subject and exist in one place, it also has a corollary placement elsewhere. At the same time. And that's okay. I understood that a book could be many things at once, without conflict or contradiction, long before I realized it about people. Or, at least, long before I admitted it.

Another thing I liked about the Dewey decimal system was that it could sometimes function as a secret code. Every once in a while during my high school years, I would hesitantly and cautiously type "gay" into a search bar in a card catalog. Just "gay," as if more specificity would kill me right on the spot. Libraries were the only space I felt remotely comfortable even acknowledging the question—which didn't yet even have words or language, just the faint outline of the punctuation. And where if not a library could I go to understand the unknown, to expand my world, to make sense out of gibberish? I would type "gay" and then survey the titles that came up and then click the window closed without ever doing any further exploring. I didn't know what I thought I might find if I actually went to the aisle where the books were. A very quiet gay bar, perhaps? I figured it wasn't worth the risk. But as I closed the screen, I memorized the Dewey decimal number of the section where, I presumed, a mirror ball sprinkled stardust across the aging carpet and the rows of books waiting to be opened.

Years later, I would learn about the work of Dorothy Porter, the Howard University librarian who devised her own classification system for library materials. In the 1930s she began building a collection of books by Black writers and volumes on Black and African history that would eventually become Howard's Moorland-Spingarn Research Center. At its inception, it was an anomaly. In 1995 she told *The Washington Post,* "When I started building the collection nobody was writing about Blacks in history. You couldn't find any books."

As her collection grew, it became apparent that Dewey reified the same sort of structural inequities that kept Black history out of books and Black books off of shelves. In Dewey, she said, "they had one number—326—that meant slavery, and they had another number—325, as I recall it—that mean colonization." The result, she explained, was that many libraries were reaffirming a Eurocentric mindset by filing any- and everything about Black life under these two categories. Porter's system, like the Dewey, classified work by genre and subject but included Black authors and Black history in every area. When I first learned about the Dewey decimal system, I assumed it was an impartial way of defining and filing the breadth of knowable information. I came to understand that the intention of the filer and the perspective that they carry play a huge role in how Dewey, and any other system, is employed.

There are probably few more interesting date options than lazily wandering the aisles of a library or a bookstore. Better if you're getting paid for it. Not that we were on dates or that we were dating. That would be untrue. But if you were inclined to get to know someone, to show them a piece of yourself, to perhaps fall a little bit in love, you'd be hard-pressed to find a better way than by spending hours picking up books, flipping them open, and talking about what you find inside.

In retrospect, we probably weren't supposed to take the entire summer to scan the library. But work is slow-going when you scan a book, show the person on the other side of the cart the cover, laugh at a joke she makes, pause for a second to discuss the O. J. Simpson trial—an obsession you both share—and then break for lunch. We were at the mercy of forces beyond our control. Every new book, every new aisle, promised different avenues of conversation and ways of seeing each other. We talked a lot that summer, we laughed a lot, but I mostly listened. I was enthralled. I stood with a book in one hand and a dormant barcode scanner in the other, taking it all in.

Electra also talked a lot about her mother. She missed her every day, in new ways and old ways, at surprising times and every moment. She talked about New York a little, but with less openness than she talked about her mother. She talked about the strangeness of her new situation. How she felt, sometimes, that she was in the way in this new life, an imposition in a house dominated by a new baby and her young uncle and aunt. She spoke about her feelings with a sort of strangeness; she was a mystery to herself then, like so much of the world. So much of what we thought about was still waiting to be filed away in its proper place: the vagaries of emotion, the substance of Blackness, the weight of grief. What we didn't know was that for some things, there is no permanent place.

Our conversations weren't only heavy things, though. We laughed a lot. She seemed to grow funnier and funnier all the time. Perhaps I was a more willing audience. She made ridiculous puns shamelessly, in English and in French. The previous year we'd both been scheduled to go on the French exchange trip, but issues with terrorism forced the school to postpone to the next year. We were eager to go, but the specter of violence and, possibly, death hung over the idea in a new way. I was nervous; she was excited. Neither of us knew what to expect.

Every day on our lunch break, Electra would drive us to the mall in her car, blasting Madonna the entire way. She loved Madonna. Deeply, passionately, wildly. She listened, it seemed, to nothing but Madonna. In retrospect, it's a period-appropriate choice but also a bold statement at odds with the rest of her personality, which while funny was resolutely subdued. Madonna was cone bras and getting censored on TV and a book about *::whispers::* sex. It wasn't an easy match. I, too, liked Madonna, but my knowledge of her work extended only to the tracks on *The Immaculate Collection* and the soundtrack to

Dick Tracy. This felt like quite a lot to me, but Electra was outraged. I was not a true fan. She was obsessed. She bought every new Madonna CD the week it came out and could list all the tracks in order. She had extensive thoughts on Madge's recent work in *Evita,* as well as past work in *A League of Their Own* and *Who's That Girl*? But her main focus was on the music. She lectured me with a professorial intensity on Madonna's most recent album, *Something to Remember,* and what it meant for her image and her career. "I'm lobbying for 'This Used to Be My Playground' to be our class song at graduation," she said to me one afternoon as we raced back to campus late and covered in Auntie Anne's pretzel butter. "It's the only choice, don't you think?" Prior to the roughly thirty times she'd played the track for me in the car, I'd never heard it, but I was immediately on board. I vowed to vote for the song even though I was not in her class and there was no voting process that either of us was aware of.

Most days at the mall, we'd quickly grab something to eat and then push the technical boundaries of an hour-long break by spending an eternity at Sam Goody, the tape and CD store. Electra would marvel at the poster for Madonna's forthcoming album, *Ray of Light*. "Sandra Bernhard got her into Kabbalah," she told me reverentially. "This album is going to be like nothing we've ever heard before. It's going to change everything." I stared at her with the same awe with which she stared at the poster.

By the time September came, we had restored the library to a state of order and everything had changed about our friendship. We were inseparable. I wonder sometimes how she would tell this story. I wonder whether the force that felt to me simultaneously matter-of-fact and otherworldly struck her as odd and wonderful, too. I wonder, also, knowing who I was then and what was happening beneath the surface, what was happening beneath the surface for her.

In February, Madonna at last released *Ray of Light* and Electra copped it immediately, cranking up the stereo in her car for the title song. "And I feel like I just got home," Madonna cries, the synthesizer shrieking in the background. "And I feel like I just got home." I bought myself a copy and I played it over and over, too, each time finding a new way to understand it and love it. And in March, with the same nonchalance that had become a touchstone, Electra asked me if I wanted to go to senior prom with her. Or rather, I think, we just decided to go. There wasn't any big to-do, no prom-posal or whatever the kids are doing these days. It just seemed like the thing we most wanted to do. "And I feel like I just got home and I feel . . ."

She wore a dark blue strappy evening gown and I rented a tuxedo. She'd hot-combed her hair and a few strands of it fell insistently across one eye to glamorous effect. I brought her an enormous wrist corsage that I'd gotten from the market my father managed. It was truly gargantuan. My father had told the florist that his oldest son was going to prom and he needed the best corsage they'd ever made. The florist delivered a creation that was essentially a bouquet attached to an elastic band. Electra had trouble lifting her arm. The corsage had its own gravitational pull. I think of that corsage a lot when I think about how well my dad loves me, that enormous wrist garden a physical manifestation of joy and pride and care.

Electra and I laughed at the size of the corsage. It seemed a bit ridiculous. Then again, *everything* about prom seemed a bit ridiculous: the awkwardness of taking photos in the vestibule of her house, the fact that my parents had followed the limo I rented in their own car with my ambivalent younger brothers and no less than three cameras, like paparazzi. We were embarrassed and happy and eager to get out of there and loving every minute.

The American Visionary Art Museum is a mosaic-covered building on Baltimore's harbor. The works inside are all by untrained artists, often dubbed outsider artists. Some of them struggle with mental illness or have experienced homelessness or been in jail. Some don't know their work is in a museum at all. It's an institution dedicated to making space for those who've been left out of the traditional art world. The exterior walls are covered by glass and metal and mirrors and found objects that gleam intensely in the sunlight. Inside, the walls are covered with art that is wild and furious and quaint and beautiful and everything in between. Each piece is a portal into an untold story. Behind the museum, in a courtyard, is a tall sculpture barn that used to be a whiskey warehouse. This is where Electra's class chose to hold their prom.

I've always found it funny that though we went to an elite, expensive private school, the prom was held in an artfully and authentically distressed old warehouse with Christmas lights hanging from the ceiling. Twenty years later, that sort of homespun reclaimed style would be all the rage; my own wedding would be overrun with mason jars holding votives in a huge room with broken stained glass and paint peeling off the walls. But in 1997 a dance in a barn seemed positively anti-establishment. These people were swimming in money, and yet when it came time for the biggest formal dance of their high school career, they went for *Charlotte's Web* chic? Some jig.

We giggled our way through a couple of dances, which were just as delightfully awkward as we thought they'd be, and then went inside to explore the artwork. She dazzled me, strolling past outsider art in formal wear, stopping and staring at a canvas, attempting to divine its truth.

Perhaps the thing that is even more overflowing with possibility than a crush is love. In whatever form it takes, from whatever context it is drawn. With a crush, after all, there are sort of only two outcomes when you get down to it: it will bloom or it will wither. But love? Love seems to have infinite possible beginnings, endings, permutations, subtle shifts, and seismic changes. Love, I've learned, is different every time you look at it. Love is every possible love story all at once. Love is a library. And nothing is as fat with possibility as a library.

The month before prom Electra had gone to France. After a semester of hemming and hawing, I decided I was too nervous to go on the exchange trip. And I wasn't certain that I actually knew how to speak French. So I opted out. She was excited about it, though. We talked frequently about what a good time she was going to have; she'd never been and she had high hopes.

On the afternoon she left, just before she was due to join the group and get on the bus to the airport, she poked her head into the library, where I was working. I stepped outside to chat. Was I on a break? Unclear. I was under the impression that talking to Electra was part of my job description.

"Are you excited?" I asked.

She looked away glumly. "I guess," she said.

"Are you nervous?"

"I've been thinking about my mom. I've been thinking about how happy she would be for me. I've been thinking about how I don't want to do this great thing without her being able to see it."

She started to cry. I embraced her. We stayed like that for a while, in the hall outside the library, while a bus idled somewhere nearby, waiting to take her away.

Finally, we separated. We agreed that she should probably get going. We hugged again and I squeezed her and whispered in her ear, "Please have the best time." And then she walked off down the hall to something new and unknown.

I really loved her. Isn't that something? Before I knew myself, before I knew that sexuality was a spectrum, before the difficulties of college and becoming and stepping out into the world, I fell in love with a young woman in high school. We had a friendship that bloomed into a prom date like the culmination of a teen romcom. It's a simple story. And one that could end right there. Except it doesn't. Or rather it won't.

Whenever I talk about Electra, the ending of the story rises up almost of its own volition and then dissolves into questions. And when faced with the end, I can't help but rethink everything we shared before it. Had I really felt what I remember feeling? Or was it just a crush? Did it matter to her like it mattered to me? What was it about that summer in the dusty stacks that changed me so? What was her experience of this period? Who had she been before we met? And what happened after she went away, going to college in Pennsylvania, responding to all of our friends less and less often on Instant Messenger, until she became a question that we asked each other from our far-flung destinations: Have you heard from Electra? Do you know if she's having a good time? Is she doing okay?

And then, the end. The question that lingers to this moment, unanswerable: In April of 2002, I got a call at my parents' house from a high school friend. She wanted to know if I'd heard the terrible news. Earlier that month, the world had lost Electra. My friend on the phone didn't know why, only that Electra had taken her life. No one knew why. And I sank to the floor of my parents' laundry room and stared into the darkness, trying to picture her face, her huge smile, the way she bounced when she walked, even when she was experiencing a mixed emotion, even as she composed herself while leaving the library that afternoon three Aprils prior.

When I was a strange, uncomfortable boy, I met a melancholy, cerebral girl. And none of that exists anymore. But for me it's not locked away in the past. It's unresolved, as if there is still a glimmer of possibility somehow. It's Christmas lights strung across a barn ceiling in anticipation of a magical night, or the release of an album that will change Madonna's life and ours; it's dusty books waiting to be put back in order.

I tell this story to get back there, to unwind the ending, despite the realities of life. And of death. When one tells a story, one has to choose where to stop. So, for every story, there's an infinite number of endings, a library's worth of endings, every book a new chance. Perhaps, for us, for all of us, there are so many endings that they can't all be heartbreaking and baffling.

There must be a place to stop that is just a step into a new possibility.

And so one time our story ends in the car racing toward the mall with Madonna blasting from the stereo, and another under the night sky in the barn's courtyard, and another while she and three others sing "This Used to Be My Playground" at graduation, just like she said she would. And yet another ends the first time she told me her name and I felt bright lights sizzle to life inside me.

I tell this story because of what knowledge it began in me—the complexity of love, the shape-shifting heaviness of grief, and the possibility of tragedy. I tell this story because she left before the end and I'm trying to find her in the darkness. And with her, a piece of myself. I tell this story because I believe that somewhere, still, two teenagers are standing outside a library, and their eyes are ringed with tears. And in this place, she hugs me, and I whisper in her ear, and anything is possible, for anyone. Forever.

Historically Black

When I started getting into colleges just before my eighteenth birthday, each big acceptance package was accompanied by a separate, smaller envelope inviting me to the special weekends designed for students of color. The names were always different—Minority Student Weekend, People of Color Acceptance-Fest, Juneteenth, Super Predator-palooza . . . I'm kidding about some of them. I think. But one college legit called theirs Third World Weekend. It was the late nineties. Things were wild.

The objective was always the same: to give you a taste of what it was like to be a person of color at Cornell or Brown or Yale or wherever. This was odd to me. Like, how Black was this experience going to be? Would there be a mac and cheese bake-off? Was it just going to be forty-eight hours of church? The only thing I knew for sure was that we would definitely be singing the Stevie Wonder version of "Happy Birthday," aka "the only version of 'Happy Birthday,' actually."

(Have you ever been to the birthday party of someone who has a really mixed group of friends and the white people start singing the "regular" version of "Happy Birthday," which, honestly, rivals "Streets of Philadelphia" for atonal glumness, and the Black people launch into Stevie's version and then everyone gets really confused because the white people have no idea what just happened? That's my FAVORITE thing, because I like to imagine that for a brief second the white people think that they've slid into an alternate reality and they have to question everything they know to be true and, honestly, that's reparations. A split second of reparations.)

I'm just saying, there are a lot of Black identities and experiences. And I needed a lot more information, as a nebbishy, sheltered high school senior, about what kind of Black experience I was signing up for during the Kunta Kinte Kollege Kampout. Would there be a place to self-disclose my particular racial experience on the RSVP card? At the time, I considered my racial identity to be "Vanessa Huxtable." So that's a "yes" for jazz, Black history, and small moments of dancing, but a "no" on Tyler Perry films and grills (mouth or backyard). I am not against them; I just don't know how to do them.

And besides, I wasn't aware that my race was going to come into play during this process. Getting into college went from being a hazy, amorphous next step to the goal that I put all of my feelings of self-worth and my parents' hope into. It was a source of pride but I didn't realize that it was also a source of Black Pride. That was a horse of a different colored.

I thought my success was dependent on my brain and not my skin. After all, that's the thing that my parents applauded me for. It would be weird for one's parents to congratulate them on being especially Black today. But maybe that's how other families operated. I wasn't sure but I began to wonder.

If it was a competition (and I wasn't sure it was a competition but it probably was a competition), I knew I wasn't the

Blackest member of my family. I mean, my mother had been involved with the Panthers and my father had taken over the student center at MIT in a civil rights protest during undergrad. Meanwhile, I spent most of my high school years memorizing quotes from *Steel Magnolias*. I'm just saying there's a spectrum.

When I started getting all these invitations for Ivy League race parties, I got really nervous. Was I the Black they were looking for? I wanted to just go to the white weekends, which were always separate. I mean, everyone could go to the white weekends, so they weren't technically white. They were "neutral." It seemed like less trouble, to be honest. I'd been hanging out with white people my whole life; was I suddenly going to become Angela Davis in college? I was doubtful. I was not quite sure how to locate my Blackness, but I knew that my Blackness was definitely not whiteness.

I wanted to be part of the experiences of my people, but a lifetime of feeling slightly uncomfortable all the time suggested that this was not in the (race) cards. I began to realize that I'd built my conception of my racial identity on neutrality and that that didn't jibe with the way the world was going to relate to me. That's why I'd felt out of place in our all-Black church, where the choir swayed in the rhythm and people caught the spirit and I quietly observed. And that's why I'd felt ill-suited to lead the Black Awareness Club (but still ran for president of it because she loves a well-stacked résumé!). Who was I to tell anyone what Blackness was? I didn't know and I couldn't figure out how to find out.

So, true to my nature as someone who literally cannot decide if he wants to be in or out (see also: closets, conference calls, the workforce, church choir, fashion), when it came to the colleges, I went to the all-students weekends at Brown and Princeton and the students-of-color weekends at Columbia and Cornell. At Cornell, my host—a student named Fredo—made me sleep under his bed and told me there was a race war on campus, so I shouldn't talk to any white people. The marching band was really great, though, so all in all it was a fine experience. A little *Malcolm X*-y, a little *Music Man*-y. What more could you want?

I know you'd like more information on this race war situation. Honey, so would I! Fredo was a light-skinned dude with skinny braids lining his scalp. He had no posters on his walls and literally the only thing he said to me was, "I have no room in here. This is a single. You have to sleep under the bed. There's a race war going on. Don't talk to any white people." So I didn't! I mean, would you? People would be coming up to me, asking me where I was from, offering to tell me about their majors and the clubs they were in, and I'd just shake my head like "You ain't bamboozling me, whitey."

It was a really rich experience.

At Princeton, I learned you had to join a club in order to eat! Have you heard about this? Many people have tried to explain this to me over the years, but I refuse to retain anything more than this: In lieu of meal plans, they have eating clubs. They're like fraternities. You join one and maybe live there and also eat all your meals there. "What if no one accepts you into their club?" I asked the tall, ruddy white tour guide on Princeton's campus. He stared at me like I was speaking French and then mumbled an answer which I also refused to retain. I kept imagining myself wandering Princeton's campus, emaciated and desperate because I had failed to find my people. I am not interested in joining anything ever anyway, and now I was going to have to die for it. This put Princeton in the maybe category.

At Columbia, where I would eventually enroll, they put a whole bunch of us in the Pan-African House, which was a two-floor dorm apartment. What I remember most vividly is sleeping on the floor of the common room while a bunch of Black people watched a bootleg copy of *The Matrix*. On the Huxtable scale of Blackness, the experience was a solid Denise.

The part of my brain that is constantly constructing and deconstructing a time machine wonders a lot about the choice I made. Ultimately, I think I was most beguiled by Columbia because of New York. I felt compelled by the city in a way I didn't understand. Its limits and its definitions were attractive but ambiguous, and I was drawn, most of all, to the mystery. I didn't have those words then, of course. All I knew was I had to leave my home and see Broadway shows and meet people who told witty stories about international travel and perhaps dye my hair or consider a piercing at once if not sooner. At this evening's performance, the role of R. Eric Thomas will be played by Saoirse Ronan in *Lady Bird*.

Having arrived on campus—in a full moving truck! God bless my long-suffering parents and their tireless commitment to their eccentric Auntie Mame son—I was unsure what I was supposed to . . . do. I was ostensibly part of a class, a school, a culture, a race, a city, but determining what that meant or where the entry point was proved to be a challenge. I realized I had never thought about what college was for. College was just the thing you did at the beginning of the montage, and at the end of the montage you're Toni Morrison. That was my whole plan: be Toni Morrison. Why didn't I just go to Princeton, where she taught at the time? Because it seemed super white, if you want the truth. And I didn't want to starve to death.

Columbia offered a regular meal plan that didn't require having any aptitude for social interactions, so I went there.

During my first week of school I received an email about the first meeting of the Black Student Union. I stared at the screen, once again not comprehending. Was this for me specifically? What did they want from me? How did they know I was Black? Was I being catfished? And for what purpose? Is this how they got my ancestors on the ships—invitations to club meetings sent by email? Plausible. I told myself that I wouldn't be joining the Black Student Union at Columbia because I never wanted to participate in any activity ever. Honestly, I was just nervous that there was going to be a quiz. Even though I'd been president of the Black Awareness Club in high school, there were few Black students in my year and one of my science classes included whale-watching in Provincetown, so it wasn't exactly Wakanda. The Columbia BSU felt markedly different from the Black Awareness Club, like I was stepping into the major leagues after hanging out on the farm team for years. There'd only been maybe ten of us in the club, a quarter of them white. The BSU filled a classroom and included undergrads and grad students. There was something about it that communicated Official Blackness to me.

When I got the email about the first BSU meeting at Columbia, I leaned out of my dorm window to look at the space in the basement of Hamilton Hall where it would be held, as if the opaque windows of the building would reveal how African American this experience was going to be. "Bring your kufi, we going in!" I ended up walking by it a day later when the meeting was about to start, searching the faces of the people walking in for a hint of acceptance or judgment or betrayal. They didn't seem to notice me.

And so I went about my year, avoiding the BSU and instead making a group of friends so diverse we could have starred in an early-2000s Disney Channel show. Looking back, particularly at the group of students that comprised my first-year suite, it's almost a parody of Benetton-ad realness. We spanned races, cultural backgrounds, nationalities, abilities, and sexual orientations. A blind Persian boy with a love for N.W.A lived next door to an out gay boy from Staten Island with a Nick Carter haircut and a stereo that constantly played club music; across the common room was a willowy French Canadian girl who seemed bemused by all of our interactions and in my memories is always in pajamas; catty-corner to her, a goth girl with a huge comics collection and a devotion to *Hedwig and the Angry Inch*. We were all, to some extent, friends by nature of proximity, and they formed the basis for the friendships I sought out as the year progressed. And in those groupings, I was nominally Black but not, you know, officially African American. Or so I thought.

However, the facts were these: I had a merit-based scholarship that was earmarked for students of color; I was, mysteriously, on the BSU mailing list; and, at some point in the application process, I had self-identified as Vanessa Huxtable and some admissions officer had puzzled over that for a hot minute and then finally marked my race down in a file somewhere. And while I thought that my race was incidental information in my friend groups and in my place at the school, as time went on it kept popping up in odd but consequential ways.

I feel like I should give you a little context right now: When I started at Columbia, the president of the university was a guy named George Rupp. This was in 1999. I never met George Rupp and I actually had to look this information up because I am not a podcaster named Alex and, apparently, I didn't pay enough attention to important things like knowing the name of the president when I was in college. Ah, well. You can't learn everything. That's going to be the motto of my college when I start one: Thomas University—you can't learn everything!

Anyway, George Rupp announced his retirement in March of 2001 and was succeeded, in 2002, by Lee Bollinger, who'd previously been the president of the University of Michigan. Neither of these men had too direct an impact on my life—in fact, by the time Lee Bollinger officially began his tenure I was already at a different school. *However,* the important thing about Lee Bollinger here is not so much what he did at Columbia but what he did *before*. In 1997, a student named Barbara Grutter sued the University of Michigan Law School, and then-university-president Lee Bollinger, because Grutter had been denied admission in 1996. She surmised that her earned spot had been taken by a less qualified student who was admitted through affirmative action. The case that she brought contended that the affirmative action policy was unconstitutional, and it went all the way to the Supreme Court. The court eventually ruled in the school's favor but, obviously, as you are reading this in a less affirmative, more inactive future, the policy would remain contentious and would continue to be chipped away at for years.

So, when I first arrived at Columbia, *Grutter v. Bollinger* had just started making its way through the lower court system and affirmative action was all anybody seemed to want to talk about. It was a hot-button topic on the news, it was widely discussed on campus, and it was a question that hung, in my experience, over every admission. Once I was walking through campus with a friend and he asked me what I got on my SATs, which is the sort of question that is only not insanely random for a few years of your life. It's odd, this period during which the prevailing assessment of your academic potential (and worth as a candidate for a successful future) is contained in a number that seems to be everyone's business. It's like there was a Freedom of Information Act request filed by all the people at your church, your parents' jobs, your school, and any random truck stop.

Anyway, even though this was late in my first year and I had begun to suspect that my worth wasn't bound up in those four digits, I wasn't totally sure about that, so I told him. Offhandedly, he said, "Oh, you must be affirmative action." And then he kept talking about the paper we had to write on *Song of Solomon*.

Sometimes I think about the nonchalance of his assessment and that stings me; sometimes I think about the haze of confusion that settled around me as we continued to walk through the sunny springtime campus and that brings me low. Sometimes what sticks is just being asked the question at all and having a simple fact be a trap that I could so guilelessly walk into. A trap that hadn't been set by an individual but rather by a circumstance.

These were the moments when I was reminded that no matter how passively I engaged with my Blackness, it was never not a force at work in my life. And, I found, the knowledge of my Blackness could be used as a weapon against me at any moment.

All my life I'd operated under the assumption that there were many kinds of Blackness. I saw the variety of experiences on campus, in the church congregation at home, at family reunions. And I assumed that eventually I'd learn how to navigate them, to feel comfortable in spaces where I felt not Black enough or the wrong kind of Black. Or, if I didn't learn to navigate them, I thought, perhaps this wider exposure at Columbia could offer me a path to change. I could be a different kind of Black. But in that passing moment, during the conversation about the SATs, it occurred to me that no matter where I was, perhaps there was only one kind of Black.

From then on, everything about Columbia had an asterisk for me. Everyone, from the faceless admissions officers to the Black Student Union to my friend, seemed to have a more accurate read on me than I did. I started to see myself in a kaleidoscope, dividing and doubling, going in and out of focus. Had I gotten in because of who I was or had I gotten in because of my Blackness? And if I'd gotten in because of my Blackness, was it an issue that I couldn't figure out how to define my Blackness or engage with it? Was it a problem that I didn't really know who I was, Black or otherwise, anymore?

When I started college, I carried with me the good wishes and hopes of the community that I came from, some who knew what an opportunity like Columbia could provide, and others—like many members of our church—who had never heard of the school before but had a blind faith that I was headed toward something extraordinary. But what I wasn't prepared for was the way the world that I knew seemed to constantly take on new definitions and features. Sometimes piece by piece, sometimes all at once. I think the simplest way of putting it is that nothing I'd arrived thinking felt true anymore. But, I suspected, if I simply tried to ignore the shifting understanding of Blackness and its connection to my sense of worth, if I never actually acknowledged this feeling, I might never have to look it or myself in the face.

Turns out I was wrong. College revealed me, suddenly, like the villain at the end of an episode of *Scooby-Doo*. I would have gotten away with it, if only it hadn't been for those meddling kids in the Black Student Union.

Disorientation

I had never seen anything so beautiful in my life as the Columbia University 1999–2000 course catalog. A thick, printed brick of possibility, it provided a blueprint for getting a degree. More important, to a new student laying eyes on it for the first time, it seemed like a Cheesecake Factory menu of potential knowledge. When you go to the Cheesecake Factory, you know that you can't eat everything, but for a brief halcyon moment, as you peruse the Bang Bang Chicken and Shrimp, you believe you *could*. Electives, it turns out, were my Bang Bang Chicken and Shrimp. Sure, you're supposed to complete your requirements first, but, like an eighteen-year-old Bartleby the Scrivener, I announced, "I elect not to." The possibilities were too alluring to wait. In my first year at Columbia, I was repeatedly drawn to electives that focused on Latin American history and postcolonial literature, texts concerned with the aftermath of imperialism, particularly British imperialism. What I know now but couldn't have articulated then was that I was searching for an understanding of Otherness outside of the context in which I existed, which I found in postcolonial studies. Surprisingly, I also found literature and histories that centered on people who had been othered inside their own narratives, despite what a Eurocentric perspective might suggest. I drank it up.

Some of these texts also challenged heteronormativity in the same way that they challenged Eurocentricity, which I was not expecting. I kept stumbling across ideas that sparked foreign feelings in, say, an essay about Orientalism and homoerotics, or a Native American fable about a two-spirit person, or *Maurice,* a British queer love story by E. M. Forster. What I'm trying to tell you is that postcolonialism turned me gay.

My memories from that time come in flashes, scenes. Like the one Latin American history professor who regularly gave us updates on her gay brother who was also her psychic. I wasn't sure how this would help me in a future career, but I found it endlessly fascinating. In another class, we read and dissected Salman Rushdie's latest novel, *The Ground Beneath Her Feet*. I'd never read Rushdie before and would stay up late into the night, poring over the unruly sentences again and again in awe. The novel is a wild, sexy gloss on the Orpheus and Eurydice myth, set to a rock beat and framed by a collision between Eastern and Western cultures. It spoke about intersection and Otherness and love in a way that felt more powerful than anything I'd ever read before. Bits and snatches of the novel buried themselves inside me, like the pithy refrain that pops up over and over again in the text: "Disorientation. Loss of the East." It was a literal definition of a term, as well as an invocation of a state of being that spoke to me. What, I wondered, was my East? And what waited beyond the horizon?

During freshman orientation week, I had to attend an interactive assembly run by a team of trained facilitators that was meant to introduce different ideas around diversity and sensitivity. The word on the street was that it was just a bunch of people talking about not saying racial slurs and that one of the facilitators was gay. Even though this was New York City in the late nineties, the presence of a gay person at this event was still remarkable enough to comment on.

This diversity assembly therefore seemed like an entertaining affair all-around and it was mandatory, so I went. Their presentation was fine; I learned all the racial slurs I shouldn't say. (I'm kidding. There's too many for one workshop.) Afterward, they had a Q&A. One student, a Black kid, asked a question about language used to talk about LGBTQ people. The (gay!) facilitator responded, "Good question! Clap it up for this guy! Okay, one of the things that gay people prefer—actually, are you gay?" The Black kid paused and then replied yes, he was. The answer went on. We were all enlightened. But, we later learned, this was the first time that the Black kid had been asked that question, and having to answer it in that way, on the first day of college, had been devastating. A year later, they were still talking about the incident in the Student Affairs Office, where I'd gotten a work-study job. They used it as an object lesson, warning us to be vigilant in all things sensitivity.

But they didn't have to tell me twice. I never forgot the way that kid had tensed and twisted ever so slightly. I never forgot the clear feeling that the room was not safe in a way that was very specific and which perhaps we both understood. I never forgot how I'd craned my neck to see his face, because I wanted to know if I'd recognize what I saw. Even though I'd never verbalized it, I knew instantly that being asked "Are you gay?" was the worst possible thing that could happen. I marveled that he hadn't spontaneously combusted. I decided on the first day that college would be a place of miracles and also of terror. I willed myself not to react as it was happening, for fear they'd poll the room for homosexuals, both known and oblivious. Although I wouldn't allow myself to put a name to it at the time, the fact that I felt a visceral kinship with this kid should have been all the proof I needed. Either that or the fact that I looked at his face and its deep dark skin and thought, *He is the most beautiful boy in the world and yet he looks so sad. I would like to kiss his eyelids.* I do not know why I wanted to kiss his eyelids; I didn't know how kissing worked. I didn't know how anything worked.

And so, to learn, I decided to do some research. During my first year, I'd clocked that there was a Queer Student Alliance on campus and also a confidential meeting called the Coming Out Group, for queer and questioning students. The Queer Student Alliance seemed too revealing an endeavor for me to even acknowledge, so I set my sights on the Coming Out Group. As I understood from reading a thirty-word description in the activities book and asking exactly zero questions of anyone, it was a casual discussion group where member identities were held in confidence to allow students the space to process their sexuality. Obviously, this was a great space for me, so naturally I distrusted it.

First of all, I kept misremembering it as a secret group. Discreet and secret are not the same thing, apparently. And because I was constantly mischaracterizing the group as akin to some sort of spy organization and not just a support group, I had some major doubts about this so-called secrecy. Like, they advertised the time and location. Any idiot could just stand in the bushes and watch people going in and know they were gay. Which is what I did. I am nothing if not any idiot.

That semester, every Tuesday around 7 P.M. I would wander over to the chapel where the meetings were held, sometimes with a cappuccino or a candy bar in hand—good stakeout food—and I would situate myself in the bushes across the walkway from the entrance. I'd observe the people going in with all the attention and all the nuance of Gladys Kravitz, the nosy neighbor from *Bewitched*. Then, after the meeting began, I'd walk slowly by the door, staring at it as if it would give up an elemental secret from sheer force of my passive-aggressive will. Then I would go back to my dorm, read *Maurice*, and listen to Ani DiFranco.

It was an interesting experiment in reconciling my outward assumptions about people and their inner truths. *That man has a yarmulke,* I'd marvel, while devouring my Kit Kat bar, *and yet he is gay.* The solution to all of my problems was to go inside. The issue with my solution was that all my problems were inside. And so I remained, shrouded in leaves, feet in the dirt.

It wasn't until I received an email from the Black Student Union at the beginning of my sophomore year that I was prompted to move my feet. As you'll recall, I'd received a surprising email from the BSU at the start of my freshman year. This was a *second* email. These people were relentless. While the email I'd received my first year had been a simple invitation that I viewed with great suspicion, this second email was completely different. "Congratulations," the missive from the faceless collective read, "you're a Black Student Union student mentor this year!"

Honestly, who were the Black people running this club? Show yourselves! I looked at the email like "Harpo, who dis woman?" They wanted me to mentor a first-year student. No, not just wanted. Demanded. I read it. I reread it. I closed the browser. I walked downstairs—still in the same building as my first year—and stared at the walls of Hamilton Hall and the little basement room where, I presumed, the Black Student Union spent every meeting figuring out ways to torment me with allegations that I was, in some way, one of them.

"You've been assigned as a mentor for first-year student Quentin Brick!" the email read.* The audacity of the exclamation point made me lose my breath. "Reach out to your mentee as soon as possible, make sure to show them the ropes, give them insight into what your experience has been like as a Black student at Columbia; share any wisdom and good guidance you've gleaned from your first year." On every point of the assignment I felt wholly unqualified. I did not know of what ropes they spoke. (Perhaps in the gym? Unclear.) In my first year, I had very intentionally not joined the Black Student Union, no offense; I'd joined a couple of writing-related clubs, made friends in my dorm, gone to class most of the time, read a lot, and downloaded a lot of Ani on Napster. Nothing about this struck me as particularly Black, let alone significant enough to pass down to someone else. What did the email see in me?

The empty Black Student Union meeting room offering no answers, I decided I had no other choice but to find this Quentin person. What I would do after I found him was still a question mark. Maybe a fist bump? Possibly.

At the time, it was super easy to stalk people at Columbia because online privacy policies were basically a shrug emoji, so I was able to look Quentin up, find his phone number, his student mailbox number, and his room number. He was in the same building as I was, situated between my room and the

* This is not his real name. I've changed it because the first rule of mentorship is "Leave me out of your book, please."

Black Student Union offices. I wouldn't even have to put on shoes for this farce. I looked him up in the actual face book, a printed book they would put out for every class that just had people's faces in it. It was really ingenious. He stared back at me—Black of course; skin tone a bit darker than mine, perhaps; a shy grin; short hair like mine. A mirror, of sorts. And a mystery.

I felt bad that he'd been stuck with me, honestly. I wished someone had conscripted some other random Black person to mentor me a year earlier. Actually! Why hadn't they dragged some Black dude, kicking and screaming, to my door to offer me words of wisdom, and give me copies of his notes on *The Iliad,* and buy me fashionable sweaters, and stay up all night, braiding my hair as we parsed the construct of race? (This is mentorship, right?)

I opened an email and began to compose an invitation to Quentin to meet, but I was immediately struck by the same question that had been plaguing me from the start: What sort of (presumably Black) experience was I to offer this boy? How does one even start such a thing? "Glad tidings! I, a Black, am to offer you guidance and wisdom for your journey, like the eccentric good witch Miss One in the movie *The Wiz*. You know *The Wiz*? It's the all-Black version of *The Wizard of Oz,* but don't refer to it like that. It diminishes it. 'Home'? Ever heard of it? At every grade school talent show ever, somewhere between 'The Greatest Love of All' and 'Hero'? It's a real delight."

I deleted the whole thing and forgot about it. If they were going to insist that I was already in community with other Black people, they were going to have to come and find me and prove it. I was busy! I was a sophomore now; I'd been elected to student government; I was in a multiracial production of *Once on This Island;* I was stalking the Coming Out Group; I was very involved in writing barely disguised short fiction about my inner turmoil about possibly maybe potentially being not totally 100 percent straight; and I'd started working for Student Affairs.

And then one day Quentin Brick emailed me out of the blue, which, frankly, seemed a bit forward. Kids those days. He mentioned that he knew we lived in the same building (a bold claim!) and asked if I wanted to meet in the lobby to chat. The lobby had a number of easily accessible exits, so I agreed. I certainly didn't know what I was going to say to him. I had very little to offer. The most unique information I could offer was which bushes to avoid because they had sharp branches, and a long list of people who, based on the rooms they walked into, were probably gay.

He was sitting alone on a sofa, staring out the glass doors of the dorm lobby, when I arrived. He sat hunched forward, his thin shoulders in a defensive sort of curl. He was slight and looked even younger than he had in his picture. I recognized him as my contemporary but I also saw in him a fragility that I knew all too well and fought to keep at bay. He saw me enter and gave a big, open smile. *Somebody really should mentor this kid,* I thought. Quentin said he just wanted to meet me. It was good to make connections at school, he reasoned. This had never occurred to me. I considered asking him to be *my* mentor. He asked how I'd found my first year. I told him I'd enjoyed it, complained about a couple of the classes, and tried to maintain the appearance of someone who was wise and yet accessible. I said, "We should get a cappuccino sometime!" I'd just discovered coffee and coffee shop beverages and was very interested in bragging about it to everyone like I was the first imperialist off the boat in Colombia. He said that sounded fun. I asked him what the Black Student Union meetings were like. He gave an embarrassed smile and admitted he'd never been. "They just emailed me with an assignment," he said. *Who were these sociopaths?!* It was starting to seem perfectly plausible that the Black Student Union didn't exist at all, but was rather a psychological experiment or a well-intentioned but aggressive algorithm. That's also a metaphor for race, I suppose, but obviously I didn't know that then.†

I became a little obsessed with talking about the invisible hand of Black Student Union. (Invisible raised fist? Maybe. Let's workshop it.) I brought it up to all of my friends, most of whom were not Black. Nobody thought it was as odd as I did that I was getting emails from them. In fact, most people were a little confused about why I didn't just go to the club.

I didn't follow through with Quentin about the coffee, because I am a flaky person. Instead, my activities, particularly Student Affairs, became a comforting distraction that kept me from having to investigate the various parts of my identity. The office had two deans with whom I was obsessed, a man named Ron and a woman named Kenya. I have only had a handful of Black teachers or administrators in my life, and I remember

† God, imagine trying to explain constructs to me at that point in my life and in the social development of the United States. I would have stared at you blankly and then called the authorities on a phone attached to a wall. "Hello? Is this Bill Clinton, who some people are unabashedly calling our first Black president? I know you've just left office but I need your help. I'd like to report a race thought crime."

(Our first Black president! The audacity of reality is stunning! The saxophone isn't even that Black an instrument. I mean, every instrument is Black if you play it right. But it's not like Bill Clinton went on *Arsenio Hall* with a djembe. Lord!)

them all with a truly terrifying level of detail. I would encounter a Black person in a position of intellectual or cultural authority and I would perform a full-body scan like I was a 3-D printer or a TSA agent, all the while gawking, slack-jawed. I wanted to memorize these people. Kenya moved through the world with a level of authority and command that laid me all the way out. She would stride into the office, give me a pleasant greeting, and then move on to whatever was pressing and I would actually get light-headed like a teenager seeing the Beatles. Kenya was also the first person I ever encountered who carried hot sauce in her purse. She was full-time Black. Once, she was headed off to some fancy Columbia dinner with, I don't know, Yo-Yo Ma and Maya Angelou, and she stopped in the doorway of her office to ensure that her little bottle of Frank's was in her bag. I literally said aloud, "That is the Blackest thing I have ever seen in my entire life." I was awed.

Kenya was definitely someone who wouldn't even *think* of allowing hateration in a dancery. She was erudite and kind and intelligent and clearly making paper and also Black as hell and I was shewk. Ron's presence was an equally stunning force in my life, though he worked with students more closely and had a more casual relationship with us. Kenya was like Mount Rushmore and Ron was like the park ranger who leads a guided tour. He had a level of accessibility and a beguiling version of masculinity that was completely foreign to me. Little details about him—his sense of humor, his aesthetic, his excellent ability to roll his eyes, his very moisturized skin—glimmered and glinted like light on sequins. Ron felt so safe. The importance and the rarity of that in a time when I felt constantly at risk, in my racial understanding of myself and in my acceptance of my sexual orientation, can't be overstated. I was obsessed with the two of them, with their takes on Blackness. I kept thinking, *If only there was some sort of culturally recognized structure whereby older people could help guide, instruct, and advise younger people. Wouldn't that be great? Ah well, maybe in the next life.*

As sophomore year went on, it got too cold to be lurking outside the Coming Out Group. I started staying in on Tuesdays and glowering at the walls while drinking cappuccino. This was not satisfying at all. In retrospect, I realize what I wanted to do was migrate inside, meet some people, kiss some eyelids. But what my brain heard was "stalk differently." The Queer Student Alliance held a dance on the first Friday of every month that they went to great pains to advertise as "for everybody." I wasn't fooled, obviously. That's how they get you: Come to this "for everybody" dance, speak with other humans, suddenly be a gay. Not on my watch!

But after a while, I got antsy. I started to wonder if maybe I could just, like, go to the dance as a representative of "everybody." Like, definitely not saying anything about myself. Just enjoying this everybody dance as a regular person.

On the first Friday of February, I walked down the metal stairs into the multipurpose space. Slashes of pink light cut across my feet and worked their way up my body as I descended. *This is just a dance party,* I told myself. *There's a lot of people here and it's dark and it doesn't prove anything.* My goal was to get in, definitely not dance, and leave after making a thorough visual inspection of who was there. My stalking had leveled up: I was willing to go on queer reconnaissance missions in service of completing my mental index of all known homosexuals. I could dress it up and say I was trying to normalize it, but honestly I was just a weirdo.

Seeing myself in the crowd proved to be a challenge at the First Friday Dance for a number of reasons, not the least of which was that there wasn't much of a crowd. Hardly anyone had shown up, even though the dance was one-third over. One of the ways I express my cultural heritage is by always being late, but, honestly, New York City constantly thwarted me. The dance was advertised as starting at 8 and ending at 11 P.M. After that, the word on the street was, people would go across to the West End, a bar that sort of carded but not really. I've never been cool enough to understand what that kind of arrangement meant, so I'd decided to just go to the party. I waited for what I thought was an appropriate amount of time in order to show up fashionably late. Literally sitting in my room, fully dressed, staring at the window until 9:55 P.M. *Should be on and popping by now,* I said to myself as I took the elevator down and moseyed across campus to the queer dance party, wearing what I'm sure were cargo pants and a flannel shirt or something equally tragic. But like my attire, my lateness was apparently not fashionable enough.‡

I stared blankly at the dance floor, dotted with a handful of people nodding their heads to club music. In the musical version of this scene, a salty drag queen appears from a crevice in a wall,

‡ Honestly, I do not know what New York City wants from me on this point. Nowadays when I go out in the city, people don't show up to places until one or two in the morning. Some places don't even get started until after last call, which is at four. Four in the morning is objectively the next day and I will hear nothing else about it. If Melanie Griffith's *Working Girl* shoulder pads are already on a ferry sailing across the Hudson to the strains of Carly Simon's "Let the River Run," then your ass should not be just paying the cover charge. It is outrageous.

smoking a cigarette. "Welcome to being gay," she spits, before working up a hacking cough. It's strange when the thing behind the door isn't terrifying or wonderful, but rather just plain. When you find your people and realize they're just people.

I didn't drink at that point but I had somehow already developed an instinct for avoiding social discomfort by going to the bar. This was an 18+ college event, so the bar in question was a juice bar. I have to say, I miss juice bars. They always sounded so luxurious, like a counter at a resort; in my mind they seemed like the kind of place you could get a papaya juice or a coconut water in an actual coconut. In reality, they were regular bars, staffed by bored people who offered you soda, water, or cranberry or pineapple juice. I don't want to blow the juice bar industry wide open, but half of those options aren't even juice. And yet, my fruity luxurious life began the night of the First Friday Dance, where I encountered my first juice bar and behind it, Quentin Brick.

"Justin!" I cried with a mix of shock and chagrin (my signature fragrance).

"It's Quentin," he corrected me. Really killing it on the mentorship front, I have to say.

"What are you doing here?" I asked, surveying their selection of sodas and canned juices with widening eyes.

"I volunteered," he said. I stared at him like the lead character in *A Beautiful Mind* trying to figure out the hidden equation. If he was volunteering, did that mean that he wasn't . . . associated with the dance and the known homosexuals therein? Or did he volunteer because he *was* part of the club? Was he "everybody"? Or was it like Aaliyah says, "Tell me are you that somebody?" How did one determine this kind of information? You know, beyond asking or having any sort of human interaction. What I'm saying is, was there a secret code of some sort?

I asked Quentin for a pineapple juice and then lingered at the bar, looking for obvious signs that he was, in fact, "that somebody." He served a soda to someone else and then turned to me. "I've heard this party used to be super popular," he said. "That's why I'm here. People used to come to it from other parts of the city. It was, like, a gay hangout for real."

I nodded cautiously. The words "a gay hangout" seemed awfully gauche; I mean, was he just openly saying what this place was and who was in it? If I had had pearls, they would have been clutched.

"Who'd you hear that from?" I asked, mentally preparing to record the name of another known homosexual.

"This guy I dated," Quentin said. "He was older."

My mouth fell open and I shoved the pineapple juice into it to disguise my shock. Quentin Brick was that somebody. Aaliyah's voice echoed through the empty dance floor, up the pink staircase, and out into the world.

Quentin Brick, my *mentee,* invited himself over to watch a movie. I felt like I couldn't say no—this was, after all, part of my duty as the most committed member of the Black Student Union—but I was also acutely aware that agreeing to it was an acknowledgment of something greater, something that was still a shapeless country over the horizon, undiscovered and nameless. At the time, I owned three DVDs and Netflix didn't exist, so we watched *The Sixth Sense*. It's a thoroughly re-watchable movie because it's so well structured and everyone in the cast is divine, especially Toni Collette. Perfect fodder for intelligent discourse that never crosses any sort of line nor resolves itself into any identity categories. I wondered if this was a date. I wondered if I thought it was a date. I wondered if he thought it was a date. I thought about asking Toni Collette but that seemed excessive.

Quentin arrived on time even though he was a New York native and I'd expected him to be fashionably late. I was prepared to watch the movie any time between 7 P.M. and 5 A.M., to be honest. You really just never know. I had also made plans for later in the evening to go see a movie with two friends from my floor. In the retelling, it sounds like I had a really full social life, but I assure you that these two events were the only things on my calendar all semester, and because I am an inveterately flaky person, I scheduled them on the same night.

Quentin sat on my bed and I was suddenly aware of him as a person in a way that I felt like I hadn't been aware before. All the things that felt personal and yet incidental played out in my senses: the aroma of his fabric softener rising off his clothes, the texture of his skin, the sound of his breathing, the curl of his lips, the shape of his teeth. I looked at him on my bed, then I looked directly at the wall where I imagined the television camera was beaming my exploits to the folks at home. I raised my eyebrows like "This is already too much."

I popped the movie into the CD-ROM drive on my computer and slid down onto the floor. Quentin scooted over on the bed but I assured him I was fine where I was. The floor is great. I love the floor. *The Sixth Sense* proceeded Sixth Sensibly. Midway through the movie my dorm phone rang. I paused the DVD. Haley Joel Osment's face filled the computer screen, terrified and tearful. I answered the phone. It was my friends calling from the lobby of the movie theater to see if I was coming. I hesitated. Quentin slid over to me and kissed my free ear. I froze. I could smell Quentin's fabric softener mixing with whatever mysterious aroma was just himself. Little molecules of himself secreted themselves inside me. I turned back to him and smiled. Well, I probably grimaced pleasantly. It was the best I could do. I told my friends I wouldn't make it. I hung up and turned back to Quentin. Haley Joel Osment continued to stare, traumatized, from my computer screen.

What followed was a full-on disaster. Quentin and I started to date in a weird tentative way that involved watching movies, kissing a little, and me freaking out and leaving. I'm not sure this is what the Black Student Union meant when they asked me to show him the ropes, but I guess we'll never know. They weren't specific. We went through all the normal things you do when you date someone early in college—hanging out, talking, eating meals in the dining hall together—but every moment felt fraught and life-altering and joyous all at once. It felt something like freedom and something like damnation. The fact that I sometimes enjoyed dating a boy was, to say the least, disconfirming information for a Christian, Black-esque straight person who spent his free time carefully curating an Audra McDonald fan page on the internet. And it didn't feel like there were two sides of me fighting for dominance; it felt like I was coming apart at some basic level, like I was becoming diffuse, like water becomes mist. And that, honestly, was too dramatic, even for me.

A part of me held on to the conservative teachings from my Black Baptist church, where being gay was such a sin it wasn't even spoken of. I didn't go to a church where the pastor delivered spittle-flecked invective about the danger of homosexuals; I went to a church where gays didn't exist and if you were one, you ceased to exist in the eyes and lives of the congregation. But despite what I knew to be true of the place I came from, I couldn't think of being attracted to Quentin as wrong. I also couldn't think of it as right. It was something else altogether. It wasn't a collision, but an expansion. I hadn't expected that. I felt like I was drifting toward an understanding of myself that I couldn't comprehend.

At least it seemed like drifting, though in the writing of this it's clear that I was also captaining my ship. Or at least nudging the helm, raising the sail, letting the wind take me. The intentions behind my actions truly felt like they belonged to someone else, not outside myself but somehow beside the person I was before college.

Quentin had dated other guys in high school, many of them older; he was experienced and savvy. He didn't seem to struggle in the ways that I did, having somehow managed to find a way to cobble together an identity that included a devout religious practice, an active queer life, and a closeted self for the sake of his family. Our dates were frequently arranged around long-planned family obligations or his regular weekend practice of religious witnessing on the street. Once I ran into him in the hall as he returned from standing on the street corner where he and another member of his church routinely gave out tracts, pamphlets made for converting people. He was wearing a simple blue dress shirt and dress pants and seemed to carry himself differently. His face lit up when he saw me, but I drew back. I didn't recognize that part of him. He got mad at me for my reticence. Despite the email from the Black Student Union, I couldn't believe that he was my people. His religious life and his family life were distinct and walled off from his queer life, necessarily so. And the distance made them seem extreme to me. And dangerous.

The world of proselytizing, as I knew it, was full of condemnation and a strict adherence to rules. The goal was to reach sinners, after all, and bring them into rightness with God. Quentin said that he was doing it as an obligation, but I assumed that he must have believed in what he was preaching as well. I think what I was shocked by, then, was an absence of shame, either for being a person of faith or for being gay. There was a defiance in him that I knew I didn't possess. Under his fabric softness, he was steely, solid. He had made a decision.

As loath as I was to admit it, I had also made a decision, however passively. A sin by drifting. But I didn't expect that once I'd started drifting, I wouldn't just float off into some indeterminate destiny. Rather, it was like an explosion had blown me out of my own life, decimating everything that I knew, catapulting me away from my East. Everything about my experience at Columbia suddenly began to fall apart. But maybe it was always falling apart, getting more diffuse, small explosions sending identities careening toward each other, definitions of self, like detritus, landing just out of reach. I was coming apart. Quentin saw that and wisely broke off our dates. It was better for us to be friends, he said. And my freak-outs had gotten to be too much. My mentee knew there were some things I had to explore on my own.

I didn't. I returned to my room. I didn't go to any more dances. I withered in my academic pursuits, too, the wide world of knowledge that I had so eagerly sought now passing in front of me, unprocessed, unlearned. I remained, in many ways, still hidden in the bushes outside the Coming Out Group, candy bar in hand, leaves in my face. But the ground beneath my feet was quickly falling away.

Someone Is Wrong on the Internet

It was accidental, and it was little by little, but at Columbia, I stopped being "good." When it became purposeful and more sudden, the only way I could understand it was to look at it from the outside, like fiction. Like it wasn't happening to me. There's this scene I can't shake from the title story in ZZ Packer's book *Drinking Coffee Elsewhere*. The main character, Dina, is attending college orientation. She's a Black woman who is maybe probably queer. She's starting at Yale after growing up in a lower-class Baltimore neighborhood. To say that Dina and I had something in common back when I read the book the summer before freshman year would be an understatement. But you couldn't have told me that then. I literally had no idea. I didn't even drink coffee back then. Honey, I was about to go through it.

There were moments I thought to myself, *Oh, baby, you are gay.* But I didn't say it like that. If anybody had spoken to me like that then, I would have set my hair on fire. Instead it was like *What if I was . . . gay?* Which is not a "good" thought for a churchgoing, pious, straight virgin to have. So I didn't have those thoughts. I thought about other things. I thought about Dina.

In the story, Dina is at an orientation icebreaker and is suddenly, awkwardly, aware of herself. The orientation leader asks the students, "If you had to be an object, what would you be?" Dina's answer: a revolver.

There's a moment of silence. The words hang in the air like a vulture. Dina, in her narration, confides in us, "I don't know why I said it. Until that moment I'd been good in all the ways that were meant to matter." Even though I didn't have a real conscious awareness of how closely my narrative would follow Dina's when I set off for Columbia at eighteen, her summation of her precollege life hit home.

I had been good in all the ways you were supposed to be good. My only predominant personality trait was "good." I wasn't sporty; I wasn't cool; I was good. I was smart enough, I guessed, but not as smart as I could be. After all, I'd been wait-listed at Harvard, so essentially I was a moron.

Like Dina, sometimes I'd step outside myself and wonder why I was even entertaining the notion of not being "good." *I didn't work so hard to leave Baltimore just to come to New York to turn gay,* I'd think. Which is hilarious because that's the reason 65 percent of people leave home and come to New York. That's the city's slogan: "Come here and tongue kiss a boy or whatever. Then write a solo show about it. BTW, the L train isn't running this weekend." Anyway, I was pressed. And my grades started slipping, which wasn't good, and I started drinking, which wasn't good, and I was sad, like, all the time, which seemed kind of normal, to be honest, but also not good. And then, at the beginning of the second semester of my junior year, I received a letter that said, "Hon, you're a mess. Take a minute, go for a soak in a tub, buy an olive grove and rediscover yourself like Diane Lane in *Under the Tuscan Sun,* something. Just. Like. Stop."

Actually it just said, "You're on academic probation." And

told me to make arrangements to spend the next semester elsewhere.

So, suddenly, at twenty years old, I was home again, in Baltimore. And I was sad and I was tired and I was maybe probably gay. And I was no longer good. I began to suspect I was a revolver.

In the absence of good, what is there? I felt I'd disappointed my parents. And my church. And my whole race, actually. Isn't that the prevailing narrative for people in oppressed groups of all kinds: your ancestors suffered so you could achieve, so you better achieve. Rosa Parks didn't sit on that bus for me to go to New York and turn gay.

I was living in my parents' basement, and I had started taking classes at the University of Maryland, Baltimore County (UMBC). I was unable to figure out how to be good again after failing my family and my race. And in the midst of all that, I accidentally pointed a spotlight at myself by going viral on the early internet. Don't get me wrong—I wanted to be famous. But I wanted it to happen when I was R. Eric Thomas, Ivy League success story, not R. Eric Thomas, basement-dwelling internet troll. But you get what you get, I guess.

In 2002 the internet was still in its Wild West days—there was no Twitter, no YouTube. It was a lot harder to go viral back in those days. Which is my way of saying you should be impressed.

I should say my experience at UMBC was very different from my experience at Columbia. I didn't make many friends, I didn't live on campus, and I was sad and I was tired most of the time. I worked an early morning shift at the *Baltimore Sun* in their delivery complaints department—you called me if your paper didn't arrive. But sometimes people called if they were angry about an editorial. Or sometimes they called if they were lonely. I worked from 5 A.M. until noon and then I went to class. I didn't do a lot of socializing. Mostly I just went to lectures and wrote movie reviews for the school newspaper and went home.

I went viral in the middle of February. I was in the school bookstore one afternoon when I noticed a Black History Month display. The sign on the display read, "From Bondage to Books: Black History Month." It had a picture of Harriet Tubman and a picture of Colin Powell. And that was it.

I looked at it; I looked around. Was anybody else seeing this? The bookstore was this big, glass-encased two-story structure. It was overcast outside and so inside everything was gray. There was no one else around. Maybe a cashier up front. I was alone. Me and the sign.

I gave it a Clair Huxtable raised eyebrow. This sign was trying it. The sign infuriated me. To me it said, "Oh, the history of Blacks in this country can be boiled down to the Middle Passage, slavery, and whatever it is that Colin Powell means to you." Which was complicated then and remains "interesting" now.

Now, yeah, you can't fit a lot on a sign. But you can fit more than that. I felt three things in quick succession: I felt a raw exposure in the middle of that empty bookstore. Then I felt trapped, stuck standing where I was. And then, as I turned on my heels and left, I felt powerful. The sign didn't have to have the last word.

I marched straight across campus into the newspaper office and announced, "I'm writing an editorial." They were like, "Aren't you the movie review guy?" I was like, "I've changed!" Because I wanted to talk about the sign and the sentiment behind it, I decided to write my editorial as a satire. (And this, dear reader, is a moment where you might quietly wish the hero of the story had another instinct. But he did not.)

For my part, I wish, for the sake of good storytelling and for my progress in therapy, that I could explain why I chose satire. I think my goal was for people to read it and say, "You are very funny, and racism is bad." I remind you now that you are holding a book in which I have written funny things. Perhaps you have spent money for it. Or perhaps you are sitting on the floor of a Barnes & Noble, nibbling on a date and chuckling to yourself. Whatever you're doing, you've somehow come in contact with this thing that I wrote, fifteen years after I sat in my student center and wrote an editorial that I considered satire. And in the intervening years I've learned how to be more, what's the phrase? Successfully funny. I didn't know that then. I thought if you wanted to write a satire, you just said everything very sarcastically and called it a day.

I called it "An Idiot's Guide to Black History Month." The article takes the caustic position that Black History Month is unnecessary, since the history of African Americans is unremarkable and, as the sign says, is really about slaves learning to read and becoming Colin Powell. It started off:

> *Another February has passed and another Black History Month is behind us. Good riddance. That whole Underground Railroad bit is going to get old pretty fast. I mean, honestly, how much Black History is there, really? We all know about "Black History." Africa, slavery, Civil War, Jim Crow, Aretha Franklin, Civil Rights, MLK blown away, what else do I have to say?*

It went on to talk about the sign in the bookstore before circling back to more incendiary thoughts on Black history. I sent it in, and the crazy white people on the newspaper staff published it. It went to print and was published online on a Thursday with my email address at the bottom for praise and compliments and my name at the top with no accompanying photos. The online component was new; we'd just redone our newspaper's website and were committed to putting all of our content up.

It's important to note: my full name is Robert Eric Thomas; I go by R. Eric Thomas in print so that you can more easily google me. (I kept the "R." because there's a motivational speaker in Michigan named Eric Thomas who would very much like to be left out of my bullshit.) Robert Eric Thomas is an intentionally racially neutral name, as my parents didn't want others to be able to see my name on a job application or résumé and discriminate against me. It was a beautiful and sort of heartbreaking gift. And, as far as I can tell, it has helped me in my life. I've had a lot of job interviews with racists.

It was, however, a problem here.

When you see an article on the internet that is maybe a satire but also not so well written, an article that says Black History Month is unnecessary, and the name at the top is, well, white, you might get your feelings hurt. That's the thing, there's no neutral.

By Saturday, I had more than a thousand emails in my inbox. And the number grew as the weekend turned into Monday and the article was passed around to the National Association of Black Journalists listserv and other mailing lists. I thought I was famous.

What was remarkable, I remember, was the speed at which it all happened. Nowadays, something going viral over a weekend is normal, to be expected. When I publish an article today, I usually know within thirty minutes whether it's going to do well based on the reaction of my Facebook friends. Back then, the speed was stunning. At home, I worked with a 56k modem, which felt like racing through time and space. Plus, there were sound effects. This was an event. I was shewk.

I had written my editorial for the school paper, emphasis on "paper." I thought I'd start a conversation on campus between scholarly people with ink-stained fingers or something. I could never have conceived of thousands of people screaming at me online, which is hilarious because that's what most of the internet is today. I mean, it's not that for me; I'm sensitive (FOR OBVIOUS REASONS). Today, I go out of my way to avoid anyone being mean to me online or assuming I am a white person. Most of the time, I don't write for websites that have a comments section, because I've learned the hard way that even if there are a hundred comments that are like "LOL, you're hilarious. You're my favorite person. You're the hero of this story," all it takes is one person to write "Meh" to send me spiraling into despair. I am serious.

The email responses to my editorial were sharper and more jagged than anything I'd ever received. People were not playing around with me, which is great for justice but was very bad for my feelings. People were writing things like "Dear White Devil" and "You are a Klansman and you should die." At one point, I got an email inviting me to speak at an ultra-nationalist rally in Kentucky. Because I have a real problem, I wrote back, "Hey, I'll be happy to speak if you'll fly me out and pay for my hotel. Also, I'm Black. Does that make this weird?"

They didn't respond. I'm not proud, but I'm also not trying to pass up a per diem.

I wrote a follow-up, which was non-satirical and said, "Lol,

I'm Black." But the newspaper was printed only once a week, and we didn't know you could just update your website anytime, so we had to wait until the next Thursday, when the printer ran again, to publish it. We literally did not know how to use the internet.

On campus, things were fraught. You remember, no one knew who I was, so everyone there thought there was some Nazi Youth running around in their midst. The Black Student Union announced that they would be holding a town hall to talk about the imbroglio. I hadn't joined the Maryland BSU, like the one at Columbia, so they didn't know I wasn't white either. I really need to start joining things. I was a little shirty that they didn't extend an invite to the town hall through the newspaper. I really am a trip; like my faux-racist ass really thought this group of Black people should've sent a telegram or evite or something.

It was held in the late afternoon, and because it was February, the sun had already set. The campus was empty and the light was blue, and I stood outside of the building where the meeting was being held and tried to will myself to just go home. What was I going to do? Burst in like it was a courtroom? "Surprise, bitch! You're out of order!" No, I was not. It had been a long, hard week of having mean things said to me on the internet. But I watched people stream in, mostly Black people, in groups, and I felt those three things in quick succession again: I felt alone, I felt trapped, and then I felt powerful. I didn't need an invitation. I could go wherever I wanted. (I was embracing my white privilege.)

These were my people. I went because, although I didn't know anybody, this was my community. We all wanted the same thing, right? We all had to walk by the sign every day. That's what this was really about. The internet hated me, but this room was full of people who believed what I believed. I felt like I belonged there. I felt like I was supposed to be there.

I stood in the back and I listened. Everyone who stood up to talk mentioned this white racist, R. Eric Thomas. Everyone was furious. Everyone was angry *at me*. That was not the intended effect. They wanted something. They all wanted an apology. From my white ass.

I was shocked but I stayed silent, which is uncharacteristic. I have never in my life walked into a room with a microphone and not planned on saying anything. Speaking, whether anyone wants me to or not, is one of my spiritual gifts. But in that auditorium, I was speechless. I got defensive all of a sudden. None of these feelings were what I intended. My intentions were good! It was incomprehensible to me. I wrote a satire! I turned to a guy standing next to me. This tall, light-skinned Black guy. Attractive. I said, "This is really something, isn't it?"

He said, "Yeah, this R. Eric Thomas is a real asshole."

I was like, "Well, he's got some good qualities. His grammar is impeccable."

I looked around that room full of Black people, my people, and I felt angry and isolated. Again. The town hall continued, but I felt myself getting flushed. I gathered my stuff and left. I wasn't feeling the way I wanted to feel. I wrote what I wrote because I wanted people to laugh with me. Except I wasn't laughing. Walking off into the night, boarding the bus I resented, and traveling back to the basement apartment my own actions had forced me into, I realized that I was furious. Had I ever been laughing? The words that I'd so gleefully dashed off ran through my head, colored now by the pain and frustration I'd heard from my classmates. I had to admit to myself what should have been plainly obvious. I didn't write what I wrote to make people laugh—I wrote it to make them angry.

Alone in the bookstore, I had read the sign that had hurt my feelings. And that hurt had acted as a flint, igniting an anger that had lurked beneath the surface for years, directionless and formless but now suddenly powerful. And aimed. I wanted someone, anyone, else to feel the way that I felt. And so I turned to the computer, and I started typing. I was the revolver.

The second article was eventually published, which quelled some of the in-person anger, though the Black Student Union did censure me, which is this sort of public rebuke. It feels like it should come with a certificate but it didn't. I received hate mail for months but I never heard anything about the sign. Anyway, it came down the first week of March because Black History Month was over.

Unsuccessful Black Hair

I am currently bald. I say currently because I am holding out for medical science. Yes, I have heard of Rogaine; no, I haven't tried it. I don't want *my* hair back. I want to take a pill and get John Legend's hair. I know you're thinking, *Have I been sleeping on John Legend's hair? Is it extraordinary?* No. It is fine. It's very nice hair. It looks good all the time without being showy about it. I'm not asking for a crown of glory; I just want a nice, unremarkable full head of hair that does its job competently and attractively like the third lead on a crime procedural. Is that too much for modern science to give?

Other people seem to notice my baldness more than me, which makes sense because I am incredibly humble and never look in a mirror. Also, I just kind of don't care. But it's still a surprise to me when little kids draw me as a round-faced bald man. Are little kids drawing me a lot? Why, yes, they are, thanks for asking. I'm a kindergarten art model. It's a living. I look at these drawings and I see Gordon from *Sesame Street* or Steve Harvey but never myself. I suppose I don't know what I look like, or maybe I'm just waiting to memorize my look after I get my John Legend treatment.

My hair, when I had hair, was no great shakes. I didn't really have a plan for my hair. I was too shy to try most fun hairstyles, and it felt like, when it was just cut normally, it didn't have any of the verve, sheen, or glow of other people's styles. I now realize that it's because I wasn't putting any product in it, products with names like Verve, Sheen, and Glow. I mean, it said it right on the tub of metallic blue gel, but how was I supposed to know?

Most of the time I don't think about my hair, which in and of itself seems like a dereliction of my duty as a Black person. Hair is integral to cultural Blackness—how we do our hair, what products are available to us, whether we let white people touch it (we don't), and the messaging we receive from non-Black people about our hair, it's all part of the experience. I know this; I'm sometimes affected by it, but I find it hard to internalize. I am proud to be Black but I've never been able to harness pride about my hair. I just don't really connect with it, or the lack thereof.

Baldness is a legitimate Black hair choice, too. Why don't I make Taye Diggs my hair idol and keep it moving? Do I look like Taye Diggs? No, but has the tyranny of facts ever stopped me before? Again, no. One year for Halloween, I went as Kanye West. Sort of. I wore sunglasses and a sports coat because I am the laziest Halloween dresser known to man. Did my bald ass look like Kanye West? No. Somebody asked me if I was Lex Luthor. This was hilarious to me because this person was obviously costume color-blind and very woke. But still, let's not be ridiculous about this. You see my bald ass walking down the street on Halloween wearing a suit, you don't think, *Hey, that's Lex Luthor! I can tell from the context clues.* You also don't think, *Hey, that's Kanye West*. More likely, you think, *That guy is dressed as Kareem Abdul-Jabbar.* Or, most likely, *Why is that bald man going to a job interview at 8 P.M. on Halloween night? And why does the suit have shorts?!*

The suit has shorts because I'm dressed up as *Sexy* Kareem Abdul-Jabbar. Also known as Lex Luthor Vandross.

Back in college (the golden age of Terrible Hair Decisions), when I had hair but wasn't putting Verve or Glow in it like I should have been, I didn't particularly like my hair, and only once did I deign to try something adventurous with it. This was after I had dropped out of Columbia, enrolled at UMBC, and after I had accidentally written something that caused a campus-wide controversy and got me briefly labeled as a white racist. Things were not going well. I didn't yet know about the concept of a depression beard, so crisis hair seemed like the next best thing.

One of the things I didn't mention in the last essay was that during the blowup over my viral Black History Month satire, the local NBC affiliate got involved. They emailed me asking if they could interview me about the imbroglio, and this fame-obsessed bitch immediately said yes. I'm the president of the Showing-Up-on-Television-Anytime-I-Can Society. Well, technically Gore Vidal is the president of that society. I'm the vice president. The Al Gore Vidal. The news crew showed up at my after-school job, which was waiting tables at a comedy club. (Just a note, if you've gone viral for writing something that a lot of people think is racist, maybe don't tell the news trucks to meet you outside of your place of employment.)

The whole newspaper dustup occurred during a period when I was between haircuts. This happened frequently, as I was very uncomfortable at Black barbershops. To start, I was a not-especially-masculine man who never successfully learned the name of the kind of haircut he wanted, so going to a barbershop was always a losing proposition for me. But there's more to it than that. There is something specifically hierarchical about my experience of a Black barbershop. The space exists for the cutting of Black men's hair, of course, but also to host overtly heterosexual camaraderie and community, which I've found most often expresses itself through machismo. The more macho one was, the Blacker one was. This showed up in topics of discussion, in grooming, in the unspoken rules of who could and could not be there (rarely any women, besides moms, and even they would sometimes drop their sons off and come back). The rule, as I understood it, was that a successful man devoted time and attention to his hair to attract women and to be presentable in a largely white society that had a limited capacity for accepting new hairstyles. But you also wanted your pride and your preening to be rooted in masculinity. There wasn't, and isn't, a wide spectrum of ways a Black man could express himself—his beauty, his pride, his love for his own being—in the spaces I passed through. This came from centuries-old external pressures on him, namely the presumption that he was a savage and therefore not actually a man at all. Having a strict understanding of how a Black man operated in the world kept us safe. As someone whose deviations from that model were always clocked by others, I understood that.

And, I should say, there were certainly barbershops that catered to men who put Jheri curls in their hair, and pretty men who always had a girlfriend, dandies with bespoke suits, fly politicos with big pockets and slicked-back coifs, high-siddity boys with "good hair," but those weren't the shops that I was going to. The barbershops I went to were full of working-class men with natural hairstyles, the whir of razors, and stacks of *Playboys* in a corner somewhere.

I was never even close to the top of the hierarchy in the barbershop. My internalized discomfort with my own Blackness seemed to be writ large, like a message shaved into the back of a high-top fade. And my hair didn't seem to want to lend me a hand, anyway. Apparently, it was the job of every Black barber to give me a stern talking-to about my razor bumps, the fact that I had waited too long to get my hair cut, the things I was supposed to do (and obviously hadn't been doing) to maintain it. The barber, with his hands in your scalp, knows who you are, which is more than I could say for myself.

So I didn't get my hair cut a lot. And I didn't know how to cultivate a 'fro, so when the news truck showed up at my job during the Black History Month satire imbroglio and started asking me questions like "What is your race problem?" I appeared on the evening broadcast with my Resting Bitch Face sitting beneath a medium-size mass of matted, dense, unpicked curls. My hair looked like the kind of hair you give a Black Muppet if you haven't taken enough cultural sensitivity classes and all your materials come from the clearance bin at A.C. Moore. But at least I got on TV.

A month later, *still with no haircut,* I got the newspaper to send me to a college journalism conference in Manhattan. I desperately wish I could remember that conversation. "Hey! So you know how I wrote a satire that no one thought was a satire and brought down the fire of the nascent internet on myself and this paper and then had the audacity to appear on the news talking about how I'm not sorry? You want to pay for me to go to New York, where I really want to be anyway, and learn how to actually write?" Whatever it was, they said yes.

I was obsessed with being back in New York. I felt I'd taken it for granted when I was there, struck dumb and immobilized by all the changes I was undergoing and all the dynamism of the city. I wanted to claim a second chance. I realized I felt freer in New York and sometimes more lovely. In Baltimore, I was inarticulate and tender-headed. Just not cute. Not cute all around.

The conference was in late March. I was still receiving little dribbles of hate mail from my unsuccessful Black History Month satire. What can I say? The fans can't get enough. I didn't yet have a smartphone, so escaping to New York also meant leaving behind an inbox that had nothing for me but insults. It meant allowing myself to tiptoe back into the life I had at Columbia, where, in my gauzy memories, I was always happy and my hair reached up to the sun in an exuberant explosion of sex appeal, like Maxwell's. This kind of delusion can carry you far in life, I've found. But you can never let it slip.

When I arrived at the Roosevelt Hotel for the conference, I got in line to check in and spied an attractive Black guy two people ahead of me. He had beautiful skin and gorgeous, Black hair. It was freshly cut, shaped up at the nape of his neck, tapered on the sides and longer on top, with waves. Waves? Is that what they're called? Sure. Honestly, sometimes I look at a guy's well-maintained hair like it's a crop circle. I marvel at the achievement but I can't for the life of me imagine how it was done. In any case, the aliens had come down and blessed this man's head.

I continued to openly stare at the back of his beautiful head the entire time we waited in line, because I am a creeper. I felt immediately self-conscious, aware of my small, unruly 'fro, and the gulf between what I looked like and a Maxwell album cover, and the fact that I could not say for sure if the waves in his hair were naturally occurring or something that a barber or someone had cut in or what. He must have felt the fiery intensity of my total confusion, because he turned around and caught my eye. He nodded at me in acknowledgment and then went about his business. I love when hot people nod at me; it reminds me that I exist. But something in me broke a little bit when this particular hot guy nodded at me. I remembered what I looked like and felt the need to shout, "Sorry to bother your eyes with all this. Work in progress! 'This Woman's Work' in progress!" It might have been the better option. At least he would have kept looking at me. Instead, I said nothing. He turned, got his key, and disappeared into the hotel.

For whatever reason, that fleeting feeling of freedom and loveliness that I'd been clinging to slipped away. I don't know why I needed more than a passing acknowledgment from this stranger. Like, I was in a city of six million people. Why didn't I go get nodded at by literally anybody else? Despite the fact that much of my self-worth was wrapped up in my rapidly disintegrating academic career and the fact that the National Association of Black Journalists thought I was a racist, I decided to hang my emotional health on the nod of a stranger.

Is there such a thing as internal validation? I know we're not supposed to hang our hopes on external validation. "Love yourself!" everyone says. "Or at least like yourself. Tolerate yourself!" But a lot of the time, being told that everyone else—or anyone else—finds worth in you carries more weight than telling yourself that you're worth it.

I weighed this as the hot guy at the college newspaper conference nodded and ignored me, as he checked in and then I checked in, as I lay across my bed and patted my matted 'fro.

And then it occurred to me: I didn't have to let our interaction die like that. I could do what anyone who needs the attention of a boy to feel complete would do: I could *She's All That* myself. You know *She's All That*-ing: it's that ancient African tradition wherein an unremarkable nerd transforms into a beautiful hottie just in time for the prom, usually by combing their hair and taking off their glasses. I didn't even have glasses! I was halfway to hot already! (Though, truth be told, I always thought I'd look better with glasses and was constantly vexed by my perfect vision. I'm a one-man O. Henry story.)

When I'd been enrolled at Columbia, I once wandered through Morningside Park to explore Spanish Harlem and came across a Dominican hairdresser. They had the same haircut chart that my brusque barber on the West Side had, but here there was music coming from within and the shop was full of women and it seemed unlikely that anyone would leave in the middle of the cut to go get lunch and buy a bootleg. I stopped in, asked them to cut my hair, didn't suffer any emotional damage, and left. Lying across my hotel bed, hands tangled in my Muppet hair, I remembered the Spanish Harlem shop and decided to make a return trip. I would have them fix my hair and in so doing fix my life. Like a reverse Rapunzel, I would be freed by having my hair cut, and I would return to the hotel a new person. A swan. And this swan would, of course, captivate this stranger who was just trying to live his life. It seemed improbable and not terribly well thought out and I was very excited about it.

The Dominican beauty shop was just as I remembered it: music, pink chairs, chill feminine energy, and no customers.

This was my idea of heaven. In a grooming situation, I really don't need to be around a lot of other people. This goes for haircuts, manicures, massages, trying on clothes, walking, talking, existing, etc. A lot of people have a therapeutic relationship with the person that does their hair. I am and have always been someone who could really use a lot of therapy but never found that safety in the barbershops. I felt safe at the beauty shop. And, as the name would suggest, I felt in the presence of beauty. So when the beautician asked me what I wanted her to do with my hair, some desire buried deep inside me rushed to the surface and leapt off the precipice of my lips. I didn't say the usual, a mumbled variation on "Can I have a low fade or whatever it's called." Instead, I said, "Can you straighten it?"

"You want a perm?" she asked, pointing to the box of lye relaxer on the counter. I charged ahead. "Yes," I said. "Just straighten it and maybe cut down the sides." So she did.

I had never straightened my hair before; I can't say I ever thought to straighten my hair before. But as I leaned my head back into the sink so she could apply the chemicals, I realized it was what I had wanted for a long time. Did I want to be white? No. Did I want white hair? Well, I wouldn't mind it. Wasn't I always absentmindedly sweeping hair behind my ear like all my friends at school did, even though there was never any hair to sweep? Didn't I spend far too much time thinking about the concept of bangs? Failing to find access to an understanding of Black male attractiveness, I reverted to the white version, which somehow felt more accessible, perhaps because of its ubiquity. *She's All That*-ing rarely happens to Black characters, after all. In lieu of a therapy session where I could work out this racial disassociation, I put my head in the hands of a kind Dominican woman who gently and expertly dragged a comb smeared with chemicals from the roots to the tips of my hair. She set a timer for fifteen minutes as I sat up, looked at myself in the mirror, and smiled.

At around minute nine it started to burn. "Is this normal?" I asked.

"You're ripping the curl out of your hair," she said. "It's gonna feel like violence."

That was a bit more lyrical than I was ready for, so I was just like, "Okay, cool. Well, um, I trust you. Also this is terrible."

She was like, "Quiet. I'm watching *Entertainment Tonight*."

I love celebrity news, so we watched *Entertainment Tonight* for six more minutes together in silence.

When the timer went off, she put me back in the sink, washed and shampooed my hair, and then dried it. She removed the towel, and for the first time in my life, my hair fell into my face and I felt an unfamiliar thrill. It was bone straight. White straight. It was like a limb had appeared in a space where there was previously just phantom feeling. It was a surrogate solution to all the conflicted racial feelings I had. And it was a lie. But I had never felt lovelier, and beauty beats truth any day. At least that's what I took from my half-remembered viewing of *She's All That*.

In the movies, quite frequently you'll see Black people going to sleep and waking up, because that's what human people do to keep themselves alive. However, very rarely in a movie do you see a Black person wrap their hair in a silk scarf or a do-rag before bed, apply moisturizer or oil, or do any of the other myriad things it takes to maintain some Black hairstyles, like, say, relaxed hair. As someone who learned absolutely everything from movies and yet also nothing, I didn't know that once you straighten your hair, you can't toss your head and go like you're a hair model in a L'Oréal commercial. It takes a lot of doing. That never came up in the beauty shop, and for twelve hours, roughly, I lived in blissful ignorance. My hair was so light and so straight. I returned to the hotel and strode through the doors like Julia Roberts at the end of the shopping montage in *Pretty Woman*. Anyone who wasn't immediately beguiled by this awkward twenty-one-year-old with J. C. Penney clothes and Prince hair was out of their damn minds. I went to bed that night like a Black person in a movie. Not a care in the world and not a thing on my head.

Like a character in a fairy tale discovering that a terrible prophecy has come true, the next morning I found that a natural curl had already started to seep out of my scalp, and my hair, which once fell gracefully, stood angrily from my head. I panicked. I didn't know that the chemicals had left my hair desiccated and that I'd need to condition and wrap it if I wanted to keep it looking nice. I thought I'd been cursed! I was late for a workshop session, so I just ran some water through it—another cardinal sin of Black-relaxed-hair care—and rushed off to the day's first workshop, a session on minorities in college newspapers, looking like Black Kramer.

At the workshop, a Samuel Clemens–looking dude recognized my name from the imbroglio I'd recently been involved in with my school newspaper. He struck up a conversation with me about the reaction and we talked about satire and race. My head started to itch and I nervously smoothed it. It resisted. The hot Black guy from earlier popped up behind Samuel Clemens. He grinned at me and apologized for eavesdropping but told us he couldn't help but be intrigued. "I edit a literary journal at Emory," he said. "This article sounds like just the kind of thing we're looking for."

Despite the fact that the entire young internet had gotten mad at me for writing a satire that no one thought was a satire and everyone thought was written by a white person, I immediately told him I'd be happy to let him read it and republish it. Maybe it was his beauty, maybe it was my white hair privilege, maybe the chemicals had seeped into my brain. All I knew was that yesterday he nodded at me and today he was asking to read my writing and if that isn't the payoff of a *She's All That*-ing, I don't know what is.

The hot guy asked me what I was doing for lunch. "Nothing," I said, resisting a persistent urge to scratch my scalp. "Let's continue this over food," he said. I high-fived my rapidly fraying split ends of indeterminate racial heritage.

We walked to a coffee shop around the corner, talking all the way about my article and his journal and what life was like for him in Atlanta and what life was like for me in Baltimore. We had an instant chemistry that I was sure must have been one of the side effects of the hair. We sat at a counter by the front window and I caught a glimpse of our reflections—he, darker than I, perfect hair, perfect skin, perfect smile, and me, overeager smile, hair berserk.

After lunch we discovered that we were going to the same afternoon session, a presentation by some folks from the Sesame Street Workshop. If I were a good journalist, I suppose a question that I should ask would be, "Say! Why are there Muppets at a college newspaper conference?" But everyone knows I am not a good journalist. I just like a good story. AND MUPPETS. And the story here is two Black dudes, one with a sort of Bride of Frankenstein thing going on with his hair, leaning into each other as they laugh at the antics of a special guest star Cookie Monster. It was amazing how quickly my life had become perfect. Here's the place, were this a movie, that the montage would kick in. Us, eating and deeply engaged in conversation, us randomly in the presence of a celebrity puppet, us getting hot dogs for dinner from Gray's Papaya . . . and us with our beautiful Black skin illuminated by the lights of Times Square as we walked after nightfall, as he grabbed my hand.

Parts of my identity that had felt unresolved and at odds with each other for years found harmony between our pressed palms. We didn't talk about what it was like to be both Black and gay in that time, or where we'd come from, or if we were out in our other lives, our real lives. I think we both knew it was temporary, though if he'd asked me to pick up and move to Atlanta, obviously I would have. What did I have to lose? What was waiting for me back in Baltimore?

As a kid, I'd never gone away to sleep-away camp or studied abroad, so the idea of a chance meeting and a sudden romance was new to me and wholly cinematic. And in movies, you live happily ever after following the *She's All That*-ing. Occasionally, you have to have a dramatic scene in which you confess that you're not really a swan—in my case, I suppose that meant admitting to the Emory boy that I did not possess naturally straight hair. (I think he might have suspected.) But everyone knows those revelations are quickly sorted out and forgiven. There was nothing standing in our way. I was also, at this point, unaware of the concept of a conference hookup. If I had known it was common practice for people to go to conferences, drink in hotel bars, and hook up with other conventioneers, I would have joined a lot more professional organizations. But isn't not knowing better?

I went to bed that night and dreamt of him. He was playing

in the sheets, pulling them over his head and then revealing himself. Over and over. We were in the hotel. I didn't know him in any other context. But I think we'd been there forever.

When I woke up, I was alone. Well, not quite—my hair, another night un-do-ragged, continued on its journey of self-actualization. It was even drier, even coarser, and even wilder than the first day. I sat in the bed and looked at myself in the mirrored closet across the room. This person was unrecognizable to me, not because the hair was transformative but because the thing that I wanted was so deeply rooted and so unruly that I wasn't even aware of its breadth. I'd told the woman in the beauty shop to straighten my hair in a moment of wild freedom that, to me, in that time, was a hallmark of whiteness, but also of a kind of Black maleness that was so different from my own experience. It wasn't about the texture so much as a loosening of external reads on my body. Well, it was a little bit the texture—hair-ography is a powerful force. But I could have flipped my hair out of my face with dreads just as easily. Ultimately, the how didn't matter so much as the result: a new me, beautiful, free.

Perhaps I was reaching for authenticity through a funhouse mirror. I didn't know. I just didn't want to be who I was. It turns out that's not a specific enough request. The natural curl had returned, a day and a half past the point when I tried to chemically rip it out, stretching furiously from root to tip, standing straight up, matted no more. A protest. It was almost inspirational.

On Saturday, the conference ended but the Emory boy wanted to prolong our time. He asked if I'd go with him to run some errands. "What errands?" I asked. He answered, "I need to get my hair cut." He'd found a barbershop up in Harlem and, despite the fact that his hair looked good to me, he wanted to get it trimmed and shaped up before going back to Atlanta. I've always believed, apropos of nothing, that Southern Blackness is the equivalent of professional Blackness, so I can see why he'd want to be vigilant about his follicular freshness.

I immediately got nervous. I pictured the barbershop, in my mind a combination of every barbershop in which I'd ever had an uncomfortable experience. I could smell the Newport dangling from the barber's mouth; I could hear the mocking laughter, feel the sidelong glances. And then I remembered what I looked like and shivered thinking of what the barbers would say about my hair. Barbers, I've found, often stand outside their shops and shout like carnival barkers at passersby about what's wrong with their hair and what they can do to fix it. In the present, I am always grateful for my baldness because it exempts me from this public critique as marketing ploy. But back then, head full of over-permed, badly maintained hair, on an errand date with a boy, I was sure I'd be asking for it. "How about we do something else?" I asked. The Emory boy insisted. He really needed a haircut but he also really wanted to keep hanging out. I volunteered that I'd walk him there, hoping to somehow convince him to change his mind before we stepped through the threshold.

We caught the subway together up to Harlem and he grabbed my hand again. I had never held a boy's hand in public before that week, and it felt magical and slightly dangerous but, more important, right. It felt safe. The neon-edged brightness of Times Square at night had been switched out for the flat, clinical light of the number 1 train, but yet we remained unharmed. No one even said anything. We were just two people, going through some things in our lives but experiencing a moment of beauty. We passed Columbia and got off at 145th Street, still talking, still holding hands. He turned boldly down Seventh Avenue and came to a stop in front of the barber shop he'd found online. I let go of his hand. "It'll be real quick," he said.

"Unless there's a bunch of people waiting in front of you like there always is," I replied. He pushed open the door. "Wait," I said. "I'm going to go hang out. Grab some lunch. But I'll see you back at the hotel before you go." He stared at me and I knew what he was asking was so little; it was so inconsequential in the scope of things. I knew that what he was offering me superseded the discomfort that a space like the barbershop had previously held, if only temporarily. But I couldn't go in. I wouldn't. It would have been easier if he'd asked me to move to Atlanta and become a professional Black person. "I'll see you later," I said, knowing that I was lying. He walked into the shop and let the door close behind him. I scuttled down the block to the corner, out of sight of the barbers waiting within.

What to do now? I turned and wandered back down Broadway, toward Columbia, out of instinct and habit and an unrequited love. I thought of rushing back to the barbershop and catching the Emory boy, but my feet knew not to waste their time turning, for it was just a thought. At the corner of 125th and Broadway, I stopped. I scratched my head and winced as I felt a sharp pain. I drew back my hand and saw a thin crescent of blood on my fingernails.

My entire scalp radiated a dull ache. I gingerly dug down through my hair with the pads of my fingertips and felt the skin. It was rough, calloused from the hairline to the crown of my head. I crossed the street to a closed storefront and inspected my head in the ghostly reflection of the window. It was as I suspected: my scalp had a chemical burn. All of it. Burnt. I had tried to kill my hair and now my hair was back for revenge.

Truth be told, I was rooting for it to succeed.

Flames, at the Side of My Face

Here is why I liked waiting tables more than almost any other job I've had: you get to have small, purpose-driven interactions; you get to talk about food constantly; in a restaurant, no one seems to mind if you're emotionally all over the place, which is great because when I worked in restaurants throughout my twenties, I certainly was; and at the end of the shift, you get cash money, baby. After turning twenty-one, I spent my nights walking the streets of Baltimore and sometimes venturing onto the dance floor of a gay bar and I spent my days speed-walking the length of the Hard Rock Cafe in downtown Baltimore, balancing burgers and mai tais. I got the job while I was at UMBC and worked there far longer than I thought I would. There came a point where I wondered if I would work there forever. This didn't seem like a terrible option, but I wasn't sure.

At the Hard Rock, I also got a great education on a bunch of bands I was too pious to listen to back in the day. Have you heard of Van Halen? Very good work, very interesting. I discovered that, as much as I'd try to stay away from the scourge of hard rock as a churchgoing youth, I'd already heard pretty much every song during car commercials. The highway to hell is chock-full of sport utility vehicles with impressive horsepower.

At the Hard Rock, I also met my future roommate Lisa. We got along instantly and shared a lot of the same interests, which at that point were primarily having strong opinions about certain TV shows and sometimes crying about them, being the funniest people in a room, drinking, making terrible dating choices, and making cash money, baby. It was heaven. Lisa and I started around the same time and were both relatively new to waiting tables, so it was a mercy that two veteran servers—Neddra and Connie—took us under their wings. There is nothing in the world like a server who has been around the block, has seen it all, and lived to tell the tale. You've got to have a high tolerance for bullshit and a good sense of humor to make it in a restaurant for more than, say, a couple of years. You've also got to be able to tell literally anyone to go fuck themselves, from the gruffest, hardest line cook to the most uppity customer. Neddra and Connie were iconic in this respect. They were Lucy-and-Ethel-like in their interactions and in their propensity for shenanigans and more mercenary than pirates of the high seas in their pursuit of money. I was in awe.

Since Neddra and Connie were two of the lead servers, they'd stake out the best table sections like lionesses on the plain, and they took care of their own. Lisa and I were their own. They quickly caught us up on the many interlocking soap operas that naturally spring up amongst a restaurant staff, and I began living my own personal *Melrose Place,* except instead of gathering around an apartment complex pool, we'd get up on top of the bar and perform the YMCA for the delight of tourists. Same diff.

The cast of characters in a restaurant is exhaustingly vast and, by nature, transitional. Under Neddra and Connie's guidance, Lisa and I went from being seen as the college-age kids who would probably blow out of there in a season to part of the regular series cast and, because of that, something shifted in the way the restaurant treated us. We belonged. I needed to belong, as much as I am loath to join things.

I was still living at home in my parents' basement and felt, in all areas of my life, adrift. I'd made a mess of my life at the University of Maryland with my Black History Month op-ed and a general refusal to participate in the community on campus. I would occasionally venture out to the three gay bars in downtown Baltimore in an attempt to meet people, but found that increasingly discouraging. Baltimore's gay scene at the time was starkly divided along racial lines, and, just as in the general community, the opportunities for white gays to socialize and advance were greater than for nonwhite. Additionally, I found that white guys would reach out to you on the nascent dating sites but often wouldn't speak to you in public. The hierarchies around race, attractiveness, and performed masculinity were at once apparent and oblique. It seemed to me, as a person who was dragging himself out of the closet, that Baltimore was a town built on a centuries-old set of unspoken rules. I found the gay community dispiriting and confusing but I also didn't have much of a choice. The options were small to start, and only got smaller when the Black gay bar, the Sportsman (essentially a speakeasy set up in a barely occupied row house), burned down, leaving only two gay bars.

The feeling of being alone, I've found, is the poison that has no taste. It seeps in slowly and easily; it never seems unusual. Isolation presents as an undesired state but nothing serious, nothing permanent, until the lonely nights become lonely months. Community goes from being a distant goal to a forgotten idea. My parents, a floor away from me, couldn't have known how disconnected I began to feel in those days; I barely knew myself.

So, to find a community at the Hard Rock was a relief and a surprise. Despite the large population of LGBTQ servers, a restaurant is not a naturally open and affirming environment. Kitchens run on bravado, machismo, and the sort of hostility that comes from being underpaid, overheated, and out of options. Front-of-house workers—servers, bartenders, bussers, hosts—often have a naturally adversarial relationship with the back-of-house ones—line cooks, chefs, dishwashers. Though the groups must depend on each other for their livelihoods, it's very easy to come to believe that the opposite side of the house is the sole cause of all of your problems in life. Your table is angry at you because their food is taking a while and they've got tickets to the aquarium they're going to be late for? Definitely because the line cook is taking his sweet-ass time with that well-done burger. Got twelve orders of a complicated menu item spitting out of the kitchen printer all at once? The servers surely colluded to end you. It was a vicious symbiotic cycle and it restarted every day. So when tempers flared, it was not unusual for someone—from either the front *or* the back of the house—to lash out with a homophobic insult. If I made a mistake on an order or slacked on my upkeep tasks, somebody was shouting down the long aisle of the kitchen about how I was an idiot faggot. It wasn't constant—Hard Rock is a corporation, after all, and there are high standards and a really impressive training program—but it wasn't rare either. This was Baltimore, this was the early 2000s, this was a restaurant, this was America. Are you surprised?

Regardless, this kind of talk absolutely did not stand with Neddra and Connie. They were fearless and all too willing to escalate their objections to incidents, whether it was through management or through verbal takedowns. They were my heroines. And during our time working together, I learned how to embrace a kind of fearlessness myself and saw the same lioness streak grow in Lisa, too. And so the community of a restaurant, the watchful eye of the veterans, the idea of a future, even the caustic relationship with the other side of the kitchen, it all rescued me.

A restaurant, however, is its own ecosystem, a temporary world of short-term goals that resets itself at the end of every shift. The larger world would remain a challenge to me, particularly as I navigated life as a gay person.

Neddra's longtime partner was a guy named Edgar who bartended at Hard Rock. They were a dynamite team. While she was short and spunky, he was tall and possessed a chill I could only dream of. They were united in their intensity; they were both about the money, baby, and their desire to have fun. The crew that they and Connie and a few others presided over grew to include Lisa and me, and as time went on, I started being invited over to their house to chill, watch TV, and have some cocktails. The community that I found in the restaurant began to form fledgling roots in the real world. We were friends, it turned out, which was a nice surprise. So it wasn't a shock when Edgar invited me to his birthday party, held at a friend's house. I knew they weren't inviting a bunch of people from work; it was more a family-and-close-friends thing, so I felt honored. I was also extremely worried because, as I mentioned, I'm not sold on the idea of meeting anyone I haven't yet met, and I find myself at a loss during conversations in unfamiliar settings. I also hate small talk. What am I supposed to do with it? Small talk is always shouted. "Nice weather we're having!" Okay, well, the ice caps are melting, so lower your voice, honey. Small talk is purposefully avoiding every interesting thing there is to say.

I feared my aversion to small talk would not go over well with Edgar's family and friends. Edgar and Neddra were also, I should note, Black, and I surmised that most people there would be Black also. Having worked through, or at least identified, some of my issues about my race, I was still unsure exactly what my Blackness was. I never felt Black enough, no matter who I was around, and this was exacerbated in moments when I felt overtly gay. It felt like, despite the evidence provided by the charred frame of the Sportsman, Blackness and gayness canceled each other out. They were both communities to which I belonged and yet for which I didn't know the rules.

The party was in a small house in West Baltimore, packed with grown and sexy folk. Music blasting: Prince, Tevin Campbell, Luther—a marked change from our workplace soundtrack of wailing electric guitars and white screams. (This is perhaps not the official way to describe hair bands, but it is accurate.) The lights in the house were low; votives dotted the walls on little pedestals; food was plentiful, drinks flowing—a scene out of a movie. And in this movie I was the awkwardly gay, small-talk-averse wallflower, wandering from room to room, trying to avoid the appearance of dancing, and mumbling facts about the weather.*

* This is one of my spiritual gifts. When I get to heaven and God pulls out the Excel spreadsheet to show all the ways I spent my time on Earth, I'm going to be most interested in how much time I spent standing awkwardly at parties and receptions. God's going to be

I should note: everyone was really nice and the only problem was me.[†] In any case, this party wasn't much different from every other party I've ever been to where I knew a handful of people and I'd psyched myself up for it. Maybe I would suddenly be possessed with the physical wherewithal to navigate a room full of strangers and, who knows, maybe meet someone I really got along with. And yeah, my idea of getting along with someone was trying to have a serious discussion about which Sally Bowles from *Cabaret* was the best, and that tended to be difficult to do over a party-volume stereo, but there was always hope. Maybe this time!

More than anything, I just didn't want to find myself in a space where my gayness was self-evident and the rest of the attendees found it to be a problem. It wasn't ever about a particular party, it was about occupying a particular space in the world and the feeling that the world was suddenly, randomly, and ruthlessly hostile to that space. I had learned how to be fearless in the restaurant because I had allies and I had a strong corporate structure and, failing all that, I had a counter separating me from the kitchen. But the world is different and I felt frequently alone. There were days I'd be walking home from work or from a bar and someone would pull up in a car beside me and start shouting at me, threatening me, just for existing. And to whom do you escalate that complaint? Once, I was almost home from a night at the Sportsman when a kid, no older than eleven, rounded a corner, spotted me, yelled "Faggot!" and then hurled a piece of a brick at me, grazing my head close enough

---

like, "Here's how much time you spent doing good works," and I'll be like, "Yeah, fine. Where's the column for creepy wallflowering and half waves to people I kind of know?" And God will sigh and scroll to column AG and show me. And I'll be like, "Huh. Felt like more than that."

† Oh! Put *that* on my tombstone.

to draw blood. I grabbed at the wound and turned around, tense and totally unprepared for a further attack. I saw him just standing there, staring me down, seething. Bare chest heaving up and down. "Faggot," he called again, and then disappeared back around the corner.

I carried the shock and the fear of that moment with me always in those times. It smoldered inside me, moving slowly but overtaking everything, like lava.

So. I wasn't always a hoot at parties.

Edgar's was great, though. The crowd was fun and welcoming. Of course, Neddra's and Edgar's personalities and big-tent sensibilities didn't stop at the restaurant door, and throughout the evening one of them would spy me lingering in a doorway or against a wall and physically push me into the action. I found myself starting to relax a little. These were just people, after all, and the drinks were strong and Luther Vandross on a stereo solves every problem, really. Oh, that all of life was just strangers floating through murky candlelit rooms, bellies full of home cooking and ears full of classic R&B, occasionally bumping into another stranger and swaying for a moment to the beat.

And just as I was beginning to sink into the vibe of the evening, the lights came on like last call and the music descended to a background whisper. Someone brought a cake out from the kitchen, set it down on the table beside me, and started lighting the candles. I realized too late that in my slow detachment from the wall, I'd managed to position myself at Cake HQ, in the quickly forming center of attention. As comfortable as I had begun to feel, as welcome as I'd been made, the last thing I wanted was all eyes on me, with the lights on, as we sang the Black Happy Birthday song and Edgar blew out his candles.

As we started to sing, I backed into the wall again, grateful for the time in a space that felt something close to normal but not wanting to press my luck. I kept my voice down, as I'm not a great singer, and tried to will everyone away from the lilac button-down with elaborate hand-printed mulberry patterns I'd decided to wear, and away from my permed hair, and away from me, again. My fingers pressed against the wall; my shoulders brushed a shelf; I couldn't be closer to the wall unless I was inside it. Was that an option? Out of the closets, into the walls, like a gay poltergeist. How long was this song? Stevie Wonder was really trying it. My face flushed; I felt a pain in my shoulder blade. The tension was constricting my muscles. No, not tension, I realized, heat. I must have been feeling the heat from one of the votives. I kept singing, as inconspicuously as possible, and turned my head to gauge the distance to the flame. Out of the corner of my eye, I spied a wisp of smoke rising up from the back of my shirt, and then a curlicue of fire. Turns out, *la flamme, c'est moi.*

When you are on fire, people tend to look at you. This was the last thing that I wanted, so I slowly reached my arm up, still singing the damn Stevie Wonder "Happy Birthday," and started patting myself on the shoulder to put the flame out. Just a regular uncomfortable gay person standing against a wall, patting himself on the back. Self-care! Nothing to see here.

Girl, I really thought I'd gotten away with it, too. The fire went out, and though I could feel my skin exposed from a gash in the shirt, I figured the lights would dim again and no one would notice. I showed up to a party hoping to disappear; I ended the night lit up and semi-clothed. A real gay experience all around.

After Edgar cut the cake, the lights went down again and I extracted myself from the wall and headed to the kitchen to say my goodbyes. Neddra's voice from behind me stopped me in my tracks. "Eric! What happened to your shirt?" I cast a look over my shoulder and saw a gash in the fabric that can best be described as "Struck by Lightning Chic."

Before I could answer, another woman called out from across the room. "I couldn't stop staring! Girl, he was flaming!" It was true, but sometimes things are just too real.

Ball So Soft

After working at the Hard Rock in Baltimore for a couple of years, Lisa and I picked up and moved to Philadelphia completely on a whim. I wish I could give you a reason beyond "her lease was up and I was depressed," but that's just the truth. We didn't know anyone there, we didn't know the city, and we quickly realized that we didn't quite know how to make friends in this new city. We started with work friends and that was good for a while. But then she got a job at an office and became a professional person, who got up at a decent hour and commuted and packed a lunch, and I remained a crepuscular barfly, waiting tables during the day and buzzing through gay bars at night. We drifted apart and then, all at once, we realized we had both changed, her for the better, me for the worse. We didn't renew our lease and that's when EJ, a gay, gym-obsessed man with a high-pitched giggle and a spare room in his house, came into my life.

On paper, EJ did not seem like he was on my team. He was a fount of bottomless joy, with pecs the size of cantaloupes and a love of Philly sports teams that elicited screams loud enough to shake the windows. While we lived in the same house, I was not sure we were from the same planet. Naturally social, he was always trying to get me to participate in the things he was into—working out, something called "meal prep," and cheering loudly for the Phillies. At each invitation I was like, "Shan't. Don't feel like that's part of my spiritual journey. Thanks for the invite." I was really into making cupcakes and going on bad dates at this point. And while EJ was a very persuasive person and did seem to be having a good life as a sporty gay with muscles and friends, I was resolute about following my values.

Physical activity had never been my bag. Gym class was abhorrent in my nascently gay youth. Sweating, competing, keeping score, knowing what a first down was, moving: they were all atrocities to me. You can imagine my horror when I became an adult, came out of the closet, and found out that one of the central tenets of homosexuality is that all gays have gym memberships. I protested to the governing board, of course, noting that I'd seen *Death Becomes Her* twenty times and I owned one of those blue HRC bumper stickers with the yellow equal sign even though I didn't own a car. Unfortunately, rules are rules and so I had to either join a gym or turn straight. I can only assume that I was on some spin-class-related endorphin high when EJ said, "Join that softball team with me," and I said, "Sure!" when I really meant to say, "That's gay."

He'd long been a member of the City of Brotherly Love Softball League. A gay softball league. Indeed, each team is allowed a maximum of two players who identify as heterosexual. Any more and the team loses league funding. This was extremely gay. Corporately gay.

The idea was intriguing to me but only in the way that television is intriguing to a cat. I was pretty sure I didn't give a shit about it, but because it was so foreign and yet so close to me, it piqued my interest. Softball? Full of gays? Every Sunday all summer long? Surely you're misinformed. On Sundays, gays go to brunch and then put together IKEA furniture. In the evening they watch *Desperate Housewives* and write checks to charity.

Against my better judgment, and the strong suspicion that this was a vast right-wing conspiracy, I signed up. There was nothing in me that believed a fun Sunday morning would be primarily comprised of an activity I neither knew how to do nor was prepared for in the least. But after paying my dues and getting assigned to a team, it did occur to me that there might be some benefits to participating in this farce, that this inscrutable thing called sports might not be so bad. I was under the impression that there was a masculine energy that I had somehow missed because all my interests are fun and have award shows. Homosexual recreational softball, I thought, would be the key to making me a man.

As the first practice approached, I went to a Modell's Sporting Goods to get all the things I needed for my first day of Man Practice. They required that I have a glove and recommended cleats and baseball pants. I love a costume, so the last two were no problem. The glove was a different story. Apparently, there are many different kinds and sizes of gloves. The sales associate asked me all these questions about size and features and I just stared at him blankly. Finally, I said, "Honey, let's not do this. I'm feeling faint. Just give me something to put balls in. That's what he said, by the way."

So I had successfully procured a glove. EJ told me that I had to prepare it before using it. "Like a cast iron pan?" I said. "You want me to season my glove?" He seemed to have no idea what I was talking about but went along with it anyway. He gave me some lotion and told me to moisturize my glove and to tie a string around it to keep it closed. "My glove is wearing night cream? Is that what's happening?"

He sighed. "Yes. Can you just do it?"

It seemed simple enough, so I acquiesced.

As I dutifully lotioned my glove every night (shockingly, *not* a euphemism), I began to panic. I really didn't know how to play softball. I really was going to look like a big gay idiot out there. So I did what I always do when I don't know something: I got on Wikipedia. After reading all night—or for a good twenty minutes between commercial breaks during *Desperate Housewives*—I had learned the following about this thing they call softball: (a) you throw underhand, (b) the balls are bigger, (c) that's what he said. Here's what I still didn't know: how to throw a ball, how to hit a ball, how to catch a ball without screaming, how to get a home run (although I'm a pro at getting to third base).

At the first practice, they made me the catcher. Probably because when they asked what position I preferred, I replied, "Seated." And it was there that I discovered my true gift. See, when you're the catcher in slow-pitch softball, you're only marginally in the game. Like Waldorf and Statler's box seats on *The Muppet Show,* my comfy perch behind home plate gave me the perfect vantage point for watching the field and making snarky comments about the game in an attempt to mask the fact that I had no idea what the hell was going on. Occasionally, I would be required to catch a ball or something—which I invariably failed to do—but for the most part I was free to make all the puns I wanted out of the comic gold that is nine gays, a big stick, and a ball. And my teammates, God bless them, actually laughed.

Somewhere along the line my behavior began to turn on me. I think maybe it was the day I was assigned to center field during a practice. The outfield can be a real bore and it's hard for people to hear you yelling "That's what he said!" from all the way out there, so I decided to stay entertained by doing a split and singing quietly to myself. I had barely registered the crack of the bat when I looked up to find the ball sailing straight toward me. I cringed and prayed *Not the face!* as it landed just behind me. As I was still in the split, I didn't know what they expected me to do, so I just shrugged and then whistled at a passing jogger.

It was in that moment that I realized I'd become the gayest member of a gay softball team in a gay softball league. I had to ask myself: Was this what I'd signed up to do? How was this reclaiming my masculinity? My shenanigans were all well and good, but what about the game? Didn't I join to be part of a team and—beyond that—part of this vast, unknowable thing called masculinity? Prancing, cartwheeling, finger-snapping, ball-dropping, curtsying, and constantly doubling my entendres, I was—in my mind—acting like a real faggot. And hadn't I joined the team so I wouldn't be a guy people called a faggot? This was true, I thought, but who was calling me a faggot, anyway? In that moment, no one but me, actually.

After practice, our team manager announced that every player in the league had been given a rating based on their demonstrated skill level and that anyone with a rating under 7 would be invited to play in a special training game the following Saturday. Knowing that I was clearly going to be included in that motley crew and feeling a bit self-conscious about it, I released that old reliable sass to deflect any attention. "A game for all the players that suck?!" I exclaimed. "That sounds awful!

A field full of old queens and nerdy faggots all scrambling desperately to get away from the ball? No, thank you. And I presume that since we all suck, some, if not most, of us are going to have to actually play in this game? I mean, they can't put us all in right field and forget about us. Count me out, ladies."

The bit got some chuckles—not enough, if you want to be frank about it—but the niggling feeling inside me wasn't assuaged. I wasn't fooling anyone with this performance. If I wanted to be a part of this game, I was going to have to do more than crack lame jokes in poor taste. I was going to actually have to learn how to play softball.

They even had an acronym for this skills game, which I suppose made it more official. They called it SAUSE, which, as far as acronyms go, is pretty adorable. It stood for Seven And Under Softball Event. Or maybe the last word was "Exhibition." I could never remember. But I chose to use "Event" because it sounded far more fabulous and far more likely to involve a red carpet.

To my surprise there was no red carpet at this "event." Just a bunch of players of varying skill levels being given positive, sound advice by more skilled coaches. What a letdown. As I did some yoga poses and ran lines from *Damn Yankees* in the dugout to warm up, I also discovered a conspicuous lack of ostracism. I was sure that the seasoned pros running this exhibition game on the island of misfit boys were going to have a blast mocking us for our lack of skills and our messy French braids.

The coaches, however, were just other nice gays who had, apparently, read the full Wikipedia article on softball. They had nothing but encouragement for us, which left the task of being a hateful bully completely up to me. After every mistake I would instinctually scold myself under my breath. And the words came out so naturally and with such vehement, muted fury that I was taken aback more than once. Who was this angry ballplayer and why did he hate me so much? After a missed catch, "Fuck!" After every swing and miss, "Idiot!" And by "idiot," I meant gay.

Midway through the event, I stepped up to the plate to bat. There was a very nice lesbian stationed there to coach players on their stances, their positioning, and whatever else one does when one hits a ball with a bat. After a couple of misses, she advised me to stick my butt out, to back it up, to wait a little longer until I tried to hit it. The jokes were coming to mind so quickly that I had to literally bite my tongue to keep from cracking wise. I really wanted to get this right. It was me holding a bat going up against the behemoth that was a flying slow-pitch softball. All puns aside, in that moment I desperately wanted to connect. I wanted to be part of this thing. I could wrap a birthday present in less than a minute and make buttercream icing from scratch, but all I wanted in the world right then was to hit a ball.

I took a breath, raised my bat, and concentrated. The ball came sailing toward me; I could tell it was a good pitch, right over the plate. I swung, hard. And missed. Hard. I swung so hard that my foot popped up like when they kiss in the movies and I did a little pirouette. I came to a stop dizzy and chagrined. The shortstop looked bored; the boys in the outfield were braiding each other's hair. The very nice lesbian approached me again. "Okay," she said. "That swing was a little gay. You need to butch it up."

And as many times as I'd told myself the exact same thing, as many times as I'd muttered it under my breath as I struck out, it didn't mean the same thing when she said it. It meant something completely different. It wasn't the derision bored teenagers casually toss at you for sport or the word I'd turned into a weapon aimed at my softest self. The one word, a simple, meaningless word, dropped into context in her comment. I knew she could say it, she could use it, because she *was* it. And it was safe. And if she was it and I was it, then she and I were us. And I was on the inside. She was gay and I was gay and my swing was gay. And it was fine and dandy and didn't have a thing to do with me hitting the ball. And my objective was clear. So, when the pitcher threw again, I followed her advice, I backed up, I waited to swing, and I hit the ball. Because that's what I was actually there to do. And I followed it with my eyes for a second, like a cat watching television, until I heard her yelling, "Don't just stand there. Run!"

I only lasted one season on the City of Brotherly Love Softball League. I had a wonderful time, and I got a great tan, but I really wasn't very good and I wasn't interested in getting better. So, when fall came, I gave my glove away and promptly forgot literally everything I'd learned about the sport. The next year, EJ was on the same team again and he said that they missed me. "You were very funny," he said, in his relentlessly positive way. "You should come back. As a cheerleader." Up until this point, I hadn't been sure that anyone appreciated my presence. Sure, they laughed and they gave me good advice, and they celebrated when I got to first base and literally never any further. But I felt that same discomfort around them that I felt at random parties or sometimes at work or sometimes just walking down the street. And I'd assumed that what I was intuiting was the truth about them—that I just wasn't man enough to be a part of their group. When, in reality, I was slowly realizing the truth about myself—that I had more work to do on my internalized homophobia.

It felt safer—and to be honest, more comfortable—to perform a kind of camp and use gayness as a punchline like a problematic eighties comedian. Better to be thought a queen than to open your purse and remove all doubt, isn't that how the saying goes? I never felt that I was particularly flaming—would that I were; I feel like I'd be more interesting! But I knew that I wasn't overtly masculine either.

On occasion, people will yell "gay" when they walk by me. Teenagers or whatever. Which I think is ridiculous. Even as I speed up my step to try to run from the sound. It's a little bit of violence, a muted fury that I still cringe at like the brick to the side of my head. But in and of itself it doesn't make much sense. It's an absurdly un-insulting insult. "Gay!" they shout, always out of context and dangling dangerously without the anchor of a pronoun. "Gay!" It's like, duh. Are you trying to tell me something I don't know? How kind a gesture that would be! Some person with really extreme gaydar just tumbling through the world alerting people to their own sexual orientations. Like a blessing.

"Gay!" people shout. For whose benefit? I always wonder afterward, as they are walking away, or in the case of one strange man in South Philadelphia, continuing to sit at a red light while I stood on a street corner and stared at him. He had pulled up in a truck, immediately rolled down the window, and started yelling at me about how I was a faggot. And also a nigger. This was an intersectional moment. I just sort of looked at him, mostly out of surprise. And then out of confusion; I was wearing sweatpants and an old T-shirt. This guy must have been a professional faggot-spotter. It was almost impressive. After letting me know who and what I was, he then rolled his window back up and stared straight ahead, waiting for the light to change.

When the fact of your being is used as a weapon against you, the process of relearning who you are and what your value is, is a long one. I don't know that I'll ever be finished. I don't know that I'll ever be fully there. But I've learned I can't be the first person out there calling myself a faggot just to get it out of the way. That's not how one stays safe and that's not how one creates community. That energy doesn't go out into the world lightly or without cost.

Years after my time in a restaurant and my brief stint on a softball field, I am more at home in myself than ever, and it's due in large part to those experiences, the people in those spaces who accepted me in all my unresolvedness and problematicness and taught me how to tell the truth about who I am, without burying it in a joke. For years, I thought that the way to keep from getting burned was to set myself on fire first or to snuff out my light. I didn't know that I was a phoenix, growing more powerful with every unsuccessful attempt at the drag of presentability, every hurled insult, every strike, and every split. The flame is not my liability but my strength. It was inside me all along.

(That's what he said.)

Fate Bursting through the Wall

The plan was to drink until the pain over / But what's worse: the pain or the hangover?

—Kanye West, "Dark Fantasy"

It was 2011 and by all outward appearances I was not Kanye. I was being paid fourteen dollars an hour at a law firm that helped banks foreclose on people's homes, spending more than I could afford to rent a room in a two-bedroom house in South Philly, and trying to figure out whether I had the pain or the hangover. A few years earlier, I'd come across an ad for a local storytelling open mic, wandered in, told a story about living in Baltimore and being adrift and sad, and, to my surprise, I won. When I spoke, the audience leaned forward; when I made asides, they laughed; when I exposed my raw, messy heart, they didn't look away. I felt like a conduit had opened up between me and a room full of strangers, and I could remix my life—the happy parts, the mysteries, the pain, the hangover—into beginnings, middles, and ends, with vulnerability and humor. I was hooked. By 2011, I was telling stories regularly and had begun hosting shows occasionally. I'd even put together an hour-long storytelling solo performance, about softball and hair tragedies and dating profiles and self-love. It was freeing and terrifying, an unexpected way to access my creativity.

Every once in a while I thought I might want to do something more with my life than work at a law firm, but it wasn't clear what. I wanted to write, I wanted to create . . . something. But besides the open mics, I wasn't finding any outlets to do so. I'd listen to The Moth podcasts all day at work as I processed legal complaints and wished that I could see my way out. In the balance, I was maybe a couple of years behind where some of my contemporaries were, professionally. But I was light-years behind the place I thought I'd be, light-years behind the person I envisioned at eighteen as I packed for college and set out on what was supposed to be a hazily sketched but still sterling life. Things weren't bad; they were better than they'd been. But I didn't recognize myself.

Sometimes I thought I was, in some small way, supposed to be the Old Kanye. I was obsessed with the Old Kanye. I was perplexed by the Old Kanye. Post-Katrina, post–Video Music Awards Kanye but pre-whatever-it-is-that's-happening-now Kanye. Wild-card-genius, mercurial-*enfant-terrible,* grieving-son, producer-savant Kanye. Despite the fact that he was one of the most famous rappers alive and I was a paralegal in Philadelphia, I sensed a kinship with him, like we'd both experienced the same creative frustration, the story clamoring to get out, the competing forces that threatened to rip us apart from the inside, the darkness at the edges.

So I started to write about it. I was fascinated by Kanye's then-most-recent release, *My Beautiful Dark Twisted Fantasy,* a furious, brilliant, sonic barrage of an album. It served as his comeback after a self-imposed exile following his Taylor Swift outburst at the VMAs, but it's also a deeply conflicted rumination on fame and fatalism. I idolized him even though I knew I could never be as bold, as self-assured, or as iconoclastic as he was. Kanye was, to my mind, the ultimate example of society's Good Black Man and Bad Black Man, and he didn't seem to wrestle with any of the duality of these harmful figments so much as delight in it. I had been good once but I wasn't so sure I was good anymore. I didn't think I was bad, but I wasn't sure. Kanye lived life in stereo and I coveted that.

My Beautiful Dark Twisted Fantasy is a masterwork, but it's also an incisive exploration of Kanye's deep depression, his substance abuse, and his thoughts of suicide. It's like if Virginia Woolf wrote bangers. And I was drawn to that because I still felt lost most of the time. There were times that I was furious at myself for hating being gay. And other times I was furious for loving myself, gayness and all. I was frustrated by the mess I'd made of college but unsure how to make it right. I felt like a disappointment, even as my parents offered reassurances. And I found that though I could take all that and turn it into good stories, they never got close to revealing my unresolved beautiful, dark, twisted feelings.

There were times when I'd be standing on the subway platform, waiting for a train that would, hopefully, get me to the office just in the nick of time, Kanye blasting in my ears, and the thought would occur to me, *What if I just stepped in front of the train?* It wasn't ever a surprise, the thought. Sometimes it showed up as the imp of the mind, the common phenomenon of obsessive bad thoughts; other times it was an honest suggestion. There had been dark periods where I couldn't dig myself out of a hole of self-doubt and misery, but this was different. At a train station, walking across a bridge, standing by a window, I'd have thoughts of killing myself that were as mundane and as pragmatic as my work life. I felt so utterly not myself, so divorced from the person that I thought I was, or the person I thought I was once becoming, that ending my life seemed almost an afterthought. Hadn't it ended a long time ago, after all?

"Now this would be a beautiful death," Kanye sings on the third track on *My Beautiful Dark Twisted Fantasy,* "Power," a rumination on his toxic relationship with his own narrative. "Jumping out the window / letting everything go." Despite its ideas, it's not a mournful dirge, and I loved that the most. It's Kanye having a matter-of-fact conversation with his darkest thoughts. I read it as a song of triumph, a dance with death. I blasted it on repeat, reveling in the energetic, cocksure way it begins, with claps, syncopated chants, and sirens heralding Kanye's arrival on the track. I memorized Kanye's self-assured couplets, like "I just needed time alone with my own thoughts / got treasures in my mind but couldn't open up my own vault." I imagined what it might be like to stare down an abyss and shout self-affirmations into it.

I struggled to figure out what I was supposed to do to change the story I was living, so I glommed on to Kanye, who wrestled with life but at least understood the context he was in. "Power" is in C minor, a key that musicologist Cole Cuchna points out is the trademark of a heroic struggle. It's the same key that Beethoven's Symphony No. 5 is in. The one that goes "dah-dahdah-DAH"; the one he wrote about battling back against suicidal thoughts stemming from going deaf. It's commonly referred to as "fate knocking on the door." Beethoven wrote about fate stalking him; Kanye used C minor to reframe his public exile after interrupting Taylor Swift's acceptance speech at the VMAs. Beethoven was losing his hearing; Kanye was mocked on *Saturday Night Live*. But they both decided, in their own contexts and in their own worlds, that they were the hero and that their struggle was heroic. When presented with the question, *What do you think should happen to you?* they responded, *I should triumph*. Indeed, Beethoven once said, "I will take fate by the throat. It will never bend me completely."

At this point in my life, I wasn't so much a hero struggling as a man immobile, trapped between who I was and who I wanted to be, between mistakes and goals, between life and death. And so I played and replayed the album, and went to work, and nothing changed. Nothing changed. Nothing changed. Until a car in Baltimore showed up out of the darkness and I felt my fingers graze fate's throat.

One night, while I was living in Philly, a car burst through the wall of my childhood home like the Kool-Aid Man and landed, as fate would have it, on a pile of my high school yearbooks. The car had lost control after leaving a speakeasy up the street from my parents' house. My mother had just had ankle surgery and was confined to the first-floor apartment that I'd stayed in after college, so when the car pierced the side of the building, my parents were sleeping mere feet above it. My father bolted awake and helped my mother get out of the house, not knowing what kind of threat they were about to face. Turns out, it was three drunk women in an Acura, not the most sinister of villains, but villains nonetheless. Emergency vehicles showed up and so did my youngest brother, Jeffrey, who was a police officer and the only one of the three brothers who lived in-state.

The scene, as my mother tells it, was the stuff of 10 P.M. cop shows: three stranded club-goers and their drunk-driven vehicle, one tire impotently spinning its way into a cardboard box, slowly sloughing off the successive pages of a stack of my yearbooks. My mother had to be carried out of our row-house home after the accident, still drowsy, but also woozy from the postsurgical pain and the requisite prescribed medication. My father, a coiled spring in every emergency situation, talked animatedly to the first officers on the scene while keeping an eye on his wife. Coming into herself a bit, my mother did what she always does: she started taking photos. My mother stood in the middle of the street, on one leg, and took photos of a car that had crashed into her house and the women who were stumbling around beside it. For posterity. She's a scrapbooker; she'd trained all year for something like this.

Jeffrey arrived moments later, his siren on, his lights flashing. I assume he then skidded to a stop in the middle of the street, body-rolled out of the car, and went to get the lowdown from the responding officer. Based on my knowledge of my youngest brother and my knowledge of expository crime-scene dialogue from television shows, I am sure that this conversation was full of quickly rattled-off jargon spoken with a menacing growl. Jeffrey, according to my mother, then approached the driver of the car, who had just finished peeing beside my parents' staircase, and he wrote her a ticket for public urination. *A ticket.*

In the family lore, the positioning of the car in my parents' wall was seen as a blessing, because if the three drunk women had careened off the road a few feet sooner, they would have hit the house-heating oil tank in my parents' basement instead of my pile of childhood mementos, and everything—our house, the car, the three drunk women, and our beloved parents—would have instantly combusted and disappeared.

Needless to say, when three drunk women drive into your

parents' house, you should probably go visit. To see the blessing. And to exclaim things like "Look at that hole!" and "That's what he said!" and "Sorry, I shouldn't have said that" and "But really, there's a huge hole in the side of our house and I'm having trouble processing this" and finally "Where is all my stuff?"

So I boarded the bus to Baltimore with a list of things that I had to say and the knowledge that the car had come to its final resting place in the spot in the basement where I deposited all of the things that weren't coming with me to college. I went to make sure my parents really hadn't disappeared, to make sure the house was still standing, to thank my brother for his service. And I went to collect the things I had left behind like Horcruxes from Harry Potter, the things I didn't need with me, but still needed, the things I wasn't done working through, the things that had survived the relentless grinding of the wheel.

If you haven't ever arrived at your childhood home to find a gash through the brick, covered with plastic and plywood, I recommend that you first steel yourself. Your brain tells you two things: (1) Objectively, this is a disaster. Like, an actual disaster. Like, FEMA. Like, shouldn't someone be starting a GoFundMe? (2) This disaster is your life. (Stitch that on a pillow.) And this thought makes you want to look even harder, to search the chaos for the things that made you feel whole, that shaped you, that nurtured you. I stood in the basement and stared at the mess of my life. I couldn't make sense of any of it.

My mother called out to me from the top of the stairs. "Looks terrible, doesn't it?"

I called back, "I don't see a difference." She was in pain, she was medicated, there was a hole in the side of her house, and her oldest son was making jokes about it.

"Take what you want," she called. "Leave the rest; we'll throw it away."

I tiptoed through some piles of bricks and knelt next to a box. Under the ruined lid, I found a collection of books with which I'd been obsessed in middle school. So, basically, every book. It looked like a buzz saw had cut through the whole collection. Ellen Raskin's *The Westing Game,* Alex Haley's *Roots,* Christopher Pike's *Last Act,* William Golding's *Lord of the Flies,* all destroyed. I stared at them forlornly, like you do when you have to get rid of a book because you're moving or you're Marie Kondo or your house has a hole in it, and you know they have to go but you want to honor them for the role they played in your life. I shifted the box to the side, into a heap of other boxes, a broken picture frame, and some lawn furniture that would all be disposed of after I'd left. I found the box with my yearbooks in it, also now wreckage. I flipped open a few of the broken spines and looked at the inscriptions inside, some of them smeared with water or oil or nuclear waste for all I knew. A teacher's note, "So excited for what's coming next for you," had been transformed into a well-intentioned smudge.

We hadn't been able to afford a yearbook my first five years at Park. Well, I think it was a combination of a tight budget and the reality that a fourth grader does not actually need a yearbook. I get that now but I was incensed when my mother informed me, during my first year at the school, that I didn't know most of these kids and I wasn't going to do anything with the book except eventually put it in a box that would be run over in a freak accident. "That's very specific," I said. "Just you wait," she said. So getting yearbooks all four years of high school felt like an accomplishment, a vote of confidence from my parents, and a sign that I'd actually come into my own in the prestigious private school where the outcomes were so drastically different from those of my neighborhood. I felt, when I graduated, that I was launching toward something phenomenal and worthy, something that would make my parents combust with pride. Like my teacher, I was also excited for what was "coming next." Over a decade later, staring at the remains of the yearbooks, I felt like perhaps I was the one who had combusted at my launch and all that was left was debris.

One of the things that so fascinated me about Kanye's return to music with *My Beautiful Dark Twisted Fantasy* was that it didn't reject the prevailing public narrative about him, even though it was negative. Rather, the album embraced it. He leaned into the sharp edges of his personality. He made them parts of his self-constructed mythology. You could never tell a more compelling story about Kanye than the one he was telling about himself.

On the album's penultimate track, "Lost in the World," Kanye raps, "You're my devil, you're my angel / You're my heaven, you're my hell." He's talking to an unnamed woman for whom he's cycled through feelings over the course of the whole album, but he's also overtly addressing his career, the public, and most of all himself. Behind the words, Bon Iver wails, "I'm up in the woods / I'm down on my mind / I'm building a still / to slow down the time." Minutes later, Kanye reinterprets the lyric by rapping, "I'm lost in the world, been down my whole life / I'm new in the city, and I'm down for the night." The two men's voices blend together and multiply, producing a chorus of loneliness. When I played the song, I lost myself in the place where isolation and company, mistakes and self-actualization intersect like voices layered over each other. "Lost in the World" is a song about resurrection. It's a song about sequestering oneself until one gets one's mind right, and it's a song about dying and being born anew. Kanye's only path to freedom is to exist in the duality of his life; the extreme lows and the unimaginable highs. And not just exist, but revel.

Due to the place I was making for myself in the live storytelling scene, I would, on occasion, teach workshops where I would try to find a way to tell people the "secret" of my storytelling, which, as I understood it, was just to tell the truth because you had no other choice. I would remind people in my classes that the storyteller gets to choose the beginning and the end, often despite what happens in life. And that you have to tell your listener what you, the protagonist, want. This connects directly to the "why" of it all. The impetus for raising your voice to speak. There's a power and a clarity in saying, "This is where it begins for me, and this is where it ends," and knowing why. The why is the most crucial. It's what elevates an anecdote to a story; it's the thing that makes people lean forward with anticipation, their pulses quickening, accepting the invitation of empathy. "Why are you telling this story?" I asked the people in my workshops. I said it over and over again, in conference rooms and classrooms; I wrote it on whiteboards in messy penmanship, but I wasn't living it.

Why are you telling this story? I asked myself now, standing in my parents' basement, surveying the wreckage of my potential-laden childhood. *If I don't know what I want, how will I know if I've got it or if it's lost forever?*

I tossed everything I'd sorted into the trash pile and peered through the blessing of the hole in the wall. I didn't know if the beginning of my story was in a promising private school and a yearbook full of hope and my ending was in here, in this ruined space, letting it all go. But I was determined to accept it, perhaps debate it, and then move on to a new story. I did want things: I wanted to express myself; I wanted to get out of my dead-end job; I wanted to feel loved; I wanted to love myself; I wanted to know that this was not the end.

I couldn't start a new story until I gave words to the why of it, even if it hurt, even if it felt too messy, even if it wasn't the story I set out to tell. It was my story and it was all I had.

I dusted myself off and left the basement.

Kramppromise

Throughout my early thirties, I loved to tell stories on first dates. I considered myself very good at first dates and I decided the stories were why. I didn't get a lot of second dates, though, so maybe I wasn't actually good at first dates. And maybe the stories were why. I'll have to take a poll. If you have dated me, please send a brief email just saying "Yes" or "No." I'll figure it out. Whatever the truth is, something was different with Jay, my first long-term boyfriend: we went out and then we went out again and, miracle of miracles, we kept going out. Apparently that's how these things happen. Who knew?

Jay and I were complete opposites. He worked nights, I worked days; he was white, I was a self-conscious Nilla Wafer; he loved horror movies, vampires, and camping in the woods, I was a God warrior whose idea of roughing it was staying at a hotel with no concierge. But you know what Paula Abdul says about opposites: you take two steps forward, I take two steps back, but when we get together we move in to a beautiful, high-ceilinged apartment in a Philadelphia brownstone with each other after dating for six months.

One of the more interesting differences between us was the way we expressed ourselves artistically. He was a visual artist—paints and sketches mostly, but also photography, makeup, sculpture, models. I worked with words—stories, plays, the solo show I was perpetually attempting to write.

At that point, because it was my first long-term relationship, I didn't know what a reasonable expectation for two people trying to make a life together was. That's the thing that rom-coms never teach you and short stories about rich white couples who live lives of quiet desperation are too far gone to cover: What is the act of making it? What's a red flag and what's just a weird personal detail that you can spin into a charming anecdote? The line is thinner than you think.

We'd had a really stunning meet-cute. He worked in a supermarket and I was in a season where I was eating all of my feelings, so I saw him multiple times a week. I had saved up for months to buy myself a stand mixer, and I was putting it to use on the regular: cakes, brownies, biscuits. I had a lot of feelings. Plus, a stand mixer had been my dream for so long, I didn't want to waste a second of our time together. There's little that I love as much as a kitchen appliance. For years, I'd dreamed of a melon-colored stand mixer and a Vitamix, the superpowered blender that can make everything from yogurt to soup. After some arduous months of saving and working overtime, I had one of the two and I was living half of my best, *Great British Bake Off* life.

This lifestyle naturally leads one to the supermarket quite frequently, and though I'd noticed Jay behind the deli counter more than a few times, I never spoke to him, because I have no game whatsoever and I was really focused on buying a bunch of ingredients for a complicated cake that wouldn't taste as good as one from a box. And he never spoke to me, because he thought I was, in his words, "a straight businessman." Honey! He wore glasses but that prescription must've needed some work. Picture me shimmying through the aisles of a supermarket, dancing to "Isn't She Lovely" on the store radio (which, remarkably, lasted my entire visit every time; that song is roughly three years long), carrying a tote bag and pushing a cart full of truffle oil, cake supplies, and a *Vanity Fair*. Move over, The Rock, there's a new paragon of masculine heterosexuality on the scene and she's ready to serve!

Jay and I eventually met in the middle of Philly's Gayborhood. He was coming from a night out at a bar; I was coming from losing a standup comedy competition. I hadn't really thought I was a good match for standup; I have trouble memorizing things and also I like to sit. Plus, I was a storyteller and not everything is funny, despite my best efforts. But a friend had convinced me that I needed to be bolder if I was going to make something of myself. "If you wanna be somebody," my friend told me, "if you wanna go somewhere, you better wake up and pay attention!" (My friend is Sister Mary Clarence from *Sister Act 2*.) The motivational advice of a Las Vegas lounge-singer-turned-nun mixed with the shame of defeat as I passed through the Gayborhood. Then I saw Jay stepping out of Woody's. "Wake up and pay attention," Mary Clarence whispered in my ear. I walked up to Jay and said, "You're the supermarket guy!" He nodded, startled, and then we made small talk as we walked down the street. He was in a rush, so he started to make his exit and almost stepped into the street as a bike came careening past. I grabbed him by the arm and pulled him back—to save him from the bike, not to kidnap him into more conversation, but really this line, also, is thin. He thanked me and went on his way.

The next day I walked into the market, pranced up to the deli counter, and told him, "I saved your life last night."

"You did?" he replied.

I decided not to entertain his befuddlement. "So I think it's only appropriate that you give me your number," I said. The boldness! In the middle of a Sunday afternoon. Who did I think I was? She's America's Masc Straight Businessmince Icon, that's who!

Jay looked stricken, probably because a random man was shaking him down for his telephone number. He gave it to me anyway, though, and told me he was off work in an hour if I wanted to get coffee. I said sure, and spent the next sixty minutes wandering the aisles listening to the second half of "Isn't She Lovely."

It was great for a while. We started seeing each other two or three times a week, and within a couple of months it became clear to me that I was in love with him. Surprisingly, he was in love with me, too, despite the fact that we were opposites and I am a little annoying and I was baking constantly (it sounds good but it gets old!). I was shocked by how easy it was to fall in love, after years of bad dates and lonely nights. I was shocked by how much I enjoyed being with him all the time. I was shocked by how perfect everything seemed. But when we moved in together, I had to reckon with some of the more striking differences in our personalities. Jay's art was primarily focused on darker themes—zombies, sea monsters, dead mermaids, ghosts; you know, the usual. He was particularly into H. R. Giger, the guy who designed the alien from *Alien*. Jay appreciated him as an artist and as a horror fan, which I could respect but did not like one bit. When we were casually dating, I'd just turn a blind eye to the canvas with the bloody undead skull chilling on his bedroom floor or the plastic replica of Sigourney Weaver's space nemesis on a shelf directly over his pillow. But when we moved in together, the apartment was flooded with horror, like the hallway in *The Shining.*

It should be said, I am very averse to horror movies. Horror movies are at the top of a very long list of things that I grew up believing were the devil. At various points in my life, that list also included fortune-telling, psychics, the lottery, episodes of *DuckTales* with the witch duck Magica De Spell, rock music, Santa Claus, particularly creepy laughs . . . I could go on. The point is, I had a scattershot but serious fear of dark forces. Besides, I don't like being scared, so what did I need to be watching a horror movie for anyway? Jay found that perplexing, but you can't really argue with your boyfriend standing in the middle of the living room screaming "The demons come through the cable wires, even if the film has been edited for network television! That's how they get you! It's in the Bible."

Nevertheless, Jay would try to find common ground, excitedly telling me about movie news concerning the upcoming *Alien* sequel (get thee behind me, space monster) and inviting me to watch something called *House on Haunted Hill* (if the house is not on HGTV, you can keep it). "You've seen *The Exorcist,* right?" he'd say to me, making a reference mid-story. I'd reply, "No, crazy. I obviously have not. What you should be asking is 'Have you seen *My Best Friend's Wedding* thirty-seven times, because the answer is yes and this conversation will go a lot better." Ah, relationships.

Keep scary movies away from me. *Particularly* if there is some sort of occult theme. I am so serious about it; I will leave the room, which I did many times during the time I dated Jay. "You can sit here and watch that possessed grandma perform a ritual sacrifice if you want; I'll be in the kitchen boiling some holy water for tea and going directly to heaven."

Jay and I didn't talk about spirituality a lot, but he knew I was a Christian and I knew that he was probably agnostic. Occasionally the Bible verse about not being "unequally yoked" would float into my head. Basically, as I'd learned in church, it meant Christians shouldn't make a household with non-Christians. However, as with much of the Bible, I wondered how much of it applied to gay life. And so I decided to just cross my fingers and hope for the best. Jay assured me that there was nothing related to spirituality in his love of scary movies. I believed this, but every once in a while I would google "How to know if my boyfriend is a devil worshipper."*

Sometimes Jay would try to make a placating compromise on a movie night by picking a film that didn't have horror elements, perhaps as a show that this was not an elaborate campaign to steal my raggedy soul. He'd pick something scary but not occult-y, like an intruder movie or something, but those were even worse. As you know, home invasion as a concept terrifies me, and then you put it on-screen with a nice family of white people and I'm in full hysterics. Bad things happening to white people is a whole genre of horror movies, and I find it deeply disturbing. Put me down as wanting only good things to happen to white people.

Jay, a white, did not see it in the same way. We agreed to disagree about movies. And the soul.

Film criticism aside, I decided it was probably best for our relationship if I shared some sort of common interest with him, so I chose his art. It seemed a good middle ground. More

* Because I'm a Christian, my enemies are Satan and Pontius Pilate. I didn't think that Pontius was trying to infiltrate my subconscious through the entertainment preferences of my boyfriend, but the jury was still out on the other dude. So I was vigilant. -Ish.

than once, I opened a closet to discover a screaming ghost or a desiccated skeleton, and that wasn't my preferred way to start the day, but I figured, *This is what he makes and I care about him, so I care about what he makes. And also I am locking that closet from now on.*

I began looking at the things that he painted, sculpted, or sketched with an artistic eye, saying things like "I love the brushwork on the blood dripping down that zombie's cheek." And these were expert opinions, mind you: I took two semesters of art history at Columbia. I'm basically Thomas Crown.

The pivot from frightened God warrior to art critic wasn't so hard. Jay, as I've noted, was very gifted. And I began to see the craft behind the image of a werewolf engulfed in flames. I even started to see how I might be involved in the work as a gift of love. Or so I thought. Jay would sell pieces at a street fair once a month, but, after some observation, I decided that "sell" was too generous a verb. He would lay out some canvases on a blanket and then lean against a wall and smoke cigarettes. "No one is going to buy this undead harpy from you if you're just standing there looking like a surly British cab driver with a corpse in his trunk, Jay! You have to *advertise*!" I decided that what his macabre art show needed was a little R. Eric Thomas sparkle! I dubbed myself his marketing manager, created business cards, a mailing list, and a contest. I bought a new blanket, printed out some signs at work, and took to standing in front of Jay as he smoked, making amiable conversation with the passersby like Mrs. Lovett from *Sweeney Todd*. "Wait! What's ya rush, what's ya hurry?! Don't you want to see a demon mermaid?!"

Alas, my tenure as the Mama Rose of Fleet Street did not last very long. My efforts netted Jay a small mailing list and a blooming resentment. We quickly learned that we weren't destined to be a family that ran a multimedia empire together, and when the street fair closed down for the winter, so did the marketing arm of the Art Ghoul, LLC. I wanted the passersby to see him the way I saw him, but in so doing I tried to change him. I didn't want him to change; I loved the person that he was.

By December, however, that aborted attempt to mix business with pleasure was largely forgotten as I focused all my mental energy on an even more monumental and important project: figuring out a color scheme for our Christmas tree.† Having a tree at all in a city is a real hassle, and this was particularly true in our case since we were on the third floor and we'd have to lug it all the way up the stairs, so I needed to make it count. Jay really wanted a tree. And when he talked about it, it seemed homey and romantic and sweet. I made him swear that before we carried it home we'd wrap ourselves in plastic like Kathy Bates in *Fried Green Tomatoes* to keep from getting covered in tree sap. He consented even though he had no idea what that meant. We picked a date for the tree.

But first! A theme! What's a Christmas tree without a theme? A busy bush, is what it is. I wasn't about to have people come into our apartment and think we just put ornaments and lights up *wherever we wanted* like a couple of *normal people*. We were a gay couple, after all. And I have a lifelong quest to make everything as complicated as possible. "Cranberry and Pewter," I declared one night, sailing into the living room and studiously avoiding looking at the person being sawed in half on Jay's computer screen. "Those are our colors. Not red and gray. Cranberry and Pewter. I've already bought the ornaments from Target. Unfortunately, we don't have any room for any old ornaments or sentimental keepsakes this year. We're just doing

† If you don't have theme colors for your Christmas, do you even believe in Christ?!

two colors, plus white lights, possibly a museum plaque on the side where I can give some background on my thought process."

Jay stared at me blankly. It's wonderful to collaborate.

The tree was, objectively, breathtaking. (Please remember my two semesters of art history at Columbia; this is classically trained objectivity.) We set up one of Jay's cameras across the room and took a warm, Cranberry-and-Pewter family photo, which got so many likes on Facebook. It was all I ever wanted.

I can't say, however, if it's what Jay wanted. I assumed it was because I assumed that's what a relationship was: getting everything you want exactly the way you want it, a melding of minds but not really a melding so much as my mind staying the same and the other person just sort of being subsumed. That may sound bad to you but I encourage you to think of it as romantic instead.

Close to Christmas, we went to a holiday party with a bunch of Jay's friends near his hometown. Many of his friends were also horror movie aficionados, and their conversation naturally veered over to old favorites, movie news, sinister fan art they'd found online, and the like. I busied myself with a plate of hummus across the room. As we were leaving, one of his friends stopped Jay and presented him with a gift the friend had been working on. It was an Elf on the Shelf doll, but the red and white clothes had been replaced by black clothes, its skin had been painted green, and its grin had been accentuated with red lips and two tiny white fangs. This was no longer an Elf. "It's a Krampus!" Jay cried with delight. He hugged it close to himself; I crossed myself even though I grew up Baptist and I wasn't really sure how to do it.

I knew what a Krampus was, because I'd read David Sedaris's essay "Six to Eight Black Men." In some Northern European countries Santa Claus has a sidekick or helper who doles out punishment for bad children. Sometimes that sidekick is a squad of Black men, like backup dancers. Other times, that sidekick is a Krampus, a werewolf-looking demon figure. And the punishment? The Krampus drags the children to hell.

"I can't wait to put this on the tree!" Jay exclaimed.

The ride home was tense: Jay amiably chatting, me having a quiet but steadily escalating panic attack, and our new addition, Santa's demon friend, radiating heat from the backseat.

One of my spiritual gifts is the ability to spiral out of control at the smallest provocation, and a creature who knows the access code to hell is no small provocation. I started rethinking our entire relationship as we drove back from Jersey into Philadelphia. *If Jay loves these dark things so much,* I thought, *who must he be? Either he is just a different kind of person, someone who likes scary things, or he is conspiring with the elf, the devil, and Pontius Pilate to try to steal my soul.* I couldn't stomach the idea of the latter, so for most of our time together I chose to believe the former. But it never really went away.

I couldn't shake the idea that my soul was in mortal danger. I felt like if I was a better Christian I would have known what to do in this situation, but gone were my youthful days of zealotry, like the summer I went to a revival and came home convinced I had to break all my Janet Jackson CDs in half. I realized that my interpretation of God warriordom had become laxer, more modern in the years since growing up and coming out. I strove to understand the Bible in context and to apply what I had just started learning about intersectional feminism to my religious beliefs. My deepest desire was to find a way to reconcile my truth as a gay person with my assurance that God not only loved me but had saved me. I didn't know if it was possible, but I was holding out hope. Still, I wasn't going to church and I hadn't in years, but I believed in God and I really didn't want to go to hell. So, it turned out, hell came to me.

We got home and Jay trotted up the stairs, burst into the living room, and turned to me expectantly. "Can we put it in the tree?" The creature was neither Cranberry, Pewter, nor *of the Lord*, but he popped it onto a branch midway up, framed it in twinkling lights, and cast me an affectionate grin. He was so happy.

When we first moved into the apartment, we'd had to sign a lease earlier than we needed to secure the apartment. So its halls, which would in my mind soon fill up with horror, sat empty for two weeks as we intermittently brought over a box or two. One afternoon, I popped in and wandered through the rooms, imagining what life would be like for us there. I had never lived with a boyfriend before, and the possibilities of our love nestled in every corner like dust bunnies, hung in the air as sunbeams, echoed off the bare walls.

I rounded the corner into the kitchen, a cramped space that had been converted from a child's bedroom. The refrigerator had been shoved into what used to be a closet; the linoleum buckled as if in protest. Our home. In the middle of the floor, I saw something new: two pieces of carpet scraps we'd found left over from the previous tenant, arranged into a heart. And on top of that heart, a Vitamix. I let loose an audible gasp. Jay had secretly saved and worked overtime for months to buy it for me. He may have misread me as straight prior to our relationship, but over the course of our years together, he consistently saw me for who I was and showed his love for that person through small kindnesses and large gestures alike. I knelt on the kitchen floor of the apartment we'd soon share and marveled at the person I'd stumbled upon.

A few months later, staring at our new roommate, the Krampus, on our otherwise Cranberry and Pewter tree, I tried to call that feeling back to mind. It wasn't working. Jay worked overnights, so we were both alone at home a lot. Well, he was alone. I was having a face-off with a doll. Jay would leave the apartment at 10 P.M. and he'd get back around 7 A.M. five days a week. We'd moved in together in October, so by December I was used to puttering around by myself after work at a law firm, watching *Scandal* on our couch, planning color schemes for future holidays, and slowly driving myself crazy with loneliness. Sometimes we'd argue about his job; I'd press him to find something that would allow us to spend any time together. He'd grow frustrated with me, rightfully pointing out that it wasn't exactly ideal for him either but that he was trapped. I was trapped in my job, too, but because it was in the daytime, suddenly it seemed less urgent. As much as we made adjustments for each other's happiness, there were some things beyond either of our controls. I wanted to spend more time with my boyfriend, to enjoy those stereotypically cozy winter nights in front of our perfectly curated tree, watching movies where everyone goes to heaven in the end, if not actually, at least by implication. Instead, I found myself fighting a squatter from the underworld.

Realizing that Jay's absence and my paranoia put me on the back foot, the Krampus quickly began to terrorize me. Sometimes, I'd be sitting on our IKEA couch and I'd hear it breathing behind me. Was it breathing? Probably not—demons don't have lungs. I think it was just making noise to mess with me. I found I couldn't even look in its direction. I'd turn it some nights, moving it to the back of the tree, or just adjusting it so it looked in a different direction. The Krampus always turned back, its beady eyes trained on the spot where I always sat, its forked tongue licking its fangs with anticipation. Sure, Jay probably readjusted it when he came home in the wee small hours of the morning, but there is no way to prove that. You'll never catch me playing the devil's advocate, honey. That's how they get you.

Krampus and I were terrible roommates. It got to the point I couldn't even set foot in the living room anymore, because you can only fight the forces of evil for so long before you go crazy. I had access to four different rooms and a whole city of experiences; Krampus didn't have legs that worked. Yet, somehow it had all the power. The living room was canceled; Krampus owned it. When Jay would leave home, I'd shut the door so I didn't even have to think about it. But Krampus wasn't satisfied. Krampus wanted more. Krampus's face would appear in the soap as I washed dishes and shout spoilers for *Scandal*. Krampus became a recurring guest star in my dreams; it was a surprisingly versatile actor. But I wasn't beguiled! You can't tempt me with award-winning subconscious performances, Krampus! I'm a God warrior.

I was, to put it mildly, completely losing my shit. And because Jay and I were, more often than not, ships passing in the night, I was doing it completely on my own. A relationship was supposed to be a refuge, I thought. I didn't know and I had no experience to judge it by, but I was highly doubtful that it was supposed to be a battle for the soul against your partner. And if I'd thought a little harder, I might have connected my anxiety around my soul to the fact that I'd never been in a relationship this long—my homosexuality was leveling up. I was, actually, afraid of the devil doll in my living room, but I was, unknowingly, also afraid that my happiness with a man was going to damn me.

At the end of one particularly grueling week of spiritual warfare, Jay and I were watching TV on the couch on his night off. I fidgeted. I had to say something. "Don't say anything," Krampus growled behind me. A bead of sweat wormed its way down my temple; my breathing got heavier. I'd found myself a captive of my own apartment and now Krampus and Jay were here together and it occurred to me that perhaps this was how it would all end. I turned to Jay. "You have to tell me the truth about something," I squeaked. "Stop!" Krampus bellowed. The room seemed to shake; I could see my breath as it escaped my lips; the lights started flashing on and off. Well, that last part was okay: they were Christmas lights. But the rest of it: not good. I grabbed Jay's arm. "Are you a devil worshipper?"

"What?!"

"Are you in league with the darkness? Are you a soul snatcher? Are you and Krampus working together to drag me to hell?!"

"You can't be serious."

"Shockingly, I am!" I felt slightly sheepish but soldiered on. "I might be going crazy. But this doll, I think it's possessed. At the very least it's really creepy. And I feel like I can't be in the same room as it. Sometimes it shows up in my dreams. It told me what happens on the season finale of *Scandal*, which is rude and—"

"Okay, I get it. If it bothers you that much, I'll just take it down."

"No!" Krampus shouted.

"No . . ." I whimpered. "You like it so much."

"Yeah, but you hate it."

I nodded. It was just an artfully painted Elf on the Shelf, but I hated it.

Jay plucked it from the tree's branches and put it in a box. He disappeared to his workroom and I never saw Krampus again. It was a kindness and I told him how much I appreciated it, but I also felt like I'd failed in some way, like I hadn't been flexible enough. I'd pinned my existential anxiety on his hobby. I had loved but I hadn't loved hard enough.

For all of love's complications, I think every couple's story starts with two strangers who, if they want to survive, must move heaven and hell to reach each other.

Comforters

When my relationship with Jay ended, it was sudden, like a fault line exposing a crevice in the middle of rush-hour traffic. We found ourselves on either side of the crack, and though we tried to put it back together, it became clear that it was made up of a thousand tiny cracks that had accumulated over time. We wanted to be together but the earth had moved. I was surprised by how quickly and completely I, too, cracked wide open. I try not to cry in front of friends, because it feels unnecessary and I'm nothing if not prudent, but I couldn't help it. I was crying in front of everyone. I was making new friends just so I could cry in front of them. I would literally scroll through my phone and ask myself, *Who haven't I cried at yet?*

I went over to my best friend Jake's house one night and, in the middle of an unrelated conversation, burst into tears and actually ironically uttered the phrase "Who . . . who gon' love me?" I then realized I'd quoted the movie *Precious: Based on the Novel* Push *by Sapphire,* and started maniacally laughing. It was a lot to process. This is why you shouldn't cry in front of friends.

Jake was a massively successful dater. I was . . . a work in progress. There's that OkCupid question, "What's the most private thing you're willing to admit here?" Sane people would write the same kinds of boilerplate answers: "I'm not telling you, LOL" (*extremely* common) or "If I drop a piece of pizza on the floor, I sometimes still eat it." Whatever, something normal. Safe. I will tell you my answer to that question. (This is 100 percent the truth. Because it's Christmas and at Christmas you have to tell the truth.) (I am writing this in April.) Anyway, my answer to the question "What's the most private thing you're willing to admit here?": "I am actually getting pretty serious about being on the *New York Times* Weddings and Celebrations page and I'd like you to be on board with that."

Massively unpopular. (Spoiler: My husband, David, and I did end up on the Weddings and Celebrations page. *And* he lets me lecture him on *Clue* whenever I want. So I guess the arc of the moral universe *does* bend toward justice.) But in the moment, there were a lot of attempts, a lot of loneliness, and a lot of unanswered missives about mid-eighties comedies. And very little cuddling.

Jake used to herald the descending temperatures by declaring it Boo Weather, as in the perfect temperature to get boo'd up and hunker down under a duvet with a warm body. And this is true. It is nice to cuddle in the late fall and winter. (Please do not touch or look me directly in the eye in the summer.) I was always 100 percent here for Boo Weather when I was single. But I rarely had a boo, and I never owned a duvet.

As Boo Weather approached, my tear ducts had dried up, but the question remained: "Who . . . who?" I tried to make myself get out there, boo up, etc. But to no avail. And when you're unboo'd and still sort of sad, the winter feels like dying.

It's easy, I guess, to look back now and say that everything turned out okay and Jay has moved on and I'm married and we all lived happily ever after, as if none of the sadness left a mark, as if winter never came, as if now is all that matters. But that place in me that compulsively cried to everyone who would listen is still in me; the bad times don't go away just because times are good. We say these things build character; they make us who we are. And that's true. But that doesn't mean they don't suck. It doesn't mean winter isn't cold.

I think the worst thing about winter is that I always think it won't be that bad, and it always tricks me. It's all gently descending temperatures and entreaties of Pumpkin Spice Lattes and then BOOM! There's a foot of dirty snow on the ground and you're locked inside a ship en route to the Island of Lost Boys.

Here are the stages of winter. Please print this out and warn your loved ones.

1. Ooh! Scarves and cardigans! Cuddle weather!
2. Yes! Kids in Halloween costumes! Cuteness overload!
3. Aw, changing leaves! Smells of cider! Let's go hiking like Caucasians!
4. Really, Christmas carols this early? Where do I store my gloves? Why don't I have a better system of organization in my own damn house? Do I own gloves? What is my life even?
5. GIVE ME ALL THE TURKEY! Give it to me! GIVE IT TO MEEEEE!
6. Christmas carols! Yay! Am I enjoying this? I am! I am enjoying this.
7. Christmas carols? Still? Oh, look, *Love, Actually* is on. All right, enough with the Christmas carols! You know, *Love, Actually* is kind of sad. Laura Linney can't have sex with the hottest man on the planet and actually, now

that I think about it, every single person in this movie is a different, new kind of asshole, and it's infuriating.

8. Oh. Now it's just cold and dark. Forever.

There is not a moment of my day when I am not irate about *Love, Actually*. It's the most nihilist romcom ever made. Every single person is making terrible choices except Emma Thompson, and she's so rightfully sad. That movie makes me so angry, and yet every time I watch it (once a week from October through May), I'm like, "This is so me. This is so true."

It's because of winter! It gets in your mind. It short-circuits you! It makes you think that Colin Firth isn't just creating a hostile work environment because he's lonely. I get it. But we have to tell the truth.

There's that moment in the late fall when you think you may have dodged a bullet, when the air is balmy but crisp and all you need is a jacket. Every year I think that maybe it will stay like this.* It was on one of those perfect balmy days, right at the beginning of Boo Season, that I went on a second date with a nurse named Franco. He was the first person I'd gone on a date with after Jay; it had been months, but Jake encouraged me to give it a shot. Franco was nice enough; he talked fast. I like fast talkers. Sometimes. Sometimes I'm like, "Yo, this isn't a pig auction in Tuscaloosa. Can I get a word in edgewise? That word would be 'some pig.'"

* Why can't it? We call it unseasonably nice, but why can't nice be in season? Why can't it be every season? Why can't life always hover in that perfect space where we feel good, and it doesn't hurt to walk around, and everything seems possible with a minimum of perspiration?

We went back to his place and made out a little. In retrospect, it was kind of a meh experience. But I was so beguiled by the *mise-en-scène* that I mistook it for romance. His place was so nice! The air smelled good, the furniture looked nice, the paintings on the wall were so pretty. And he had this gorgeous white comforter, so fluffy and pristine. At that time, on my bed, I had the blue checkered number I'd gotten when I moved to college. It was, admittedly, a little worse for wear—its synthetic stuffing was creeping out of a tear in one side and its colors had faded. And it was full-size; at that point I had had a queen-size bed for years. But all throughout my move into adulthood, in my three apartments and during my relationship with Jay, I had kept warm under that thinning, blue checkered sheath from the 1998 Sears Campus Essentials collection.

Franco did not have anything from 1998 in his apartment. Everything was pristine, chic even. (I admit now that I have developed better taste in the years since, and much of what he had was your standard-issue IKEA bachelor nonsense. But I am always here for nonsense, regardless.) That comforter, though, I couldn't get over. It rested on his bed like a low-lying cumulus system, at once weightless and cumbersome. The (IKEA) lamp light bounced off its rolling surface; it seemed to illuminate the whole room. As he gave me a tour of the apartment, I lingered in the doorway of his bedroom, staring hungrily at the comforter. He may have thought that my amorous looks were more focused on what happens under the comforter, because he started making out with me again. This was fine.

We quickly realized that we were boring to each other. Does that happen to everyone? It happened to me a lot.

I'd be kissing, or worse, talking, when the thought would just walk into my head, *This is dumb.* Franco was nice but he talked too fast and his apartment was freezing. Why did he have the air conditioner going full blast in November? Didn't he appreciate a perfect day? This was not cuddle weather. And besides, I didn't want to cuddle with him. Just his blanket.

I excused myself to the bathroom. He had a peach candle burning in there that smelled just like an actual peach. It was stunning! It wasn't one of those candles that smells like a peach Jolly Rancher or peach body lotion. It smelled like biting into that perfect peach you get on that first truly warm day after a long, hard winter. The peach that reminds you, as juices run down your hand, that being alive is generally a good and pleasant thing and you should keep doing it.

I tried to find a label on the candle but it had none. So chic! I sniffed the air and realized the peach was mingling with another smell. Was it just clean in there or did he have an air freshener? Or was it the expensive basil soap he had by the sink? I was so overwhelmed by this olfactory experience that I forgot to snoop through his cabinet.

I finished washing my hands and decided that I was not leaving this apartment without getting what I came for: the names of all his products. I licked my lips like a movie heroine who is trying to project her steely determination. I realized that even my lips smelled good. What flavor Burt's Bees was he using? This was like a gay Wonka Factory. I stepped out. *Try to be casual, keep it chill, Eric. Don't frighten him; he's a nurse, so he probably has access to sedatives.*

I strolled into the living room and ran my hand along the arm of the sofa. "Nice apartment you have here . . ." My mind immediately filled in *Be a shame if someone trashed it!* because

I am apparently possessed by a stereotypical movie mob thug. I shook my head; threats were probably not a good look.

"Say, what flavor of lip balm do you use?"

He looked at me quizzically as if it's weird to just know that information. I maintain that that is not weird information to carry around in your head. I will not defend this point.

He fished into his pocket and took the tube out. "Pomegranate?"

Why is there a question mark? I wondered. *Can you read? This is going to take all night.*

"Cool," I replied. "Nice. Good." *Yup, keep it to one syllable, my friend. Lure him in.* I grabbed my coat. "I should be going. Oh! Say! That's a nice candle. I want to buy one for my . . . girlfriend? No. Sorry, for myself. Masculinity is a prison, amiright? What flavor is it?"

He cocked his head. "Peach?" I was probably going to resort to violence.

"Nice. Cool. Do you know where you got it?"

"Yankee Candle?" Was everything in this room a surprise to him?

"And, haha, this is weird, but is there another air freshener you have going? It just smells really good. Also, where did you get that shirt? Also, that comforter, is it a duvet cover or just a comforter? What's the brand? Do you mind if I take a photo of the tag so I can remember? I'm just going to go take a photo."

It wasn't pretty but I got it all out of him. And I marched off into the perfect evening with a shopping list and a spring in my step. That weekend, I went out to IKEA and to Bed Bath & Beyond and to Target and bought it all—from the air freshener to the body spray to the Burt's Bees lip balm that made his lips seem less like a stranger's. Everything. Everything but the comforter. The comforter I couldn't find. You've heard of spring cleaning? This was fall hoarding.

When Jay moved out, he, naturally, took all his stuff with him. And the empty spaces, where his artwork or his favorite chair used to be, haunted me. For months after he left, I would wake up every morning and refuse to get out of bed until I'd managed to convince myself not to get the lyrics to "Where Do Broken Hearts Go" tattooed on my body that day. Like, I was sad in so many creative ways.

BRAIN: Okay, what are we not going to do today?

ME: Eat healthily.

BRAIN: What else?

ME: Go to a tattoo parlor . . .

BRAIN: That's right.

ME: But—

BRAIN: *No.*

ME: But the lyrics are so evocative!

BRAIN: You're going to regret it in, like, a week.

ME: You don't know my life.

BRAIN: Girl, I am serious right now. You can't get that song tattooed on your body.

ME: Yo, but what if I get it tattooed in Chinese so nobody knows?

BRAIN: Listen, you are Batman villain crazy right now and I'm going to need you to sit on your hands. Just for today.

ME: But I'm sad!

BRAIN: You'll get over it.

ME: What if I don't?

BRAIN: Then you can get the tattoo.

ME: So, like, tomorrow?

BRAIN: Boy, you testing my last nerve! Get out of this bed!

ME: Who you think you yelling at? You better take that bass out your voice when you talking to me! I brought you into this world and I will take you right out!

One morning, I felt the pull of inking my entire body with Whitney lyrics a little too strongly. I rolled over and grabbed my phone, intending to look up tattoo parlors. Instead I logged on to Amazon.com and started clicking. If I couldn't get my comforter in reality, maybe I could find it online. And unlike love, fluffy, cloud-like, expensive blankets were available in abundance online. And they all wanted to go home with me. I added a couple of options to my wish list, decided all were too expensive, then realized I felt a little better and got out of bed.

A few days later I logged back on and bought some more of Franco's air fresheners. *My room should smell nice,* I thought. *Like a hotel lobby!* I felt better and got out of bed.

A few days later I went on a candle binge. *If I'm going to get over this breakup, I'm going to need fire. Preferably peach scented*. It turns out there are many accurate fruit smells that a room can have. I bought them all. And I felt better and got out of bed.

Then I bought a new set of pots and pans, bright red ones with smooth white insides. Franco, the nurse, hadn't had pots as far as I could see. But they came up on my Amazon page and I liked them. I decided I'd hang them from the rack in the kitchen and told myself one day I'd start cooking again. And I felt better and got out of bed.

Then I decided that the reason it was so hard to get out of bed sometimes was because my bed was old and saggy and sad. So I went to brunch one day and on my way back popped into a mattress store. I rolled around on beds in an empty warehouse while a teenage sales associate looked on dispassionately and flurries whipped around the window. I flipped onto my side on a Tempur-Pedic and muttered, "But what will really make me happy?" Then I bought a double-sided pillow top, paid for delivery, and got out of bed.

Finally, I decided to revisit the comforters, the impetus behind this spending spree. I weighed the attributes of a couple different brands; I read every insane online review; I called my friend Jake, crying. And then I hit "Buy." And that was that. It came in a couple of days; I spread it across my new bed on an early winter morning just as the temperatures started to threaten that cold was indeed going to come again this year.

I went on one or two dates a week that winter. I always came home by myself. To that apartment full of stuff: Brené Brown books, cardigans, IKEA tables, cleaning tchotchkes, pots that seemed expensive to me then, wall art I knew was cheap, every good-smelling thing, a DVD copy of *Love, Actually,* and a CD of Whitney Houston's greatest hits. The apartment that Jay and I picked out together. Our apartment that felt half empty and echoed after he left. My apartment that I slowly filled back up, with new stuff: a painting over the spot where a picture once hung of me throwing my head back, guffawing at something he'd said; a set of colorful bowls in the bare cupboard shelf; boots on the unbalanced shoe rack; a new comforter on the empty bed.

I still have the comforter. It's fine but I don't think I ever really liked it, actually. It looked good but it was lumpy where it should've been fluffy; it didn't look as pristine in the light as I remembered. But I kept it and, for a while, pretended I did like it. Because it cost me $150 at a time when I was kind of broke and kind of broken. I kept it because I thought money could buy me happiness and for a while I was right. I kept it because it made me feel warm.

The Preacher's Husband

The night I met my husband, David, a Presbyterian pastor, I went back to my apartment in a South Philly brownstone, sat on the front steps, and decided that the minute we got engaged I would announce it on Facebook by changing my profile picture to Whitney Houston in *The Preacher's Wife*. I saw the future clearly and, apparently, that future was on Facebook. You've got to be always thinking of how you'll turn life events into #content, and it's a known fact that engagements, the *first* baby, *some* new jobs, winning *Big Brother,* and photos with celebrities are the gold standards of social media reaction-getters. Squandering such gifts is a scandal and a sin. And I wasn't trying to sin, because, honey, I was about to marry a preacher. I was about to be Mrs. God or whatever. Mary Man-delene? Possible. I was a little unclear on some of the details, like (a) how to contact David, (b) what male wives of preachers were called, (c) what a Presbyterian was per se, and (d) if enough of my friends were familiar with the complete Whitney Houston film collection for my reference to land. It was a stressful time; prayers were requested.

On the night we met, David had been on a panel about LGBTQ people of faith, alongside representatives from other branches of Christianity, Buddhism, Judaism, and Islam. I'd been asked to moderate for reasons that I am still unclear on. I suppose it was for my personality and the fact that I had a standing appointment on my Google calendar that read "Go to church, you asshole," which I consistently ignored. In any case, David delighted me so thoroughly that midway through the panel I stopped talking to all the other panelists and peppered David with personal questions. Please invite me to disrupt all of your events for a small honorarium.

Afterward, I mumbled awkward conversational things in David's general direction and tried to fend off someone else who wanted to badger him with long-winded anecdotes disguised as questions. *What is a good way to flirt with a pastor?* I wondered, and my brain answered "TELL HIM HOW CHRISTIAN YOU ARE." It's like when you're on a dating profile and you write that your favorite book is *Less* by Andrew Sean Greer and then you see someone else who lists *Less* by Andrew Sean Greer as their favorite book and you send them an all-caps message that's like "WHO COULD IMAGINE TWO PEOPLE IN THIS WIDE WONDERFUL WORLD WOULD BOTH LIKE THIS BOOK WHICH IS UNIVERSALLY BELOVED AND WON THE PULITZER PRIZE? We must be soul mates, you and I! Shall I schedule a spring wedding?" Except instead of a comic novel about a late-middle-aged gay man's existential crisis, the thing I was trying to bond with David over was the life, death, and resurrection of Jesus Christ. I was determined to highlight our mutual interest in the niche subject of Protestantism.

It turns out, when you are a pastor, everyone wants to talk to you about God. I did not realize this. I imagine that launching into a long, personal quixotic monologue about spirituality is something that people can't help, and it's something, I've found, that pastors don't mind. That's ministry, after all, and it's not only their life's work, it's their calling. It is not, however, a great way to flirt.

"Jesus, what a pal, right?!" I shouted at David. He nodded. Perhaps through natural development or perhaps through years of studied admiration, David has the friendly, patient countenance of his hero, Mr. Rogers. It always sounds cliché to say a person has kind eyes, but sometimes clichés are true and that's a real paradox for a person who is trying to write interesting things. His eyes look like they give to charity? Anyway, you get the picture or you don't, but don't blame me. Blame eyes.

Kind eyes are always a surprise to see in the flesh, because not everyone has them. I certainly don't. I have side eyes. In addition to his eyes (two of them! So kind!), David has a round face and, at that point, had shaggy brown hair that curled up on the ends, giving him the joyful, boyish look of a camp counselor or a campus tour guide or an Eagle Scout—all of which he has been. (Or, in the case of the Eagle Scouts, still is.)

Our post-panel conversation going swimmingly, I decided to wrap things up by asking him out. "I'd like to visit your church sometime," I said without a hint of intrigue. I put the single in single entendre. David nodded and smiled and handed me his business card with his work email address on it. *How am I supposed to text nudes to this?* I wondered. Modern love, what a scam.

What I didn't realize is that by saying I wanted to visit David's church, I had inadvertently put myself in the category of congregant and not fiancé. If a person has a need for ministry, he does not get the minist-D. (I'm sorry; I'm trying to delete this.)

We didn't talk for two months because, despite what I said, I wasn't trying to go to church. I was just a liar who was trying to go Dutch on an Italian dinner and eventually name him as the beneficiary of my life insurance plan.

At that point, I had been in Philadelphia for about a decade and I'd spent much of it searching for a church home, with varying levels of commitment. I knew that spirituality was something that I wanted in my life (Jesus! What a pal!), but as I came more into myself as a gay person, I became resolute in my desire to never sit in a pew and be told I was going to hell again. It's the little things. I'd found myself in a number of open and affirming congregations, but most of them were largely white and their style of worship was so dramatically different from what I grew up with it was hard to take seriously as capital-C Church. Some of these people were wearing shorts. Jesus didn't die on the cross for you to be exposing your knees like it's Casual Friday, Mark.

I love Church. It's theater, it's high camp, it's cabaret. What's not to love? You get to dress up like you're going to the Grammys. Literally every word that everyone says in Church is a very compelling story that frequently involves both scandal and magic. There is *so much* gossip. It's Pay-What-You-Wish. *There is a choir.* And musical numbers. And choreography. And when things really get going, people yell, shout, jump up and down, and *stop the show*. HONEY. Church is very gay.

Honestly, I see very little difference between Church and a Beyoncé concert. Maybe that's the core of my theology: if it makes you feel something ineffable, if it's bigger than you and yet deeply personal, if it sometimes involves a fog machine, it's

Church. Jesus is in there somewhere, swaying to the music, saving you a dance. What a pal.*

The church I grew up in was a small building around the corner from the racetrack where the Preakness is held. One narrow room with maybe fifteen pews and wood paneling on the walls. It always smelled of perfume and old books. The floor was cold in the wintertime and in the summer there were fans. You know the fans I mean—card stock on a big Popsicle stick with an illustration of Dr. King on the front and an ad for a funeral home on the back. You had to leave through the front door and walk around the back to get to the restroom. And every Sunday, Sister Jackson sat in the front row and stopped the show. When Sister Jackson got to thanking and praising the Lord, well, that was a wrap on service. Our church was one of those that went from eleven-ish to "until," so Sister Jackson taking two minutes, twenty minutes, a decade to get her everlasting life was par for the course. It was almost as if she was the minister of praise, though the church was never much for putting women in positions of authority, so that would've been a no-go. But at any moment, Sister Jackson could get worked up, shouting, standing, waving her hands, and the show would not go on.

I was deeply intimidated by that but I loved it. Because in church I was a spectator. Praise seemed to involve both an unabashed spirit that I never possessed and an earthy Blackness

* One time, in New York, I went to see a musical called *The Wild Party*. It starred Toni Collette (superb) and Mandy Patinkin (absent on the day I went). It also co-starred the legendary Eartha Kitt, who floated in and out of scenes pretty much whenever she wanted to. At one point, midway through the musical, they closed the curtain, Eartha emerged in front of it, sang a song, walked off, and then they opened the curtain again and the show continued. They literally stopped the show for Eartha Kitt. And that, too, is Church.

that was a mystery to me. Even though we were a simple, one-room church in an impoverished Baltimore neighborhood, it was one of the most extravagant, confounding, and dramatic experiences I'd ever had.

Church in Philly didn't compare. The churches that felt like home weren't here for the gays, either overtly or covertly. The churches where everyone wore a rainbow pin on their lapel seemed oddly calm about the Resurrection. I wanted an experience where people were shouting but not shouting at me. After some years of itinerant worship, I just called it a (Lord's) day and spent the Sabbath blasting show tunes and going to brunch. Another kind of church.

There was one church that always came up when I googled "Who will love me church lol gospel prayer hands emoji?" It was a Presbyterian-affiliated faith community that met at 4 P.M. on Sundays (after brunch!) in a huge old sanctuary with flying buttresses and sun-drenched stained glass but peeling walls and no pews. They were open and affirming; they sang hymns and also Stevie Wonder songs. The congregation was diverse across all manner of demographics. During the week, the space was used to serve daily gourmet meals, prepared by Chef Steve, a former corporate chef at Comcast, to people experiencing homelessness and food insecurity. A theater company that produced forgotten works took up residence in the Sunday school room. In short, it was a little bit like heaven. It seemed perfect for me; so, of course, I never went.

It should come as no surprise that the card that David handed me after the spirituality panel bore the name of that same church from my Google searches: Broad Street Ministry.

There was one church I could go to in Philly to fulfill my spiritual needs, but if I went to the church I couldn't date the surprisingly appealing pastor. It was a real Catch 3:16.

So, I did nothing.

I would make a terrible disciple, I think.

When David and I tell this story, it's here that we switch off, like a reliable double act with choreography as easy as breathing. He gives some background on why he was on the panel in the first place (he was stalking me), and then we fast-forward a few months to when I was performing a one-man show called *Always the Bridesmaid* about how I was very single and I had questions about God and wanted someone to date me and also explain theological ideas to me. Look, you have to ask for what you want. Some people pray; some people write hour-long theatrical monologues. *We all do church in our own ways, okay?!*

One of David's congregants, Colton, suggested to David that they go together. Colton had been conspiring to get us together since he saw me hosting The Moth the month before the panel. He'd nudged David in the audience and said, "You should marry the host." David had demurred, claiming I was too famous for him, which is my favorite quality in a person. Anyway, undeterred by my fame, they continued to stalk me until they ended up sitting in a small cabaret space watching me struggle to remember lines I had written myself based on events that had happened to me and thoughts that had actually passed through my head.

We started dating soon after, but I wasn't allowed to go to his church, because it's kind of weird for a pastor to be trotting his trade through the sanctuary willy-nilly. He wanted to wait until we were sure we were serious. He was also looking for guidance for how to do it. Not divine guidance (although he may have inquired to the department upstairs), just a how-to for being a gay, single pastor and introducing your congregation and co-workers to your new boyfriend who hasn't been to church since the Bush administration.

Initially, I was fine with this, but it eventually started to wear on me. I'd worked so hard to emerge from every closet in my life, and being kept a secret like a plot twist on *Game of Thrones* felt like a regression. It became a sticking point in our nascent relationship. All things church did. He was staying in a manse beside another church and would invite me over to hang out or watch TV and it never stopped feeling like I was sneaking around, sipping the communion wine, and breaking some sort of covenant. Eventually, I'd had enough. I decided that I was going to tell him we needed to take a break. But before I could do that, he told me he'd decided the time was right for me to be introduced at church. "I'd love it if you came to Ash Wednesday service with me," he said.

"That sounds awesome," I replied. "What's Ash Wednesday?"

I was vaguely familiar with the concept of Ash Wednesday and I've worked in an office before, so I knew that sometimes some people came to work with a smudge on their foreheads, but I thought they were all Catholic. In retrospect, I thought that all forms of Christianity boiled down to Catholic and Whatever I Am. I knew that there were variations on worship styles from church to church, but I hadn't ever parsed the differences between denominations. My parents met in an African Methodist Episcopal church but had joined a Baptist church by the time I was born. Though I'd been to services at both, I couldn't tell you how—in theology or practice—they differed. Frankly, I thought the biggest predictor of difference in a church service was the race of the people in the pews. There was white church and there was Black church.

After the invitation to the Ash Wednesday service, the thought occurred to me for the first time, *Does David work at a white church?* The congregation was very diverse, but the way they worshipped was so foreign to me. They ended after a brisk forty-five minutes! Every time! No one caught the spirit and laid on the floor. Not even on Easter! Eventually, my brain short-circuited and I just started labeling everything white. So, when I write "white" here, know I mean Presbyterian. Unless I actually mean white. In that case, I mean white.

In any case, Whitney Houston never encountered this particular issue in *The Preacher's Wife;* she was at a Black church. I was on my own.

We realized rather quickly that we were serious about each other. The Ash Wednesday service debut had gone over just fine; when offered ash I simply replied, "No thanks, I'm trying to quit." The music was nice; the congregants were friendly. And, for David, that was one of the last hurdles. Somewhere along the line we started talking about marriage and so I started googling things like "What do Presbyterians believe?"

"What is my church lady hat size?" and "Does this mean I have to stop cursing?" David wasn't the lead pastor of Broad Street, but I knew that eventually his path would lead him to his own church and I wanted to be ready.

I started searching in earnest on Amazon for books about being a pastor's spouse. Every single thing that I found was exclusively directed toward women and seemed to assume that I would be playing the piano for the choir, teaching Sunday school, and definitely not working. I understood this kind of life but I was shocked to find myself stepping into it.

I began to wonder if I was supposed to be giving up parts of myself to fit into a mold of a pastor's spouse. Should I learn to play piano? David assured me that he didn't expect it and that the church he envisioned for himself didn't require me to teach Sunday school if I didn't want to. "I want you to feel free to be exactly who you are," he said.

As his time at Broad Street came to an end, David began putting out his CV on a site that's basically LinkedIn for Presbyterian pastors. Pastors looking for "calls"—invitations to lead a congregation or a specific ministry—would post profiles, and churches looking for pastors would fill out profiles of their own. Imaginings of life in exotic locales like Ohio and A Dakota started popping up in our evening conversations. Once, he read me a profile of a church that had a laundry list of duties for their new junior pastor: "lead the youth group, perform couples ministry, preach twelve Sundays a year. Also, in keeping with the traditions of the church, the pastor will occasionally wear colonial garb."

"Excuse me?"

"Apparently, George Washington visited this church once, so they celebrate by dressing up in clothes from colonial times," David said. This was white church. David clicked to another profile and then turned to me with a new thought. "If I got that, what do you think you would wear?" he asked.

Visions of Crispus Attucks in a church hat danced in my head. Hard pass.

I replied, "Oh, honey. I'll be the pastor's wife-husband. I'm going to wear whatever I want."

Dinner Guests

In a box in my parents' dining room sits a stack of five-by-eight-inch index cards with photos and profiles of important Black historical figures. At every meal during Black History Month, they'd set a card up at an empty space at our dining room table and we'd spend the meal talking about the person profiled in a tradition they dubbed "Dinner Guests." Some people save a place for Elijah; we saved a place for Shirley Chisholm. The conversations always centered around achievement rather than overcoming. In what I would later realize was a stunning bit of narrative alchemy, my parents taught us Black history lessons that weren't remarkable because of all the oppression they involved but because of the extraordinariness of the Black people at their center. This would prove to be dramatically different from the rest of reality, which is, let's be honest, an oppression-fest.

On our first date, David and I went to a charming little Italian restaurant in Philadelphia, the kind that was designed within an inch of its life to project homespun warmth and familial charm. And it worked. We talked for four hours about the best dinners we'd ever had, about the boisterous, convivial parties his aunt and uncle threw at their home, and about my parents' Dinner Guests tradition. He recommended to me the poem "Perhaps the World Ends Here" by Joy Harjo, which begins "The world begins at a kitchen table. No matter what, we must eat to live." I now know that we were setting an intention for ourselves, for the way our lives together would play out, and the places that we would find comfort, belonging, and transformation. But we didn't know that then. All we knew was that we liked to eat and we liked to talk and we wanted to keep doing those things, preferably simultaneously, for a long time. Which is as good a foundation for a relationship as any.

As I prepared to bring David home to meet my parents for the first time, I thought of the empty setting at their table that had once held space for Dr. Charles Drew and Gwendolyn Brooks. David was in Baltimore for a conference, and my mother had told me I should come down and bring him over, even though it was Valentine's Day and it was snowing heavily. "But it's Valentine's Day," I said. "Won't you be busy?"

"We don't have plans, boy! We've been married thirty-six years. I'll make spaghetti."

My mother welcomed David into the house and asked if he had enough time for a tour of the family photos. He said yes, because I hadn't warned him how many family photos there were. She ushered him into the dining room. On one side of the table my parents have hung a painting I'd commissioned of my mother's grandfather N. A. Smith baptizing her uncle in a river. Opposite that painting hung two photos of the slave cabin where N. A. Smith was born. "This is where we begin," my mother said.

This was my second time bringing a boyfriend home. Soon after Jay and I moved in together, my mother called and demanded that I bring him down for Thanksgiving so she could meet him. This was a reasonable request that, naturally, sent me reeling with anxiety. I had never brought anyone, of any gender, home. So a boyfriend introduction at a large family dinner seemed, frankly, beyond the pale. But I will do anything within my power to please my mother—and it didn't seem practical that Jay and my parents would just never meet for the rest of their lives—so I agreed. Before we ended the call, my mother said, "Oh, and Martin is coming, too. I just thought you should know."

Martin is my cousin. He's twelve years older than me. He's always been very good-looking, macho, and cool. I guess it runs in the family. For a while, Martin existed largely as an idea, a character in our family story that was oft referred to but rarely seen. Right after high school he went into the military. He served in the Gulf War and then was stationed in Europe. Afterward he came home, got married, had two extraordinary daughters, and continued to serve the country for over a decade.

Memories of him float in this half-light that seems fantastical. During the Gulf War, when I still lived at home, I remember we would occasionally get souvenirs from him. Not like cultural artifacts, just "I'm thinking of you" stuff. Like once he sent us a VHS copy of *Die Hard*. Could this be right? If so, awesome. But I remember we were told we couldn't play it because it was full of sand. I don't know if that was actually true or whether that was just something my parents said to keep us away from an R-rated movie. I prefer for the sand to be real; I imagine it pouring out of the cassette case and filling up the room, a billion particles from across the sea bearing the message "Yippee-yi-yo-ki-yay. I miss you. Love, Martin."

Anyway, Martin was back in the States and my mother

wanted to give me the heads-up about him coming to the same Thanksgiving dinner as my new boyfriend. I didn't really understand the issue, so my mother launched into a long story about someone else's controversy. My favorite kind. Apparently, when we were all kids, one of my brothers remembered Martin saying something homophobic about me behind my back and had carried the memory with him, at some point relaying it to my mother. Hearing this, now far into the future and irreparably gay, was embarrassing, which is a strange emotion to have about the whole thing, but this plotline made me feel like a bit of a rube.

The night before Thanksgiving, I talked with my mother on the phone again. She said, "I called Martin and I told him, 'Listen, Eric is bringing his partner and it's a man and that man is white and you just have to be cool, okay? Just be cool!' "

The next afternoon, Jay and I caught the train to Baltimore. When we arrived, I texted my dad, who said he was parked outside. Every time I go to Baltimore, my parents have new cars, and I realized as we walked out of the train station that I had no idea what I was looking for. I told Jay to just look for my dad. He said, "I've never met your dad," and I was like, "Just use your imagination."

We eventually found my father. He is warmth, he is authority, he is a preternatural rootedness. He hugged me and shook Jay's hand and we drove amiably for the five minutes it takes to get from the train station to my childhood home.

At the house, my mother answered the door, petite, with smooth skin, cheeks just a bit rosy from the heat of the kitchen. A light dusting of flour sat atop her busy sweater and also on a scarf holding her hair back. I am always surprised for a moment when I see my mother. She looks exactly the same way I've always remembered her. How has she not aged? Does time stop in this home? I marvel at her whenever I see her.

My mother gave me a hug—heart to heart, she always says—then hugged Jay and then turned around and went upstairs. "Come on up!" she said to me. "I need you to stir the gravy." My dad pulled Jay aside and told him that he'd be helping grab sodas from storage. Fifteen seconds in and we're put to work.

When my brother Stephen brought his girlfriend—now his wife—home to meet our family, everything was very different. I could tell he was tense because he told me over the phone, "Don't make any racial jokes." His wife, Kathleen, is also white. Stephen has never been one to shy away from the edge, comedically, so this was a surprise. I teased him, "You know that racial humor is my bread and butter. Or, I should say, my fried chicken and Kool-Aid." He was less than amused. I promised to bite my tongue.

When they arrived, though we were on our best behavior race-wise, Mommy and Daddy were extreme whirlwinds of activity. My dad's charm was up to an 11; he was making jokes with Kathleen and running around remodeling the house (that's what he does when they have guests; he built a deck during dinner). Meanwhile, my mother had me drag out all her scrapbooks and led Kathleen on a tour of my brother's youth. Everyone was just vibrating with excitement and anticipation. It was like in *Beauty and the Beast* when Mrs. Potts warbles, "It's a guest, it's a guest, saints alive and I'll be blessed!" The silverware danced, we toasted to the enduring power of love, and, like in *Beauty and the Beast,* no one said the N-word.

There were no scrapbooks at Thanksgiving, just gravy to be stirred and sodas to be put in the fridge, and a house that seemed eerily empty. It's a big house and I knew it was full of people, but I felt disconnected. Jay had been swallowed up by unpacking more soda than we'd be able to drink in a week; my mom was upstairs changing. My uncle was in the living room watching TV. My aunt was in the kitchen waiting for me to relieve her of gravy duty. My youngest brother, Jeffrey, was sleeping. And Stephen and Kathleen were at her mother's house and weren't coming.

And just as soon as I realized I felt adrift, everyone converged, like the dinner bell at Golden Corral had been rung. My mom, my dad, my youngest brother, my aunt, my uncle, my boyfriend, and me. With an empty chair right next to me. For Elijah. Or Martin, whoever got there first.

We were just commencing that period of life when the last of us who had been defined in the family system by being children were now undeniably adults, and that kind of thing always takes some getting used to. Roles realign, stories shift, people must reintroduce themselves. So, we were all strangers for a moment, peacefully making a new world at a table. Reaching over each other. Having polite conversation. Filling up our plates. As a family, we were sometimes quiet, sometimes funny. We didn't mind silence, even though most of us were talkers. We had the easiness that comes from knowing the same stories and knowing which parts you're supposed to say at what time. I often wonder who the audience is for those stories, the ones everyone gathered has heard every year, the ones most of us lived through. Maybe they're not for anyone outside of the circle. Maybe the telling is the metronome by which we set the beating of our hearts.

When I think of our family at that point, I think of the ease, the placidity. Which is why the frenzy around Kathleen had been so remarkable; a potential in-law had been a new story for our immediate family and we had all still been learning our parts. Thanksgiving dinner with Jay, with its comfortable disjoint and frequent pauses and my low-level anxiety, was more normal. It felt good to be home.

Then the doorbell rang. Martin.

Martin came lumbering up the thirteen stairs from the front door to the dining room and filled the frame. He's jacked, with a shaved head and light green eyes. He's unmissable. He sat down next to me. I didn't speak. *Should I introduce Jay?* I wondered. *I think process of elimination will let him know which one Jay is. But one never knows.*

Martin had already eaten, so he was just there to keep us company. The meal continued at its comfortable, herky-jerky pace. I nervously shoveled food into my mouth and prayed for silence. Martin pulled out his phone and started scrolling through memes. *I like memes. Should I talk to him about memes?* Jay and my mother started talking to each other, so I shifted in my seat so I could ear-hustle their conversation and listen for land mines. Martin started telling a funny story to the rest of the table. I tried to will my other ear to listen in to that. Was I expecting something that would offend? Maybe. I really didn't know. Everything that was being said at that moment was totally new for me and potentially dangerous.

I couldn't really make out what Jay and my mom were saying to each other, but no one had stormed off in a huff, so I guessed that was a good sign. And I couldn't really tell what Martin's story was about, but when I looked back at him he was brandishing a hunting knife to punctuate a point and everyone else was laughing. I decided to accept it all as a new normal.

When it was time for Jay and me to leave, Martin turned to Jay and spoke to him for the first time: "Jay, you're part of the family now, so you should know we're crazy." Which just floored me. This macho vet, this stranger from the desert, was supposed to be the liability, and he was the first person to refer to my boyfriend as part of the family out loud.

Martin then looked at me. His eyes shot up to my closely shorn balding head. "You and Jay are rockin' the same haircut. You oughta just shave it off. You're not fooling anybody. If you're bald, you're bald."

His face pulled into a mask of incredulity as if to say, "Who has time to hide who they are? In this economy?!" And then he went back to looking through pictures on his phone.

I hadn't wanted to go home, because I felt like a liability, a story that came with a warning label. As I rode the train home with Jay, I realized that my parents had replaced the flurry of activity that surrounded Kathleen's arrival with a hug for Jay and an invitation to get to work as an offering of normalcy. The scrapbooks had stayed put away and my mother had instructed everyone to just be cool. They were expending the same amount of energy not to put on a show. As if to say, "This is home and you're welcome here as you are." I think it's important to note that that takes work: family doesn't just happen; welcome isn't a neutral state. We have to tend to these things.

And that's what Martin did, too. With his invitation to Jay, with his too-true aside to me, with his presence itself, he offered a gift of not being a guest, but rather a member of the family.

I must admit, I've never taken the photographic tour of my parents' house that my mother commenced when David came over on Valentine's Day. How often does one ask for explanations of things that they should just know about through the osmosis of family history? I knew the people in the photos and I could call to mind most of the anecdotes that they'd provoke, though I could never do it like my mother. My mother has the memory of a griot. Our family's story spills out of her, spontaneously and authoritatively, a life force all its own. She has spent a lifetime piecing together the threads of family tales, anecdotes, controversies, mysteries, and secrets into a cohesive, growing whole. This isn't something I take lightly. The stories of Black life in this nation and prior to this nation have never been as well kept as the stories of white life. We inherit a narrative that is full of sand. There are so many on the outside who want our stories, our histories of achievement, erased, so we have to save the space for them—in ourselves and in our midst.

"This is where we begin," she said to David, pointing at the photos of the slave cabins mounted on the dining room wall. She doesn't mean this is the start of the family—she's researched farther back than that, as much as she can with the purposefully spotty records of slaveholders and kidnappers. She means these cabins are the first words of the story.

N. A. Smith, my mother's grandfather, was conceived in slavery but born in freedom. It's a sentence I know by heart, as every year we celebrated his birthday as N. A. Smith Day, the day our story began. This is the start of our America. I mouth the words along with her as she tells David. I am struck by the gift she has decided to give him and by the welcome she is sharing with this person, this stranger, this white man who also happens to be the person that her son loves.

She led him into the living room, taking care to give the background of every photo—family vacations, class photos the subject was not interested in sitting for, wedding candids, the painstakingly restored images of Black people in sepia tone and formal wear: N. A. Smith, his wife E. P., and their children. Free. Arching toward the future.

We rounded the living room, pausing at every bookshelf and side table, dozens of frames on every surface, and then down a hall back to the dining room. She ended on the other side of the dining room, with the painting of N. A. Smith baptizing his son in a river, a painting that I'd commissioned based on a photo that was nearly one hundred years old.

At dinner, my father—the most encouraging person in the world—chatted with David about his ministry, his plans for a future church, and his ambitions. Then my mother and I got to talking about memorable funerals we had been to and made ourselves cry from laughing and then cry from crying. We told the same stories over and over, retracing the lines, committing our existence to memory. My mother pulled out some scrapbooks and David was an enthusiastic audience. It reminded me, all of it, of so many dinners that had come before. There were moments I would look at David animatedly talking to my parents in the warm light of the dining room I've eaten in my whole life and I'd fall out of time. All of this was new, but also so familiar—in both meanings of the word.

Every family's story is a tale of becoming, sometimes through oppression, sometimes through achievement, and sometimes simply through the current of time. We were born grasping after freedom, in a house that could not hold us; every day we get closer and closer to our destination, until our features come into view. Soon, everyone further on down the family line can see us from their seats at the table; we're coming home.

Set a place for us. We're hungry, we have so much to talk about, and we're coming home.

Eggquity

Church #1: Genesis

"Robbie went home sick because his head split open in gym class. I saw it with my own eyes. I saw his brain. So, he had to go home." I was giving my mother the latest updates from kindergarten at Genesis Baptist School. She'd picked me up from the school bus, as usual, and we were riding in our car the five remaining blocks home. I stared out the window, working my way down the mental checklist of mottled brown buildings, painted brick row houses, and yellowed storefronts we always passed. Nothing much of note ever happened at school: Bible verse memorization, naps, recess, music class, learning words. Slow news days. Except the one time my best friend, Robbie, had run into a cinderblock wall and his entire head had split open. Like a hard-boiled egg.

We'd been playing Marco Polo in gym, a game I'd never heard of nor truly understood. The gym teacher, a trim woman with frizzy Meg Ryan–in–*When Harry Met Sally* hair and a permanent uniform of a pale blue sweat suit, had explained it to us with the same air of utter resignation with which she approached everything. Sis was over it.

Meg Ryan, like many of the teachers at Genesis Baptist

School, seemed to have found herself standing in front of a dark multipurpose room full of kindergartners as a result of her lifelong devotion to Christ. Most of the staff at Genesis were also members of the affiliated church and found themselves employed as an act of service. We knew this because teachers were constantly going on sabbatical to work on mission trips and because we prayed before everything. I hadn't been in any school before—save for a brief period in which my mother tried to homeschool me and we decided we were better as friends—so I just took it as natural that all instructors were kindly white people who didn't dance and had read the Bible cover to cover and would sometimes get teary-eyed when talking about "the situation in Africa." All that being said, it was clear to us and to the gym teacher that instructing young Christians on the finer points of physical activity was not one of her spiritual gifts. She also played the guitar in chapel. Maybe that was more her speed. The evidence was inconclusive.

In gym class, she sighed through directions as if leading a breathwork instructional video. "You put the blindfold on and then everyone has to chase you," she wheezed, the world's most ambivalent kidnapper. We all rushed forward to obediently blindfold ourselves. For fitness and, ostensibly, for Christ.

"No," she moaned. "Only one of you. Robbie. Robbie? Robbie, right? You'll put the blindfold on and everyone else will chase you. Wait, no, you'll chase everyone else. That's it. It's like tag."

We all stared at each other quizzically. *Help her, Jesus.* Robbie, a round-faced, red-cheeked boy, dutifully stepped forward and tied a strip of cloth around his face. Meg Ryan stepped back against the wall and then jumped forward suddenly. "Oh! You have to say 'Marco.'"

"Marco!" we all replied in unison.

"No! Robbie says 'Marco' and you say 'Polo.' " By that point, we were all fairly soured on the idea of global exploration in general. The gym teacher blew her whistle. Robbie's head swiveled blindly. "Marco?" he called out warily. "Polo?" we replied suspiciously. "Run!" the gym teacher called. So we all scattered and Robbie spun around in a circle and then ran full-speed, headfirst into the wall. Seeing my nearly decapitated friend, Meg Ryan sprang into action. And by sprang, I mean she sighed heavily and pushed herself away from the wall.

It struck me as odd that someone so lethargic would dedicate her life to physical activity, but I was five; what did I know of the motivations of adults? I was not then, nor have I ever been, a particularly physically engaged person. A lot of writers talk about their bodies as being cars that drive their brains around, but I never felt like that (I'm special!); I always felt like my body was a turtleneck that was too small and a pair of corduroy pants that was a little too big. I felt like my body was always tripping me up, squeezing me in; itchy and noisy, too hot and too leaden and too hard to move. All this is to say, I was an anxious, awkward kid but I had not yet discovered that some of those feelings could be alleviated by eschewing gym and all forms of movement beyond typing and talking.

Seeing Robbie's brain immediately come popping out of the gash in his forehead, however, was the first hint that movement was not necessarily something I should be incorporating into my life going forward.

"Anyway," I said to my mother as we pulled up outside our house, "we had to stop the game."

At this my mother interrupted my laconic retelling. "His whole brain? Are you sure?"

Obviously, I was sure. It was red and fleshy, what else could it have been?

"Are you sure he didn't just cut his head?"

I grew huffy; if I had *known* I was going to be treated like a hostile witness, I wouldn't have told this story at all. Besides, all of this happened last week. This was *prologue*.

"Why are you like this?" my mother asked.

I knew it was Robbie's brain because I saw it and he got sent home and I couldn't imagine anything less drastic. He was back the next day with a Band-Aid holding in his frontal lobe. "But," I told my mother, "the point of all of it is that *today* in chapel we didn't have anyone to play the guitar and they announced that the gym teacher was on a missionary trip to Africa! Isn't that suspicious?!"

My mother seemed less than convinced by my conspiracy theory, but I'd seen it. They shipped Meg Ryan to Africa to keep her from sending the rest of us careening into cement walls. The wages of sin is death and the wages of causing a five-year-old's brain to come falling out of his forehead is having to go tell people in Ghana about the everlasting love of Christ. Amen.

Discussion Questions

1. Cinderblocks aren't the best thing to build a gym's walls out of, but we didn't know that; it was the past! What kind of dangerous hellscapes did you grow up in?
2. My neck hates turtlenecks. Or perhaps turtlenecks hate my neck. Either way, I'm no turtle. What kind of clothing makes you want to burn your entire closet to the ground?
3. It's interesting, isn't it, that the missionary trip to Africa was both the gym teacher's higher calling in service of the Lord and also a tool of punishment. What instruments of our devotion are also used to make us suffer?

Church #2: Exodus

We were in a season of meetings. In the mid-1990s, I was a preteen, and our Sunday morning church services were expanded to include frequent congregational meetings about church business. These meetings were never joyful, they were never good news, and they were never short. As an adult, I've decided I can't sit in a meeting longer than an hour; I become antsy and argumentative. I'm sort of a nightmare, to be honest. Count me out of any Constitutional Congress, I guess. I discovered this about myself in church.

Time moved like molasses in those days. The stretch between summers was an endless, dry expanse, birthdays and holidays were mirages that were perpetually out of reach, and every Sunday we spent an eternity at church. The normal service included Sunday school, an 11 A.M. service that lasted two or three hours (depending on the Movement of the Spirit), and sometimes dinner. The meetings tacked on another hour, at least. In service, an eternity of church was characterized as a good thing; that's what heaven was supposed to be like. I was unconvinced. I was twelve and I had discovered skepticism.

I wasn't skeptical about Christianity, per se. I was too obedient for heresy. Jesus was born of a virgin, attended a trade school to learn carpentry, quit his job to start a small faith-based nonprofit with some friends, did a couple of well-received TED Talks, and then was persecuted, crucified, and rose again. But a lot of the conversation around the whole worship concept gave me pause. So, the goal of this whole "Life" thing was eventually to get to heaven, where there were streets of gold and everyone got a mansion and we'd worship God forever? Was it mostly singing or was there also a very long sermon? Because, if we're being frank here, the latter seemed a little less than ideal. See my earlier note about meetings. Were there breaks for food or would you not need food anymore? What if you just wanted food?

I had a lot of questions. For instance, these mansions: So we each have a mansion on a street that's made of gold? Who is polishing the gold? Will I live in the same neighborhood as my family? Will we recognize each other? My brother Stephen and I were bickering a lot during this period; would he be across the street from me, teasing me for eternity? Could I put in a request to the neighborhood association?

And circling back to the sermons on Sundays: is it heretical to say sometimes they were boring? Women never gave sermons; I found that odd. I began to notice that we seemed to always be talking about suffering. The suffering of our forebearers, the suffering of the saints in the Bible, our own suffering. It seemed, sometimes, like the message was that we deserved it, that we were bad, and that that was the point of life. But soon, we'd be in heaven, where a preacher would helpfully remind us that once we were bad, but Jesus loved us, so now we had a mansion full of shiny surfaces covered with fingerprints.

Also! When were we supposed to be at home in our mansions if we were worshipping God all day? Was heaven like those churches you can stream live online while you feed your baby or vacuum or whatever people do? I just needed some clarification around the *logistics* of heaven. Not to be critical; it just seemed like the plan wasn't fleshed out. Perhaps we should call a meeting. Under an hour, please. With snacks.

On Earth, pre–Second Coming, our church congregation was completely Black, and, while I couldn't prove it, I began to suspect that this also informed our experience and the way we talked about life, destiny, sin, and suffering. I tried to discern a connection between the all-white worship leaders at Genesis

Baptist School, their tears over the situation in Africa, our one-room church full of lower- and middle-income Black people in a poor Black neighborhood, and the kingdom of heaven with its streets of gold and high real estate values, but I couldn't figure it out. Fortunately, church was very long and I had a lot of time to think.

One night, on the ride home from church, I asked my father, "Why does God give us free will if He's just going to punish us for doing bad things?" My father answered that free will gave us the opportunity to make choices and, in so doing, to show our devotion. "Yeah, but why?" I responded. My father patiently reiterated his point. He quoted Scripture. He gave his theories. I responded, "Okay, I see what you're saying but also *why*?" This went on for quite a while. We arrived at home and walked up the stairs and somehow never got past the landing at the top. There we stood, for an hour or more, as the sun went down and the darkness crept in, and he gave me a spiritual education—one that was kind and thoughtful and questioning in and of itself—and I asked over and over again, "Sure, sure, I see your point. But why?" It was the best meeting I ever had and the best church service.

The meetings at church were also about sin but there wasn't time for discussion. Something had taken ahold of our congregation—some in leadership might say it was evil, others might say it was a natural development based on social and socioeconomic conditions. Either way, like the town of River City, Iowa, in *The Music Man,* we had trouble. Young women in the church kept getting pregnant, magic-like. Or at least it seemed like magic to me, because at every meeting a girl I'd grown up with was forced to stand in front of the church and tearfully read a letter confessing what she'd done. Sometimes she'd be alone; sometimes her parents would stand gravely behind her. Every once in a while a boy would stand with her. *Perhaps this is the magician,* I'd think.

The meetings were meant to confront sin, to call it out, and to provide a venue for the girls to ask for forgiveness from the community. As far as agendas go, it wasn't the most boring I'd ever encountered, but it was troubling nonetheless. I saw what they were trying to do, yet I couldn't help but ask, over and over again, "But why?"

The meetings seemed to escalate. Once, there was no pregnant girl at the front of the church, only the leadership, looking ashen, telling the congregation that we had to vote on the serious matter of excommunicating the music minister. He'd served in the church for years, but I suddenly realized I hadn't seen him in a few weeks. There was no discussion about why he was being excommunicated, which fascinated me in the moment. It was a meeting about something everyone already knew, to perform a task that had already been decided. The people around me wept as they raised their hands to vote yes. And I never saw him again.

I was too young to vote and it wasn't until years later that I thought to ask what he'd done to warrant such a strict punishment. None of the girls had been excommunicated; no one else, to my knowledge, ever had. Perhaps you already know this tune, but it was my first time hearing it. He'd struggled with his sexuality for years, the answer came. He'd even gotten married to a woman, thinking that could solve his problem. But something in him had broken. He annulled his marriage, he confessed to the pastor that he was gay, and he'd been sent away. They hadn't even needed to count the votes.

The last meeting I attended was in the summer. The church was full and warm; the air-conditioning units at their limits, the humidity pushing in through every crevice. There was no girl up front, once again, but no grave church leadership either. I shifted uncomfortably, like a suspect in a murder mystery trying to figure out why the detective has called us all here. The problem was itself a mystery, as the pastor relayed it. He stood in front of the congregation and told us that we needed to make a decision. People who had AIDS were trying to join the church, he said. How many remains a mystery. Was there a mass migration? Did we, a one-room church with a music ministry that was markedly less joyful, seem a beacon for those with HIV/AIDS? I didn't know. In any case, the question had come up and the pastor was putting it in front of us. How did we want to proceed?

You are reading this in the future and so debating this seems wrong to you. I assure you, in the past it was also disturbing. I listened intently as members of the congregation expressed the sorts of fears about AIDS that come from the intersection of a lack of sexual health education and a pervasive paranoia that has come to define Reagan-era America and the years thereafter. People wanted potential congregants with AIDS to identify themselves before joining; they wanted to take steps to ensure the safety of our social gatherings and dinners. One person suggested that we discourage people with AIDS from joining because there were children in the church. I, a child, wondered what I was being protected from.

The consensus seemed to be that letting them join was a dangerous idea. "But why?" I murmured under my breath. I never spoke at church meetings. I was a child and therefore not a voting member. Besides, this level of conversation was rare. The pregnant girls never had to endure a Q&A. Something had gotten out of hand in the congregation. We'd lost church. I raised my hand and felt my face get hot before I even got called on to speak. The pastor pointed to me. "I don't understand what we're talking about," I said. "I don't understand why we have to know anything about anyone. It's not like they're going to bleed into our macaroni and cheese at church dinners," I said.

After church, the pastor pulled me aside. "You have to understand that people need time to come around to some ideas, son." I nodded. I said nothing. I was not his son. My father was the man who puzzled through questions with me for hours, whose house had open doors and open arms inside, and who welcomed the doubt that is necessary for true belief.

Discussion Questions

1. Who are you most looking forward to seeing in heaven? Who are you trying to avoid?
2. In church, God is our father and Jesus is our brother. Who are our cousins? Does heaven have an eccentric aunt? Do you have an eccentric aunt? I hope you do.
3. The thing is, the promise of church is community, salvation, and a relationship with God. If the gay music minister and the person with AIDS cannot be part of the church, where do they find God?

Church #3: Resurrection

David was freaking out. It was ten minutes till eleven on Easter Sunday and he was running around the big-steepled Presbyterian church at which he was serving as a pastoral associate. He'd spent weeks—honestly weeks—planning the Easter egg hunt and it had suddenly and dramatically all fallen apart. He'd stuffed hundreds of plastic Easter eggs with candy the night before and then lugged them all to work, leaving them in the church's parlor so that he could come back and set them up in the morning. He had carefully worked out a plan for hiding them that ensured that every child would receive an equal number of eggs. It was meticulous. But a church volunteer had arrived before us and, not knowing about his plan, had hidden over half the eggs randomly, and started dismantling what she thought were extras. Suddenly what was supposed to be a measured game with enough prizes for everyone looked to be a mad dash with no guarantees. David was melting down.

"I worked so hard," he lamented after the volunteer left to take care of other duties.

"It's just Easter eggs," I said, realizing almost immediately how unhelpful this was. His plan for the hunt was a reflection of his abilities, his labor of love and of sacred service. It was, perhaps most important, the difference between a morning full of happy new childhood memories and a lackluster event that probably ended in tears. As he furrowed his brow and tried to think through a solution, the full picture of the competing interests revealed itself in my head. He was dealing with an age-old church tradition—that most precise and fickle of things, one of those things about which everyone has an opinion. He was also dealing with a daycare issue—parents were entrusting their children to his care and expecting that when they emerged from service, they'd be able to pull out their iPhones, collect their offspring, and capture the unbridled joy that can only come from finding a plastic egg under a bush. Lastly, he was also dealing with a justice issue—behind the candy-crazed pursuit by hordes of pastel-clad children was a metaphor for access and inequity. The children were to be presented with what they were told was a level playing field—there are enough eggs for everyone, we'd say—and David was facing the possibility that that premise would be a lie. The children might never have known it, but we'd know it. Worse, we'd be the architects of this debacle. I may not understand Easter eggs, but I wasn't about to let my husband become the villain of Easter.

"You're right," he conceded. "It'll be fine. Some kids will get more eggs than others and that sucks, but it'll be okay." Having successfully talked him down, I was now ready to re-escalate the crisis. There was a metaphor at stake.

"Not on my watch," I declared, still unhelpful but determined. "You go take care of the kids. I'll sort out this egg imbroglio." The organ in the church began to play in the distance; I had exactly forty-five minutes to bring justice into the world on Easter Sunday. White church is very prompt.

I surveyed the ruin of the parlor, the empty plastic bags, the basket of surplus eggs, and the pile of mini chocolate candies. I unwrapped a Krackel and ate it as I tried to figure out how to go about righting this wrong and also what a Krackel is and why there are no full-size versions of it. This is an entire candy brand that exclusively exists in miniature; what's the business plan here? *Deal with this later,* I scolded myself. *We have a holiday to save.*

We never had Easter egg hunts in church growing up. We were Baptists and that bunny didn't die on the cross, did it? No, it did not! Our Easter baskets had chocolate crosses nestled in fake grass; I haven't done the math, but I think from a square-inches perspective you get more chocolate from a cross than a bunny. So chalk one up for crucifixion, I guess. To be fair, I do recall my mother hiding Easter eggs around our house when we were little, but there were just three of us doing the searching and so there wasn't a complex system of organization. David had plotted a hunt that happened in two shifts; there was a set change involved! The eccentric in me delighted; the logistician despaired.

Here's what I knew: the littlest children were to do the hunt first. In his plan, they'd each be assigned a color and told to pick up only those eggs. Parents would help; joy would break out. After they were done, we'd collect any unfound eggs, then grab the second batch of eggs and hide those for the older kids, who also would be assigned a color. Maybe this makes sense to you, but this was my first white Easter, so I marveled at the intricacy. The more I thought about it, though, the more I wondered how anyone managed to plan a hunt without a strict set of rules and regulations, and possibly a clipboard. To celebrate the death and resurrection of Christ, we hide treasure and then release children of varying developmental levels and abilities in a desperate, clamoring pursuit. Remarkable! It's *The Hunger Games* in pastel. It's a Black Friday sale at Walmart. The last biscuit at Golden Corral. We don't expect other humans to act sanely or with any sort of grace when they perceive scarcity, so it's foolish to expect kids to. Perhaps this is where they learn it. Perhaps the yearly tradition of American children tearing across the White House lawn, dodging and diving over their peers, trying to snatch up as much as they can, is a metaphor itself. Or a precursor.

I'm just saying, everybody wants candy.

I walked out to the yard to take stock of what had already been hidden. These eggs were just sitting everywhere in plain sight. This was a shock, as well. Apparently, you don't actually want to hide the eggs. You just put them where the kids will find them and pick them up so that the process isn't unnecessarily impeded. My mind was blown.

The first step, as I saw it, was to take an inventory. I rummaged through the parlor until I found an actual clipboard. Years as a bar manager taught me that it was a fool's errand to try to do this kind of work without one. Clipboard: essential. There was probably a clipboard at the tomb when Jesus rose, to be honest. He emerged, filled out some forms, and went about his day. (Literally his day. Because it was a Sunday.)

I went outside to count the eggs that were out there so I could figure out how to adjust the inventory to achieve equity. Just a man in a suit standing in the dirt, counting Easter eggs by color like a middle-management toddler. David had bought a lot of different colors so that he could ensure every child got one. I realized I needed to list each color as I came across it and tally them. I may have spent far too long ruminating on what exactly each shade was, but honestly, if you're not going to be thorough about this sort of thing, it displeases the Lord.

Twenty minutes later, I had an inventory. There were 176 eggs and the counts were all over the place. I was sweating. I had way too few "grass green with stickers," "daffodil yellow with stickers," "cerulean," and both turquoises—"turquoise prime" and "turquoise cheeky." I had way too many neon greens, whites, and sky blues. Honestly, I considered running into the church and shouting, "Easter is postponed due to issues on the factory floor!" But I'd made David a promise.

The best way to level the playing field was to take the color category with the lowest count and then remove eggs from the other categories until they all matched. (Perhaps this is a metaphor for taxation, but don't ask me. I'm just a middle-management toddler.)

I realized that to do that, I then had to go on another Easter egg hunt. I had to find the same damn eggs I had just found. *Call Jesus and tell him to hit the snooze button; I have to go digging around some underbrush for a cotton-candy-pink egg.*

As I went through, I realized there were some categories that I'd just called even. The orange had eleven instead of twelve but it was close enough for government work. The grape had fourteen. I had a basket full of extra eggs and I'd perspired through my jacket, but from the sounds of the church service inside I knew I still had about fifteen minutes. I could make it absolutely even. I grabbed some extras from inside and I embarked on my third Easter egg hunt of the day.

Finally, it was done. Every single category had a dozen eggs, like God intended. Finding myself with a little time left, I went back outside and shook every egg to make sure there was candy. This is also a metaphor for justice work, I'm sure, but mostly I have food insecurity and my worst fear is for someone to not have chocolate when they want chocolate.

David came cautiously down the ramp. "How'd it go?" he asked, eyeing my drenched shirt and my clipboard.

I smiled at him and gestured dramatically to the garden littered with very poorly hidden eggs in a truly stunning variety of colors. All had been made right. All had been made whole. Heaven was at hand.

Discussion Questions

1. Does Easter have a villain? Is it Pontius Pilate? Is it Barabbas? Is it Death?
2. What's the deal with Krackel? Seriously. Please email me about this.

3. Easter is about salvation, and salvation is free and available to everyone. Yet so many churches put barriers around it. If our religions aren't about the business of achieving justice in our time, in this world, for everyone, what are they doing?

The Past Smelled Terrible

My friend Kristen and I are sitting at a café on a spring evening in the year 2017. She is finishing a glass of sparkling rosé and a cheese platter. I am downing detox herbal tea and picking at a small bowl of fruit. We are both eating and drinking what we are eating and drinking because, after a dark, seemingly endless winter, we have both decided to live. Please hold your applause.

On Election Night 2016, Kristen and her husband (also named David) came over to our house to watch the results. My David prepared an elaborate cheese platter. Kristen brought a bottle of vintage rosé by Veuve Clicquot with which we'd planned to celebrate. (We were a roomful of intersectional feminists, and half of the room was an interracial gay couple, so you can probably guess what we were hoping was going to happen.)

But by the time we were able to get together, it was already clear that the world we had imagined was crumbling around us. Kristen sat quietly in a corner, wiping away tears. My David jumped up suddenly, radiating anxiety, and ran to another room. That left Kristen's David and me, making casual conversation, pretending that the world that we knew was not ending.

I like this about Kristen's David very much. He's always polite and hospitable; I love decorum. This is probably surprising if you know me, because I am prone to yelling sassy things. Also, I know that I have a very expressive face that cannot tell a lie, and I have no problem deploying it to project my displeasure in literally any situation. But deep down, I believe in a certain order. I like RSVPs, good service at restaurants, and polite party talk.

I was suddenly seized by the realization that this was, indeed, a party, at my house no less. I became obsessed with the idea that everyone should have fun. Yes, a megalomaniacal moron was being elected in a soul-shaking rebuke of all my hopes for this country, but I was worried people would give the evening low marks.

"How was Eric and David's on Election Night?"

"Nice cheese plate, but kind of a meh mood. A little bit apocalyptic maybe?"

"How gauche."

I'm a better party planner than that.

I leapt up and declared, "I'm changing the channel! This is depressing." I flipped until I found something that would lighten the mood: *How to Train Your Dragon* 2 on Nickelodeon. Perfect for an Election Night party. And then we sat there in silence while everyone stared blankly at animated magical beasts sailing through the clouds until, finally, I burst into tears and told my David we had to move to Canada because I couldn't bear to lose the right to marry.

As far as parties go, it wasn't my best. But it wasn't my worst.

Kristen and I were spouses before we were married to either David. I mean work spouses but I'm sure it's still a legally binding union blessed by God and Ruth Bader Ginsburg. After she and I had been together for a blissful couple of years, I got antsy about what I was doing with my life and left the company at which we worked. This was my second work divorce and, let me tell you, they never get easier.

Years earlier, I had a friend, Rob, who was my cubicle mate and first work spouse. His real-life wife also worked at the company, so maybe she was his work spouse, actually. He and I sat next to each other, though, so the jury is still out. This was corporate Big Love.

One morning Rob just up and quit, and I was so distraught I had to take a personal day. Okay, not a whole personal day, but I did come in super late. Okay, I always came in super late, but this time it was with a purpose.

Years later, when it was me who up and quit, I was shocked by how hard it was to be apart from Kristen after working six feet from her every day. We started meeting for weekly wine dates where we would rail about intersectionality and theater, and the bartender with the purple hair would make great wine recommendations and laugh at our jokes because we were actually hilarious and she liked us and not just because it was her job.

Kristen loves wine. When she gets a new glass of wine, she attacks it with her nose, taking a deep breath to start the experience. Then she'll take a sip, and if it's good, she'll let out a rattling moan. She'll then turn to me and excitedly describe what's happening. "It's like a damn raspberry, Eric. With a little bit of cut grass and a . . . is it? Yes, by God, it's red pepper!"

Then she'll hand me the glass and, every single time, I'll take a sip and say, "Yup, that tastes like wine." Because I am a terrible friend. And husband.

We are a great match, even though I don't know how to smell wine (I have sinus issues!). We also have great actual spouses. My David performed Kristen's marriage to her David. Then Kristen spoke at my wedding. And then we were two work spouses with spouses, and we were in each other's lives forever.

Anyway, I tell you all this to say that Kristen and I are two friends who care deeply about each other and a better world full of nice things and people. And so, after a dark winter, we're sitting in a café, and she is having wine, and I am having tea, because we've thought about it, and we've decided we're going to live, today.

At this particular moment, I am on one of those detox diets because I'm the heaviest I've ever been and I kind of don't feel good all the time, and it occurs to me that maybe they are related and if the world is going to end, do I really want to pass on without having tried one of those fad diets at least once?

Anyway, just in case we don't go to war, I want to look as good in my fifties as Angela Bassett does, so I've cut out sugar and dairy and pretty much everything great for a month. I have decided to live, everyone! I'm living! Put me on the cover of a magazine.

Kristen is eating the exact opposite of my meal, because wine and cheese are actually what living tastes like. I will enlist in any army that fights to protect vineyards, and wherever it is that cheese is made. Cheese groves? I will fight for them.

In this moment, we are really happy. We are talking about the things that we love—theater, wine, cheese, baked goods, Beyoncé. And the conversation slides effortlessly from the deep and meaningful to the slight and ridiculous. We talk about our love of relatively frivolous things like our record players or Kristen's fantastic new haircut.

There is a moment, when things slide back to the more serious, that we feel a little guilty. Who cares about our little joys in such a time as this? Aren't there more serious things to talk about? Have we called our senator today?

I always feel weird about thoughts like that. In such a time as this, shouldn't I be more serious? In such a time as this! (As if time is ever anything but serious and potentially grave.)

I think it's important to revel in the small things that make us joyful, to indulge when possible and not problematic, to steal laughter and hoard it. I wasn't kidding when I said I'd fight for a cheese grove's right to exist. Because if there's no cheese grove, what are we even fighting for? (I believe it was Winston Churchill who said that.)

I call my senator, a lot. Just to chat. I write letters and commentary to stake a claim for the things I believe in. I vote. I march. I tap-dance for justice. And, in the end, I know that we are not at war with our terrible leaders. Instead, we are fighting against nihilism itself. We are fighting to care. What makes you happy or sad or brings you joy or makes you feel anything at all—it matters.

Yet despite our issues with the present, Kristen and I acknowledge that it's probably the best time yet for us. We've had many an office conversation about time travel (haven't you?) and decided that, if given the option, we would only go forward, because there's literally no time in human history when it was great to be a woman or a gay Black man. So, if you're selling time tours to the past, it's going to be a no from us.

The other thing about the past is that it stinks. Not colloquially. It smells bad. Everything in the past smells. We have access to so much body spray and cologne, yet the present is still kind of ripe sometimes. Just imagine all of that funk, but without deodorant and with crossing the Great Plains on horseback. No thanks, ma'am.

I'm obsessed with how bad the past must have smelled. I can't watch period drama because I become fixated on how every single person on-screen must reek. I love *Hamilton*, but even sitting in a Broadway theater, watching Lin-Manuel Miranda and Phillipa Soo and Daveed Diggs and Leslie Odom Jr. tear the roof off, I still had the thought, *All of these characters smelled really bad in real life*.

It's not just early America that smelled either. Everyone in the fifties and sixties smoked constantly, according to the extensive research I did by watching two movies. Remember when you used to go out to a bar and maybe six people were smoking and you still couldn't wear your coat for a week until it aired out? Well, imagine that all the time everywhere for your whole life.

Cave people stank. I can't even write about it. It grosses me out.

Louis XIV didn't smell good at all. Sorry—it's true. I know the French aristocracy was obsessed with perfumes and wigs and generally acting like rich drag queens, but I guarantee you that Louis XIV ended up smelling like your teenage cousin who got some cheap cologne from Rite Aid and thinks splashing it around after playing basketball won't fog up your car windows with funk. Louis XIV, I'm sorry, but you have to walk home. I just had this leather cleaned.

Going back in time isn't worth the aggravation. The scent will never leave your nostrils. That's also one of the issues with the present: a collective refusal to acknowledge the stink of the past. Rejection of time travel is one of my core beliefs for olfactory reasons and also as a form of social justice protest.

Which is why it's such a shock when Kristen, on her second glass of rosé, tells me that despite all this, she has this fantasy about time travel to the past.

"Hear me out," she says, waving her hands in the face of my disgust. You think you know some people. She continues: "I've been trying to figure out ways I can go back and warn Hillary."

Okay, I am on board the train now. I'll bring my smelling salts.

Kristen says, "I keep thinking if I go back to the beginning of the campaign and I say, 'You need to just release all of your emails right now,' it'll be fine. But then I think I should go back further, so I go back to when she's secretary of state and tell her, 'Oh, girl, a private server, no.' But then I remember, LOL, misogyny is the reason we're here, so I need to go back to whenever that didn't exist and I keep going back further and further until I'm all the way back before the Big Bang, and when I get there I whisper to the cloud of dust, 'It's not worth it.' And then I fade away like I'm Marty McFly's siblings."

I applaud this plan, because I am not sure if space stinks, and also I am a sucker for any plan that invokes *Back to the Future*. The possibility of changing the present is never so alluring as when it comes about by changing the past. There's a certain poetry to time travel. In the place of the hard, incremental work of effecting change in reality—calling your senator, voting, drinking detox tea, and then waiting—you get to see your impact appear in an instant, fully formed, functional, for better or worse. You get to find out how it ends. You get to see time unspool before your eyes and then knit itself back together again, hopefully better, hopefully brighter, hopefully overflowing with cheese groves.

Of course, there is the danger, as explained by Doc Brown, that traveling through time will rip a hole in the space-time continuum. Attempting to fix the past breaks the future; isn't it ironic? Don't you think? This is going to sound morbid, but if someone invents time travel and then accidentally breaks time, I just hope I die the day before. Like, in my sleep or something. Because, ultimately, I'm not end-of-the-world material.

I can't help but think constantly about the end of the world. I don't want to. I want to prepare cheese platters and drink champagne with friends. I want to live my life. But I cannot escape the end of the world. Headlines declare the end of everything from democracy to the climate itself. Disaster movies and post-apocalyptic movies are all the rage. And I don't want to alarm you, but I am aging. Our time will come to an end.

And I find it very annoying. The thing is, a catastrophic end to the world as we know it sounds like a lame experience. I am not interested in the least. It's scary, yes, but mostly dumb. And the way we've been taught to think about it is so improbable. We are not going to band together and listen to a bunch of scientists to save humanity like Jake Gyllenhaal in a disaster movie. Sorry. You know how I know? Because a bunch of scientists are telling us how to save the world right now, and half the world isn't listening to them.

We may very well be living in the montage at the opening of some climatological disaster flick. I'm the one idiot holding up a sign that reads "Stay hydrated!" as the sea levels rise on the beachfront property I just bought. No one is interested in humor during the apocalypse, but I don't let that stop me. It's all I have to offer in this scenario. Because I am not end-of-the-world material.

Listen. Here's my living will, okay? I have no desire to survive the apocalypse.

The minute the cable goes out, I'm gone. If I can't watch rebooted versions of television shows I used to love, what even is the point? What even?! I do not understand the people in disaster movies who want to survive so that they can rebuild society. That sounds terrible. So boring, and yet so much work. Haven't these people ever worked at a small nonprofit? It's that. But with, like, zombies. No thanks.

I don't want to shoot a gun. I don't want to figure out how to make fire. I don't want to have to dig deep to find hidden reserves of resilience. Ugh. I don't want to form a new system of government with a bunch of other idiots. I've only memorized Angelica's part in *Hamilton;* I wouldn't even know where to start with creating a constitutional convention.

I am not post-apocalypse material. I melt down if they don't have the shade of fabric I want at Crate & Barrel. I certainly don't want to forage through what used to be Seattle in search of materials to make my own crates and barrels.

And if the post-apocalypse comes about because of a massive plague or something, I have no useful medical or scientific skills. Once again, I'm out. I would like to be Patient 15. Maybe Patient 20. No higher than 50. I don't want to be Patient Zero, because then everyone would blame me, which is rude. What you're not going to do is besmirch my fair-to-middling name in your dystopian digest. I'll tell you that much. I don't want to go first. I just want to go early, while they're still doing nice tributes to the victims on television and I can get my own grave plot.

In terms of worst-case scenarios, dystopia is even more annoying than apocalypse, come to think of it. I am definitely not making it through to fight in the resistance if it involves anything more than retweeting things I agree with. I'm not surviving the takeover by some power-mad weirdos dressed in all their monochromatic shapeless dystopian haute couture. I am mouthy, and I get easily annoyed, and I don't know how to shoot a bow and arrow, so dystopias are a solid no from me. I'm basically Peeta from *The Hunger Games,* except gay. I am here for the baked goods and then basically I'm going to be dead weight. Cut your losses.

There's always a huge, complicated system for subjugating people in dystopias. There's always an oppressive hierarchy. And the people at the top, well—the bureaucracy is astounding. Do you ever think about that? Who is pushing paper in the Capitol? Who is the Housing and Urban Development secretary in Gilead?

Who is copyediting all the dystopian newspapers? Do people still recycle? On what days? Is it the same schedule or a new one? Do you still file taxes or is it just pillaging? Are there still stamps? Do they still release the special Valentine's Day stamps? Who do I speak to about my 401(k) in the dystopia? Who is updating Google Maps with all the new dystopia fortresses? These are important questions.

Our government, old, creaky, barely continent, is hard enough to run as it is now. The dystopian government wants to, like, enslave all women or set up a national murder game? We can't even get single-payer healthcare, so I feel like this is overreaching.

Governance is hard; why would I stick around after all of our infrastructure crumbles and they ban all the good TV and try to be a mayor or city council member or head of the jury duty commission or whatever? The only thing that appeals to me about that scenario is the possibility of a cape. I feel like in four out of every ten dystopian governments, once you reach a certain level of power, you get to wear a cape.

Do you ever worry that, given the opportunity, you'd help to usher in a terrible world to save your own skin or to provide for your loved ones? Everybody thinks they're the time-traveling hero, but deep down do you ever think, *Actually, though, I would totally murder Katniss Everdeen if it meant I could eat well forever*?

I never ask myself these questions.

Any time I start to wonder, *Am I dystopian*? I laugh and remember that I'll be dead before dystopia really starts to take hold. I exist in flashbacks only. I'm that guy in the soot-covered photograph that the ragtag band of resistance fighters stare at fondly in the flickering light of the gasoline fire. "He was funny on the internet," they say.

When it all goes south, I want to be remembered, not relied on.

The problem is doomsday isn't coming. And I don't think we can turn back the hands of time or whisper to the cloud of dust, as much as I'd like to. I think we're obsessed with dystopian or apocalyptic scenarios because, despite their darkness, they're comparatively easy outs. Kind of like how sometimes you wish your company would just go out of business so that you'd have to go on unemployment and finally finish your novel or paint the study or hike the Appalachian Trail like you've always wanted. Actually living, getting up every day with all the fears and tragedies and challenges and potential joys of being a human in regular old neutral-smelling, depressing times, is hard enough.

But it's what we're given: flowers and sunshine and push alerts on our phones and midterm elections; pop-up restaurants and flawed history books and strangers in offices who become parts of our lives. There's fighting for social justice and being brokenhearted about deaths that could have been avoided and being terrified about bringing a kid into this world and being even more terrified about leaving a kid in this world and trying to figure out how to wake up every day not thinking that the world is going to end. Even though it will. I'm here for that. That mid-topian life.

How are we supposed to live without a meteor bearing down on us? How are we supposed to find the best parts of humanity without a brutal regime at the door? How are we supposed to tell the people we love that we love them if we're not five minutes from being destroyed?

That's the challenge of being alive.

Unsubscribe from All That

For the second time in my life, a lot of people on the internet were talking about me. For the first time in my life, this was a good thing. An article I had written a month into my time freelancing for ELLE.com about Rep. Joyce Beatty at the 2016 Democratic National Convention had caught on online, and the profile of my Eric Reads the News column started to rise. Articles kept going viral. Not always, and without any particular pattern, but enough that the people at ELLE were excited about what I was doing. It still felt a bit like magic, which is to say unruly and confusing, but apparently good.

My boss at ELLE.com, Leah, told me they were raising my per-article pay rate. At my day job I asked for a raise and got turned down. I was not very good at capitalism, but it seemed my luck was improving. I left my day job and got a job at a university. Friends who've known me forever would sometimes stop me on the street and say, "Do you know, people who don't even know you are sharing your articles on Facebook?" And I'd say "Maybe?" because I'm not sure how I would know this information but also maybe I *do* know this information?

Late in the winter, I got another raise; I was making two hundred dollars per article, which was an absolutely gargantuan amount of money compared to what I'd earned for my entire life up to that point. I got offered a job writing for a new television series, but I would have had to move to New York just after the first of the year to take it. The offer came the day before winter break at the university, and I would have had to quit on the spot. I turned it down. I got laid off from the university my second day back from break. I continued to not excel at capitalism. Leah decided I should start making videos of my columns as well and devised a way to pay me more. I decided not to get another job. Accidentally, I was A Writer.

Pivoting to writing full-time seven months after a viral Facebook post scored me a plum freelance gig, I found that I had reached a point at which the facts no longer made sense in the narrative of my life. It's like those stories about people who came to New York in the sixties with nothing but a guitar and a dream, stepped off the bus and plopped themselves down on a street corner in Greenwich Village, and—bingo-bango—next thing you know, they had a record contract. That's how I felt when I'd explain to people what was going on in my life and why their aunt in Florida was sharing my posts and why I spent all day in a coffee shop and yet was still able to pay my rent. I'd say, "I wrote something funny on Facebook and now I am a comedy journalist? Like Lois Lane—but the Teri Hatcher Lois Lane, I think?" It would have made more sense if I had just pulled out my guitar and started in on my latest hit. I know a woman who, as legend has it, came to New York in the sixties and sat outside the Public Theater until Joe Papp gave her a job. She squatted for a job! This was, in my mind, just how things worked in that time. New York City stories from that period sound both utopian and horrible. On the one hand, isn't it everyone's dream to pack up and move to a new place and find everything they've ever hoped for? On the other hand, what are the rules? Why are people sitting on street corners playing guitar? How long is the period between stepping off the bus and winning a Grammy? What was Joe Papp thinking? (To be fair, that woman is a bit of a legend now, but how could he have known that? Did she shout her résumé to him every day? I have so many questions about this story and yet every theater person I've ever met has told it to me, so it must be true.)*

I think that when we talk about our present, in the future, the internet will sound just as lawless and boisterous and random as sixties New York, where you could rent a room above Carnegie Hall for five dollars a month and Marlon Brando would sing you to sleep. These days people get production deals from Vine accounts, a very funny guy can film himself commenting on recipe videos and suddenly he has a job on *The Ellen Show,* and writers—like yours truly—get their big breaks from a joke they thought no one but their friends from college would read online. It feels very much of the moment and also something inherent to the culture, like an old routine in a new telling. And it feels lucky and it feels undeserved and it feels hard and it feels right on time and it feels like the thing you've been waiting for. It feels like hope fulfilled. That guitar-toting sixties hippie didn't buy a one-way bus ticket to New York to *not* find success.

It also feels unsustainable in the long run. I thought a lot in the winter of 2017 about Joan Didion, quintessential sixties New Yorker and also, paradoxically, the author of the ur-text on leaving New York. "It is easy to see the beginnings of

* I will not tell you who I'm talking about because although I had the chance to ask her about it once, I didn't because I was too busy taking shrimp cocktails from a buffet. So, sorry, I have no further information for you. Ask a theater person. Call Audra McDonald.

things," Didion writes in her essay "Goodbye to All That," "and harder to see the ends." For years, I had that quote in my Facebook profile, along with the next bit where she talks about first seeing New York at twenty, getting off a bus, wearing a sundress that had seemed smart in Sacramento but already seemed less so. I read that for the first time right around my unceremonious exit from Columbia, and I was like, "My wig! I feel so seen!" And so it lingered, on my Facebook, this open parenthesis, completely ignoring the rest of the essay, which is to say the whole "wanting to leave New York" part. "It is easy to see the beginnings of things," Joan Didion wrote.

"Ah, how true. What a wonderful complete thought," I replied.

I considered the essay in its fullness years later, as I tried to navigate a Facebook feed suddenly full of reactions to my articles from strangers, the occasional celebrity, and your aunt in Florida. I pondered Didion as I sat in a coffee shop all day staring at an ever-darkening news cycle and poking at it for jokes. I thought of "Goodbye to All That" the first time I went to the ELLE offices at the Hearst Tower in Columbus Circle and felt like Annie when she arrives at Daddy Warbucks's house. I was in a pair of slacks that felt smart in Philly but started feeling downright stupid somewhere around Metuchen, and a black shirt because that's fashion, and a sweater-type jacket that I thought was black but in the harsher New York sunlight turned out to be navy blue. There is a waterfall that greets you when you walk into Hearst. The lobby is like Frank Lloyd Wright designed heaven and heaven is a mall. I pushed through the revolving door and came face-to-face with Gayle King. "I think I'm going to like it here," I said to the side of Gayle King's head as she continued on her way. "Walk faster! This is New York!" the waterfall responded. This experience, too, was magical.

Unruly and confusing. Apparently good. I can remember how all of it began for me. That's easy. But I find it hard to put a finger on the point when it changed.

The internet is a mouth, gaping, always hungry, teeth gnashing, broadcasting hot takes, spittle-flecked with outrage, drooling prejudice. It's always on, it's always changing, it's always producing. Despite the success I'd found, I was becoming exhausted by the internet. I wondered how long I could keep this thing up—sitting online all day, finding humor in darkness, navigating social media response—all from the isolation of my home. After a year of full-time writing, and after the election and inauguration of Donald Trump and all that came next, I was lonely and I was weary. I started to cherish the weekends, when I could put my phone down, ignore Twitter, leave headlines unread. I started to miss the days, before all of this, when I'd walk around Philly, running errands, and something odd would happen on my journey, and I'd write about it on Facebook and forty people would like it and that would be that. The Tia and temerity of my longing for this other period at a time when hundreds of thousands of people were reading my writing is not lost on me. I wasn't ungrateful. I wasn't unhappy. I felt, though, that perhaps the inherent nature of the internet was too grueling for long-term exposure, particularly at a time like this. I felt like one of those people who come to the Big Apple with a Big Dream and then leave five years later complaining about the cynicism and the noise and the constant crush of people and the hard edge that your dream must be sharpened upon, the almost unreachable bar, the cost.

I always wonder what those people expect. Every "Goodbye

to New York" essay includes a list of complaints about the city that are not a secret. There's a lot of people, the subways are a real scandal, rent is too high, and everyone is trying so hard—yes, we know; they put these things on the tourism campaigns. It's sort of the whole thing. Many essays about leaving are about the huge gulf between the romantic ideal of the city and the gross reality. As someone who has only a passing interest in acknowledging reality, I can understand this. But the question comes, for the New Yorker, for the citizen, for the participant, are the things that now seem unbearable the same things that made this place attractive? Didion perfectly encapsulated the despair of a particular paradox, but it was in her particular moment, 1960s New York City, a time and place of promise and turmoil in equal measure. And, ultimately, her decision to leave was internal and therefore ultimately not about New York as much as about the self. Or New York as a projection of the self. The writer saying, "I am not the romantic I once was."

I couldn't help but wonder, to call to mind another iconic New Yorker, Carrie Bradshaw, was I once a romantic about the internet? Sure; I guess we all were, right? All of us have, at some point, logged on and thought, *This seems like a good idea!* And sometimes that changes when you discover that the internet is actually just other people, and other people, scientists say, are terrible. Was I once romantic about this particular relationship to the internet—the one that pulled me out of my job and slid famous people into my DMs, the internet that connected me to a world that I'd only imagined, both literal and cybernetic, this internet that had made me A Writer? How could I not be romantic about that? What is more romantic than the sudden revelation of the thing you didn't even dare to hope for? The internet was a place that made so much possible for me. My complaints about the comments section or hate mail or the relentless news cycle were the same as a once-hopeful New Yorker's grouses about the cost of rent: what did we expect?

I've come to think, actually, if you're leaving New York, you shouldn't be allowed to write a leaving–New York essay at all. You should have to make the "New York is over" speech that Kristen Johnston delivers in *Sex and the City* before her character accidentally falls out of a window. That's New York—terrifying and macabre and hilarious and embarrassing. And that's the internet, too, for better or worse.

As much as New Yorkers talk about leaving New York, people on the internet announce they are leaving the internet far more often. Everyone you know has, at some point, said—loudly or privately, for attention or just for their own sanity—"I'm unplugging!" When people make declarations about leaving the internet, like weary go-getters buying a one-way ticket from JFK to anywhere, more often than not they are Kristen Johnston speeches and not Joan Didion essays. The internet becomes an external force, a pulsing id, humanity's dark pit, rather than a projection of self. I think this is interesting because while so much of the internet is consumption, we are sharing—either willfully on social media or unknowingly through cookies—who we are and what we want. We despair at the state of the internet, like we sometimes despair at the potholes in a city street or an ugly building that went up where a cute bakery used to be. But how much are we despairing at ourselves? We mourn our inability to find the humor, or the joy, or the wonder of discovery, or the energy. Or we rage at the algorithms and the people acting in bad faith and the ad that follows you from site to site, like a ghost. But, again according to science, the internet is other people. It's us, alas, not some sentient robot that is conspiring to steal our data and leak our nudes. (I have no nudes. Nor data. Pass me by, Mr. Roboto.) We are the internet that we bemoan; we are building this city ourselves.

The day before the 2016 election, I mentioned Trump in my ELLE.com column for the first time. There was a photo of him peeking at Melania Trump's ballot and it was too good to pass up. So I wrote it up in a sort of "Farewell to this shit show" column. (Little did I know, the shit show would be given a full series order. Oops.) Through the end of the year, I was able to keep a certain kind of content at bay. I wrote about the Obamas and Bey; I wrote about Mariah Carey's Christmas obsession; I wrote about how much Phylicia Rashad loves caftans (so much; she loves them so much). But I also couldn't help but write about some of the other things that were happening as Trump prepared to take office. He had dinner with Mitt Romney and took an ominously lit photo that looked like a production still from a horror movie. The internet was talking about it and I had jokes, so in it went. "This is a freeze frame from an instructional video on stranger danger," I wrote. " 'Hi, I'm Mittchard Romney, a politician who looks pretty good in retrospect. I'm here with my good friend, The Eye of Sauron, to talk to you about workplace harassment.' "

In late January 2017, just before the inauguration, Congresswoman Maxine Waters of California gave a terse, fiery press conference in which she said that then FBI director James Comey had no credibility. Watching the twenty-second video, I felt the disparate streams of my writing voice come together and I pounced on it with glee. She was Black, she was confident, she was extra, and she wasn't mincing words. Honey, I lived. The internet responded vociferously. The article was read hundreds of thousands of times, the most of anything I'd written up to that point. A month later, she appeared on *All In with Chris Hayes* on MSNBC and let that place out, reading a list of people in the Trump administration that she thought were colluding with Russia. I wrote, "Where does she find the energy, y'all? She is trying to single-handedly strap this country to her back and carry it to safety. And, no, she doesn't care if the country wants to go or not. Rep. Waters is that Auntie who attacks your face with a wet wipe at every cookout and has a ninja-like ability to whip a comb out and run it through your hair before you can ever protest." Close to a million people read that column. People started calling her Auntie Maxine. I struggled briefly with a question of authenticity in what I'd written. Was I treating her with respect? I thought so, but not everyone online agreed. Some took me to task for using Black and gay vernacular for a "white magazine." I felt that my context was the internet, not necessarily ELLE.com's average reader, who may or may not be white. I didn't argue about it, though. I did make sure to correct people when they said I was the first to call her Auntie Maxine. (I'd said she was *like* an Auntie but I hadn't gone as far as to dub her Auntie Maxine. It may have risen from my column, but giving her a nickname would have been overreach. I felt this was an important distinction.) Ironically, she liked the moniker and started using it herself. That April, she invited me to an event she was hosting concerning Trump's tax returns (we know how to party). I thought I was just going to be hanging out, watching her rip the president to shreds. I arrived and her chief of staff ushered me onstage for an intimate conversation between Rep. Maxine

Waters, activist Brittany Packnett, and R. Eric Thomas, Deer in the Headlights.

For a while after that, I became "the Maxine Waters guy," which is not a bad way to start a conversation. When I moved away at the end of the year, *The Philadelphia Inquirer* wrote an article about it entitled "The Creator of 'Auntie Maxine' Meme Says Goodbye to Philly." I had gone from Internet User to the meme creator, which has to be some kind of internet leveling up. Professionally, it was extraordinary. But the real value for me was in how it lifted my spirits. After months of wondering how much longer I could lurk on the internet, mining the news for comedy, Maxine Waters's determination, her presence, and the sheer force of her will spoke to me deeply. It woke a voice up in me that was rooted in cultural traditions I valued. It gave me the opportunity to write exuberantly, joyfully, and, yes, with hope. It made the city of the internet new for me. Or if not new, more familiar, less severe. Something like home.

Spoiler alert: I did not leave Al Gore's internet. I did not sing an angry aria about how it has ruined our country and our psyches before pitching my computer out the window. I did not write an introspective farewell post about how I knew that the internet I perceived must, at least partly, have been a reflection of what I was putting into it. More practically, I did not quit my job on the internet and pack it in for some other burg where things are simpler and the subways don't smell like pee. I thought about it, obviously, but I wonder now if I ever could have. I wonder if the things that the internet brought me ever could have been overshadowed by the things it took from me. I log on to the city of the internet every day. (Listen to me: "log on." Like I'm cranking up the 56k modem and making sure no one else is on the phone line.) I am in the city of the internet all the time. And it isn't the romantic idea that, to paraphrase Didion, I can remember with a clarity that makes the nerves in the back of my neck constrict. But I understand that this place, for all its complexity, for all that it costs, for all that I fear it pulls out of me, is not a place I want to abandon. I feel this in a way, perhaps, that is far clearer than any feeling I've ever had about a physical city, or community, or even this nation. I'm a native now.

Hi, I'm R. Eric Thomas; I'm from the internet.

Here for It, or How to Save Your Soul in America

It turns out, there's very little I love more than marching in a Pride Parade. Or not even marching—dancing, strutting, Queen-waving (Elizabeth or Freddie Mercury, dealer's choice). I believe that you can mark the various phases and stages of your life by what kind of Pride experience you're having. Not to say that everyone at every stage experiences Pride in the same way. But if you're looking for a rubric, Pride works. In the beginning you're just showing up. It's exhilarating and you can't find enough rainbow gear to wear. There. Is. So. Much. Glitter. Maybe you took the train in from some suburb with a drive-through Starbucks. Maybe you snuck out of the house. Maybe you're drinking wine out of your backpack. All you know is you're thrilled to be there and you go home late in the evening, sunburnt and ebullient.

Later, you get acclimated; you feign being over it. Pride becomes that place where you run into all your exes and first act shady to them and then act friendly to them, depending on what's going on in your therapy sessions. At some point maybe you even march in the parade. The first time I marched—with a website I was writing for—I was just over thirty, single, and was briefly experiencing the hint of an ab. I wore a fedora for some reason and at the last minute I decided to take off my shirt because that's basically what you do at Pride. So, that year I didn't so much march as Display Abs (One Ab) to Thirteen Blocks of Center City Philadelphia.

Maybe at some point you march with your workmates in matching T-shirts that advertise your very open and affirming corporate banking conglomerate. At another point maybe you're carrying a kid in a Björn in Pride, and pushing a stroller in Pride, and holding a sign that says "Free Mom Hugs" in Pride. And eventually, if you're lucky, you become one of those queer elders, riding a festively decorated trolley that has been chartered by a community center, waving from the window, marveling at how much has changed and how familiar it all seems.

I love Pride. I love a party, I love a family reunion, I love getting flyers and magnets from local vendors. I love Pride, too, because it began as a riot. That's important to me; every step, every shimmy, every wave, is a gesture of triumph but also defiance. The first time I went to Pride, I wasn't legally allowed to get married. I could be fired from my job because of my sexual orientation. My future husband couldn't be ordained in the church. And yet we were living in markedly better times than we'd lived in before. There was so much to dance about.

•

By the time David and I decided to get engaged, marriage equality had become the law of the land, the Presbyterian Church (U.S.A.) was ordaining LGBTQ ministers, and David had become the first openly gay Presbyterian pastor ordained in Philadelphia. The first time we experienced a Pride Parade together was just before the engagement; we knew that we were going to get married, we'd even talked about it at length; we just needed to go through the formalities, by which I mean posting about it on Facebook. That year, I marched with Philadelphia's LGBT community center, as I was the program director at the time. David, as he is wont to do at Prides, celebrations, and protests, donned his white pastor's collar and black shirt and watched from the sidelines. I was wearing a tank top and shorts that in their shortness should embarrass me but obviously do not. After the parade, I met him near the judging stand and we walked back home, me toting a sign that read, "I Love Bread." (Pride is about love and this is who I am, okay?) I was wearing every strand of plastic beads I could collect; he was looking like the young priest from *The Exorcist*. People kept stopping us to tell him they loved his costume. A friend flagged us down and took a picture. "Kiss!" my friend implored us. I froze. I finally registered that walking around Pride with my pastor husband-to-be was making me uncomfortable. On the one hand, I was relieved that I derived no psychosexual enjoyment from his priest-like getup. On the other hand, I saw for the first time that the person I wanted to spend my life with was not only an individual, but an institution. He wore his shirt and his collar to represent himself and also to invite passersby to consider that the church, as a monolith, wasn't all hostile to LGBTQ people. He wore them as a witness and as a small missionary act. From afar, it was noble, beautiful even. It was exactly what I'd been looking for all those years when I didn't have a church. But in the frame of my friend's camera, our bodies side by side, holding hands, I felt trapped inside something that I didn't understand. My Pride reached a limit; my gestures of triumph were unconvincing. Was this right? Was this holy? Was this really for me?

I stopped showing up to church so much. I had searched for so long and worked so hard to get to a place where who I am and who I love and how I understand God could coexist. And having arrived at that place, instead of celebrating, I became deeply uncomfortable and promptly turned around and left. When I did show up, I would sit in church and feel nothing, watching my fiancé perform his job like I was observing a bank teller counting cash. The choir at Broad Street Ministry would sing Aretha and Whitney and Stevie and I'd clap but I'd feel hollow. I knew that most of the work of church is building a community, participating. I knew that if you withdrew, church couldn't make you join in. I tried to put on a friendly face because I was representing David, not myself. I couldn't bring myself to be more open, because that meant revealing that I felt more isolated than ever. That didn't seem the kind of thing a pastor's spouse was supposed to say.

To make matters worse, when we got engaged I forgot to change my profile picture to Whitney Houston in *The Preacher's Wife* as had been my intention from our very first date. My plans: ruined! All those Facebook likes, squandered. What a time of turmoil.

One of the things I forget about *The Preacher's Wife* is that Whitney Houston's character, Julia, the eponymous spouse, spends much of the film lonely. The film is driven by her loneliness, and the supernatural solution to it. I certainly didn't think of that on the steps of my South Philly brownstone after our first date or sitting in the church a year and a half later, watching my future husband perform communion. I thought of Whitney herself, grinning, eyes cast heavenward on the soundtrack album cover. I thought of her singular voice, a perfect instrument in its finest form, elevating every song. I thought of the lead single, "I Believe in You and Me," which I secretly thought should be our first dance because this dude loves a theme. I thought of her cover of Annie Lennox's "Step by Step," which has provided the tempo for every workout I've ever done. I thought of her energetic "He's All Over Me," a gospel anthem with Shirley Caesar that will have you jumping around your living room, sweating through your Sunday best, every time you blast it. I thought of the way the film made me feel, which is the way that everything Whitney touched made me feel: light and complete and hopeful. There's something about Whitney Houston's voice that communicates the inner workings of joy, the thrill of hope, and the exuberance of love. Listening to her taught me about being a human who feels deeply and lives fully. Her voice is like throwing your arms wide and taking in the sky, it's like walking into heaven on a Sunday morning, it's like being born again.

When I was a child and I shared a room with Stephen, we used to listen to tapes as we went to sleep. After *The Bodyguard* soundtrack came out, I would insist that we listen to that (side A only, please) on repeat. I hadn't seen the movie; it was rated R and I was eleven years old, what a scandal! But I'd been allowed to buy the album because even then I was obsessed with Whitney Houston. More than any other artist, more than Mariah, more than Celine, more than Bette (these were the only artists I knew), Whitney's voice spoke to something blooming in me. And *The Preacher's Wife* soundtrack was, for me, a perfect Whitney creation—a little bit of pop, a lot of gospel, and through it all that voice that sang me to sleep in my youth.

What I don't ever remember about *The Preacher's Wife,* what perhaps would have been handy to recall, is that besides providing a backdrop for what would become the highest-selling gospel album of all time, it's not a movie in which everything goes well for everyone. It's about a woman whose husband (played by Courtney B. Vance, aka Mr. Angela Bassett) is struggling to keep a church afloat. Her future is uncertain and her marriage is on sandy land. The pastor prays for divine intervention to save his church, and heaven answers, as it often does, in the form of Denzel Washington, an angel who begins setting things right. The pastor being caught up in the complicated and difficult business of ministry and unable to receive his blessing, Denzel the angel spends most of his time hanging out with Whitney Houston. This, in and of itself, is a blessing, as she finds in Denzel someone to talk to, someone with whom to sort her problems out, and someone who can help her understand what her husband is going through.

I did not have a Denzel. I had not found the miraculous solution to a life beset with questions about church and my place in it simply by becoming engaged to a pastor. Indeed, it had made it harder. I had a choice, the same choice that rose up over and over again—do I stay in this hard place, stuck, or do I turn the page, even though it hurts, even though I'm afraid?

"There's a road, I have to follow," Whitney sings in "Step by Step," "a place I have to go / Well, no one told me, just how to get there / But when I get there I'll know. . . ." Maybe Whitney was *my* Denzel. The fact was, I was in church, on occasion, after years of being away. And this was, yes, where I wanted to be. And stepping through the door, remembering the times of welcome and the times of rebuke in my past, felt like triumph and defiance. It certainly didn't feel as good as marching down the street on a Sunday in June, glitter-covered and abs (ab?) out. But it was a start.

Yes, I felt alone; yes, I still searched the air above me for God's voice; yes, I prayed for transformation without knowing exactly what that meant. But I'd taken a step on the road. "Come on, baby," the chorus chants behind Whitney, "got to keep moving. Come on, baby, got to keep moving." An incantation, a wish, a prayer. I loved David and I loved God and I didn't believe anymore that those things were in conflict. I felt something like love for myself. I also knew that the way forward wasn't any less complicated, but no one ever promised me less complication. If anything, it's always going to become more complicated. Better but more. Better and more. Pride is a party *and* a riot, after all. And I was here for all of it.

"Marriage is a gift from God," David's hometown pastor, Ken, said to open our wedding ceremony at Broad Street Ministry. They were words David had written, borrowed from a Unitarian ceremony. The pastor continued, "No union is more profound than marriage, for it embodies the highest ideals of love, fidelity, devotion, sacrifice, and family," this time borrowing words from Justice Anthony Kennedy's opinion in the *Obergefell v. Hodges* case, the one that made same-sex marriage equality the law of the land. I realize now that I didn't really know what those words meant then; I didn't understand their gravity, their importance, their scope. Everything I did or said that day was a leap of faith, but when you're in a church, all you need is faith, isn't it?

I'd left the ceremony up to David. "Just make sure we get

married," I'd said. I'd busied myself with planning the reception, which included a cabaret featuring a live band. We'd hired a couple of musicians and singers, including one woman, Ashli Rice, who sounds just like Whitney Houston. I was only going to get married once and Whitney was going to get me there one way or another. I asked Ashli to perform a medley of three Whitney songs that David and I both liked. Originally, when David and I discussed it, I'd suggested that she perform the entire *Bodyguard* soundtrack followed by *The Preacher's Wife* and close it with Whitney's version of the national anthem. This just seemed appropriate. David is always far too willing to follow me on flights of fancy and actually considered having someone sing the national anthem at our wedding. Bless his heart. Can you imagine, "The Star-Spangled Banner" at an interracial gay wedding in the heart of a Sanctuary City with attendees ranging from a World War II vet to the mayor's Black LGBTQ liaison to Martin, my cousin who did multiple tours of Afghanistan, to our nephew Michael, a mixed-race boy, then three years old, growing up in South Carolina? Child, that place would have looked like a game of whack-a-mole, with some people standing up and some people taking a knee and some people looking around like "Honey, what is happening in this place on this day?" Now, that's church.

It isn't that we have a particularly deep love of the anthem. We just love Whitney. But thinking back, I almost wish we had introduced the chaos of patriotism to the proceedings. It was there already. Love is political. Church is political. Our friends and family—queer folks, trans folks, straight folks, white folks, Black folks, Latinx folks, Asian folks, baby boomers, Gen Xers, millennials, Democrats, Republicans, Socialists, and at least a couple Libertarians, Christians, Jews, Buddhists, Muslims, agnostics, questioners, and atheists—are political. This act—

daring to say that we believe in each other—is political. Daring to say that we believe in something, anything, is political. Daring to believe that we'll exist in the future in America is political.

At one point in the ceremony, as is common in the Presbyterian tradition, Ken asked the congregation to stand as he read vows that our community was making to us. "Do all of you pledge your support and encouragement to the covenant commitment that Eric and David are making together? If so, please say, 'We do.' "

"We do," they all replied as one. Michael's tiny voice followed a second later: "We do!" he cried. And if ever there was a time to play the national anthem, it's then. It's in this place where something new is being built, where people are united in one goal, with one voice, where the future is hard to make out but, yes, it's there. We're there. Better and more complicated. That's the only country I can survive in.

I don't live in that country, but every day by existing, by speaking, by loving, by writing, I make a vow to get there, step-by-step. To knit together the pieces inside that don't coalesce; to find a community that is generative, or, short of that, to make one; to see the future. This is why I treasure Whitney's "Star-Spangled Banner." It does the miraculous in that it finds something beneath the words that is true and halcyon and greater than the failings of the nation it represents.

Hearing Whitney's voice, the response is automatic, it is soul-deep and centuries old. It is the awakening of a piece within you that dares to be optimistic, a seed that was placed there by the prayer of an ancestor. It is never a guarantee.

We commonly only sing the first verse of the anthem; it's comprised of four sentences and three of them are questions. The singer wants confirmation about what is seen, what is perceived, and what it means. And that lack of surety is America most of all. America is never a set notion; it is an ideal scarred from battle, perceived through smoke. The people must cry as one, "We do!" Is that what patriotism feels like? I feel that I should know, but patriotism, too, is always a question. It's a concept that has been hijacked and beaten up, sold out and ripped to shreds by those who want it only for its surface rush, and not its arduous roots. Anything good in this country has had to be wrestled free.

Some say that's the beauty of the nation; that's the American dream, as if we are all Jacob pummeling the biblical angel for a new name. But the tribulations that tinge every victory in pursuit of simply being American—and all that that supposedly entails—are the worst of us. They are a national shackle, a dark mark across the soil. And so it is a shock when the crisp, bright, free voice of a Black woman elevates our national anthem from the dirgelike bottom of rote recitation to something otherworldly, something spiritual, something that dares to hope. The fact that it's possible is a miracle. It lifts me up; it transforms the song; it builds the country from ash.

Ashli starts her medley by singing "I Believe in You and Me" from *The Preacher's Wife*. The crowd, a couple of hours into our reception, is a noisy conference of joyful murmuring. They grow silent at the sound of her voice. I get chills because I know what is to come and I know what has come before. As she reaches the crescendo, people are shouting like it's church. And maybe it is. Maybe this, too, is holy. Maybe this, too, is heaven. Ashli segues into "I Will Always Love You" from *The Bodyguard*. My mother leaps to her feet like Sister Jackson. A queer couple finds their way onto the dance floor and sways in each other's arms. And this, too, is church. We have all caught the spirit. We lift our voices up. Couples flood the makeshift dance floor that we've made purposefully small because David and I are awkward dancers and we wanted to discourage that kind of thing, like the dad from *Footloose*. The couples are undeterred; love is not a respecter of borders.

Oh, and it is a sight. My parents are dancing; my brothers and their wives are dancing. Our friends of all genders and races and sexual orientations and many nationalities, they're dancing. They are holding each other; they are making a new world. Ashli's final note on "I Will Always Love You" pushes the buttressed roof of the church into the sky; the stained glass is a constellation now, points of light drawing us back to a place where we once found belonging and leading us on to a land we can call our own. The drummer taps the cymbals, that sizzling sound that means something's coming. The horns and guitar start to vamp. Ashli launches into "I Wanna Dance with Somebody" with wild abandon. And this is church. For this song is about keeping alive the hope that you will find someone with whom you can express your joy. And isn't that worship? Isn't that a declaration? Isn't it?

The dance floor fills. The singers belt with the same boundless exuberance with which Whitney wants to know if the banner yet waves. Does it? Does this nation we've made have a flag? A name? A home?

I catch sight of our nephew Michael and a crush of other children—those of our friends and David's congregants—darting through the crowd with glow necklaces on every appendage. I realize that this night in this church is the world that they will know, this is the world they will see as normal, this is the world they will inherit. A world made by people of all colors and sexualities and ages and faiths and gender expressions who have traveled many roads toward hope. And though we crowd the dance floor in the space that has been made specifically for us, our presence seems to create even more space, for those like us, for those yet to be. All heaven has broken out.

And this is why, I think to myself as past and present and future collapse on themselves. Hope. This is the liberation that waits for us through the smoke. And isn't that holy? Isn't that love? Isn't that worth living for?

Epilogue

The End Is ~~Coming~~ Running about Fifteen Minutes Late

(A cruise ship off the coast of Nova Scotia, late at night. Summer 2000. R. Eric Thomas, a nineteen-year-old wisp of a thing, barely a notion really, sits alone near a buffet that never closes. Eden as an island, on the sea, offering every possible culinary delight the ship's chef has it in their budget to prepare.

It's almost midnight. The sounds of the ship's casino echo from a distance—the tintinnabulation of winning, the vacuum of losing. A door at the far end of the room opens and R. Eric Thomas, age twenty-seven, enters. R. Eric Thomas, at nineteen—hereafter called Nineteen for clarity's sake—looks up but does not nod or wave for fear of seeming overly eager to an apparent stranger also roaming the high seas in search of all-you-can-eat king crab legs.)

TWENTY-SEVEN

I have some news.

NINETEEN

Sorry, is this area closed?

TWENTY-SEVEN

I have no idea. God, you're skinny. What year is it? Is that a lobster tail? I'm famished. Why don't you have more on your plate?

NINETEEN

I'm not that hungry.

TWENTY-SEVEN

That is literally the last time you will ever say that.

NINETEEN

Are you going to kill me?

TWENTY-SEVEN

Why would I kill you?

NINETEEN

We're on a cruise ship in the middle of the night. That's where these things happen. Also, you are talking to me and honestly that's a little weird.

TWENTY-SEVEN

Don't you recognize me?

NINETEEN

Why would I recognize you?

TWENTY-SEVEN

I'm you. Don't you see any resemblance?

NINETEEN

To what?

TWENTY-SEVEN

To what?! My God. To yourself. Hello! I honestly thought this would be easier. Eric, I am you. From the future.

NINETEEN

Is this theater? Are you acting at me right now?

TWENTY-SEVEN

I'm R. Eric Thomas. Age twenty-seven. I'm you.

NINETEEN

That's a stretch, Meryl. But okay.

(Another R. Eric Thomas, this one thirty-five, enters the room. He looks fine, thanks. He's moisturized. It's fine.)

THIRTY-FIVE

He's not an actor.

NINETEEN

Well, not much of one. But give the guy a break. He seems like he's had a rough go of it.

TWENTY-SEVEN

I can hear you, you know.

NINETEEN

I'm just saying, that extra-"medium" shirt isn't doing you any favors.

TWENTY-SEVEN

Wow. Am I an asshole?

THIRTY-FIVE

Eric! We are both you. From the future. Isn't this what you wanted?

NINETEEN

I wanted another one of those blueberry muffins that they served at breakfast, actually. That's why I came up here. Do you know that you can eat from this buffet any time of the day or night? Isn't that beyond? This is totally worth the price of the cruise. Not that I have any idea how much this cost. My parents paid for— Oh. My. God. Are you me from the future?!

TWENTY-SEVEN

I was never this much of a mess.

THIRTY-FIVE

You still are.

NINETEEN

All last year—I'm a rising junior at Columbia; but you know that, I guess—I would wish that a version of me from the future would come through the door and tell me what happens. It's just been really hard and I wanted some help. Everything seems to be falling apart for me. It seemed really hopeless for a lot of it. I wasn't even really sure I was going to survive it, to be honest. So it's good to see that I get old.

THIRTY-FIVE

Oh Jesus.

NINETEEN

You're a little late, though. I mean, the school year is over and my parents took me on a cruise, so it all works out. I'm not sure what you came to tell me. Actually, when I thought about what it would be like in my head, we were making out by now.

TWENTY-SEVEN

You're a disaster.

NINETEEN

Accurate. So, it all turns out great?

TWENTY-SEVEN

No.

NINETEEN

Oh no!

TWENTY-SEVEN

Yeah, you're going to drop out and things are going to get really sad for a long time.

NINETEEN

Why are you telling me this?!

TWENTY-SEVEN

You asked, dum-dum.

NINETEEN

What about you? The other one. Surely things get better by the time you're around. What are you, like fifty?

THIRTY-FIVE

I'm thirty-five.

NINETEEN

Oh no!

THIRTY-FIVE

Things get better. You get married! To a man! You become a writer!

NINETEEN

So, you both came back in time to tell me that things only get better-ish.

THIRTY-FIVE

And also to eat. I'm famished.

NINETEEN

Is this good news or bad news?

THIRTY-FIVE

It's fine. I wish I could tell you all the mistakes you're going to make that I really wish you wouldn't make, but I don't think it works like that. However, I think it's important for you to know that you're here. In the future. And it's whatever.

NINETEEN

Wow. A glowing review.

THIRTY-FIVE

Maybe the next guy will have better news?

(Another Eric, age forty-three, walks through the door. Wow, has he been working out?)

FORTY-THREE

I do not have better news.

THIRTY-FIVE
(mouth full of food)

Oh no!

FORTY-THREE

I mean, it's kind of the same thing. I hate to break it to you all, but life is a mixed bag.

TWENTY-SEVEN

Am I happy?

FORTY-THREE

I don't know how to answer that question. Are there things that make you happy? Absolutely.

NINETEEN

More than there are now?

FORTY-THREE

Yes. Definitely. Life is better.

NINETEEN

See, it gets better.

(Another Eric, fifty-one, very rich, enters.)

FIFTY-ONE

I have bad news.

NINETEEN

Oh no!

FIFTY-ONE

Yeah, the future is very yikes.

THIRTY-FIVE

That's a very expensive-looking suit, though.

FIFTY-ONE

Oh yeah, I'm rich as hell. But things are still sort of figuring themselves out.

TWENTY-SEVEN

How do you mean?

FIFTY-ONE

Uh, like destiny.

THIRTY-FIVE

(mouth full of food)

What are you talking about? The planet?

FIFTY-ONE

Sure. The planet. Things do not magically transform.

FORTY-THREE

How are the ice caps?

FIFTY-ONE

Drinkable. But we're turning it around.

(Eric, fifty-nine, enters. Same suit, but worse for the wear.)

FIFTY-NINE

I have some bad news.

FIFTY-ONE

Oh no!

(Eric, sixty-seven, enters. Rich again!)

SIXTY-SEVEN

I have some bad news.

TWENTY-SEVEN

Does it ever get better?

(Eric, seventy-five, enters. In a caftan.)

SEVENTY-FIVE

Eh. It's fine.

NINETEEN

What are you wearing?

SEVENTY-FIVE

It's a caftan. Is that a lobster tail? I'm famished.

NINETEEN

Why?

SEVENTY-FIVE

I had an early breakfast. Plus, time-traveling really makes you work up an appetite. Is there drawn butter anywhere? It's fine. I don't need it. My arteries!

NINETEEN

No, I mean, why the caftan? Also, there's drawn butter in a little urn over on the condiments station.

THIRTY-FIVE

Oh my God.

(Erics Twenty-Seven, Thirty-Five, and Fifty-One go to the drawn-butter urn.)

SEVENTY-FIVE

Why the caftan? The breeze for one. Also, who likes pants? Do you like pants?

NINETEEN

I do, actually. The right pair can really accentuate my butt.

SEVENTY-FIVE

You know what a caftan accentuates?

NINETEEN

What?

SEVENTY-FIVE

How happy your butt is to not be trapped in pants. Look at me: I'm basically lying in bed, wrapped in a blanket, but also upright. I am living my full Nancy Meyers–heroine truth right now. I haven't worn a pair of pants in at least three years. You wish you could be me. Pass me one of those cookies.

NINETEEN

So, listen, I kind of just wanted someone to come back through time and tell me that if I came out, my parents wouldn't hate me or that I'd graduate and get a job or that maybe one day I have a boyfriend. This is like an Eric conference and it's a lot. Three of them are standing around the condiments station screaming about the woman from Destiny's Child.

SEVENTY-FIVE

Do you not know Beyoncé?

NINETEEN

Yeah, I know Beyoncé. But why are they screaming about her? Does she do something special in the future?

SEVENTY-FIVE

Oh Lord. You have so much life left. *(Pause. He looks at the doorway.)* I guess I'm the last one through. Look, I don't know what you want to get from this. Things are going to happen, some of them good, a lot of them bad. People will die. People will break your heart. You'll disappoint people. You'll disappoint yourself even more. You'll try things that don't work. You'll dare to hope and sometimes that will be rewarded and sometimes it will be mocked. You'll write a book and end it with a short play for some reason.

NINETEEN

Yikes. Seriously?

SEVENTY-FIVE

The important thing is you'll live. Isn't that really what you wanted to know? That's the question, for all of you, "Do I survive to the end?"

(Pause)

NINETEEN

Yes.

SEVENTY-FIVE

Well, then I come bearing good news. You will not kill yourself today. Or tomorrow either. You will find a way to gather yourself up and push yourself into the next day. And sometimes that will feel like a blessing, sometimes a burden. But we will not go quietly into the night. We will not vanish without a fight! We're going to live on! We're going to survive! Today, we celebrate our Independence Day!

TWENTY-SEVEN

I think you got a little lost in there.

NINETEEN

Is all of that from the movie *Independence Day*?

SEVENTY-FIVE

The what? No, that's all an original thought.

TWENTY-SEVEN

It's objectively not.

THIRTY-FIVE

Bill Pullman.

SEVENTY-FIVE

What?

THIRTY-FIVE

Said that.

SEVENTY-FIVE

Doesn't ring a bell.

SIXTY-SEVEN

At a certain point, you forget where you end and pop culture begins.

SEVENTY-FIVE

Well, who cares if I didn't think of it. I meant it. Be inspired.

NINETEEN

This all seems depressing.

SEVENTY-FIVE

Okay, well, be depressed then. I could have stayed my ass in the future. You gonna finish that cake?

NINETEEN

Yes.

SEVENTY-FIVE

So salty.

NINETEEN

It just doesn't seem fair. Like, what's the point of going on?

SEVENTY-FIVE

Do you want to hear about all the good things? Or do you just want someone to coddle you and tell you there's a happy ending?

NINETEEN

Isn't that the same thing?

SEVENTY-FIVE

No! It absolutely is not. If you asked any of these versions of yourself around this room to stop screaming about Beyoncé and list what's good in their lives, we'd be here all night. But you have this idea that what you're headed for, what the world is headed for, is some sort of resolution.

NINETEEN

And I guess you're here to tell me that it's not.

SEVENTY-FIVE

At the end of the story you die.

THIRTY-FIVE

(mouth full of food)

Oh no!

NINETEEN

Are you here to kill me?

SEVENTY-FIVE

Eric. Get yourself together. No one is here to kill you . . . *(Pregnant pause; he looks at the doorway.)* Okay, yeah, no one is here to kill you.

FIFTY-NINE

You've gathered us all here today. It was a lot of work; I hope you know that. This excursion. I had to rearrange a lot of things.

THIRTY-FIVE

Oh, she's busy! She's a businesswoman in the future!

NINETEEN

So, that's it? We live. We go through things. We die. For what?

SEVENTY-FIVE

You say you want a happy ending, but neither of those words is really what you're searching for. For instance, you will not live to see a just world. But you will live to see acts of justice.

NINETEEN

And that's good enough?

SEVENTY-FIVE

That's extraordinary. Life will take your breath away. Life will— Oh! Chocolate éclairs! Grab me one of those.

NINETEEN

Wow, we really are unbearable.

SEVENTY-FIVE

You're exactly who you need to be. Each of you. It may not feel like it; it may seem like it would be much easier being anyone else. You may look back at the person you were at one point and wish that you could instead be the person you are now at that far distant, unreachable point in the past. But you had to be who you were to get to who you are.

Every page in the story is successive; they're all numbered and bound like a book.

THIRTY-FIVE
(mouth full of food)
I'm a spoiler kween.

SEVENTY-FIVE
This one you have to just be present for.

NINETEEN
What you're saying seems harder than life is supposed to be.

SEVENTY-FIVE
Well, I don't know how it's supposed to be for anyone else. The only story I can tell you is my own. And in that story, you keep turning the pages. That's hope. We hope with words and we hope with deeds. And in so doing, manifest the things that we need, the things that fulfill us, the things that give us life when we fear that all is lost.

(A burst of smoke, a flash of light, a squealing horn. Another Eric, impossibly old, comes through the door.)

ERIC ANCIENT
I have some news.

(A confetti cannon explodes behind him.)

END OF PLAY

ACKNOWLEDGMENTS

First of all, I think we all ought to acknowledge Beyoncé. Don't you?

What order am I supposed to do this in? Alphabetical? That sounds stressful. No thanks. Here are some great names of great people:

My therapist, Brian Edwards, will never read this because he has something called "boundaries" so he never googles me even when I insist that being googled is what I need for my therapeutic process. Nevertheless, Brian is a wonder who worked with me through two of the most confusing and lonely years of my life, which also happened to coincide with the writing of this comedy book of happy jokes. I doubt I could have done it without him and I'm very grateful. He also recommends books that are always excellent. What a great experience all around. Thanks also to my previous therapists Brianna Belkins and Kristina Furia. Go to therapy! Everybody!

My phenomenal agent, Anna Sproul-Latimer of Ross Yoon, came all the way to Philadelphia, bought me a Reuben sandwich, and asked me if I had a book in me and I said yes, which felt like 60 percent of a lie but I really wanted to finish the Reuben sandwich and also I thought perhaps I could find a book. Instead, Anna found the book, with brilliant editorial notes and great questions and many drafts. Thanks for changing my life.

My editor, Sara Weiss, and Elana Seplow-Jolley at Ballantine masterfully picked up where Anna left off, shepherding and shaping this book in a way that, to me, is miraculous. Thanks for knowing it was there and knowing how to help me find it. Thanks to everyone at Ballantine and Penguin Random House who worked on this book, including Taylor Noel, Emily Isayeff, Kara Welsh, Jennifer Hershey, Kim Hovey, Kelly Chian, Diane Hobbing, and Rachel Ake.

As you know, Leah Chernikoff, formerly of ELLE.com, started this whole thing and redirected my life. I cannot thank her enough. Thanks also to the whole team at ELLE.com/Hearst, past and present, including: Sally Holmes, Estelle Tang, Katie Connor, Brooke Siegel, Chloe Hall, Nikki Ogunaike, Whitney Joiner, Jessica Roy, Kat Stoeffel, Mia Feitel, Yoursa Attia, Kristina Rudolpho, Mariel Tyler, Hannah Morrill, Ariana Yaptangco, Madi Feiler, Leah Melby Clinton, Gena Kaufman, Emily Tannenbaum, Angel Lenise, Bree Green, Anna Jimenez, Jimmie Armentrout, Alina Petrichyn, Kameron Key, Alyssa Bailey, Alysha Webb, Justine Carreon, Nojan Aminosharei, Nerisha Penrose, and my close personal friend and co-worker, Gayle King.

I wrote this book and assorted other things, including my daily column, concurrently over the course of a year and change. Some of that happened at home or at Baltimore coffee shops, but most of it happened while going from one gig to another. So thanks to the following transportation companies for existing: MARC train, Amtrak, Southwest Airlines, Lyft (please make your drivers full employees not contractors), Bolt Bus. (This bit seemed funnier in my head but it's true.)

The folks at The Moth have been incredible to me and I will

literally do any show you want any time, any place. Thanks especially to Jenifer Hixon, Paul Richards, Natalie Amini, Aman Goyal, Mojdeh Reziaporah, Kyrie Greenberg, Meg Bowles, Sam Hacker, Michelle Jalowski, Sarah Austin Jenness, Kate Tellers, Catherine Burns, Sarah Haberman, Inga Glodowski, Jodi Powell, Chloe Salmon, Patricia Ureña, and every single person who fills our sold-out shows in Washington, D.C., and Philadelphia every month, shares their stories, and creates a vibrant and vulnerable community.

This is going to sound weird but thank you to everybody who has been nice to me. Like, the people who see me out and come up and say things like "I don't want to be a stalker but I love your column." I spend most of my time sitting by myself, injecting Twitter into my head, and trying to figure out what there is to hope for ("the cheese groves, the cheese groves . . .") so to have those random encounters in public or at a play reading or even in DMs is wonderful. Thanks to the people who read my newsletter and sorry I'm so bad about responding. Thanks to the OG fans and friends on Facebook. Thanks to the people who are nice on Twitter. Thanks to everyone who has retweeted me and said I should win a Pulitzer. Keep it up; we're wearing them down.

Oh! That reminds me: sorry to everyone I owe an email to. I don't know what to tell you!

I miss my friends and I love them very much. Kristen Norine makes me believe that a better future is possible. Jarrod Markman told me I was a story jukebox, which is incredibly encouraging and I appreciate him deeply. He is mad at me that I didn't put him in this book, so if you see him tell him you read about him in my book and just convince him that his copy is missing a chapter. Andrew Panebianco and Lansie Sylvia have been #goals for me for so long: friend goals, civic engagement goals, work goals, Philebrity goals, vacation goals, couple goals, writing skills goals. I love them. Jake Bowling held my stupid, weird queer heart. Lisa Schanberger led me on the greatest unknown leap of my adult life and helped me when I stumbled. Sean Simon is my favorite youth and is so incredibly funny it's amazing I don't want to destroy him out of envy. Jackson Howard! Sis! My publishing wunderkind fairy godmother. My longest friends, Lisa Warren, Cristina Watson, I love you. Melissa Koenig: what if we never met?!

Keina Staley, thank you for introducing me to Prince.

(Is he going to just list everyone he knows? MAYBE. I don't know how this works. Is this an Academy Award speech? What is happening?!)

Rebecca Adelsheim, Rajib Guha, Jason Peno, Josh Kruger, Donald Harrison, Jackie Goldfinger, Quinn Eli, Erin Washburn, Miranda Rose Hall, Peter Spears, Haygen Brice Walker, Colton Mabis, Nimisha Ladva, Sarah Longson, Kyle Toth, Alejandro Morales, Arielle Brousse, Nate Eppler, Jack Tamburri, Michele Volansky, Dany Guy, Carl Clemons-Hopkins: you've each encouraged and improved my writing in a permanent and meaningful way and I appreciate you. ANNA GOLDFARB, a true friend-tor. I adore you.

The city of Philadelphia will always have my heart. Thanks to First Person Arts for giving me my storytelling start. The William Way LGBT Community Center, 1812 Productions, Azuka, Simpatico, Interact, Act II, and the Arden: thank you. Thanks to the wonderful congregation at Maryland Presbyterian Church, and love to the folks at Broad Street Ministry in Philadelphia.

Every teacher is a blessing and every teacher I've ever had has been a blessing to me. Thanks especially to those who taught me English literature and writing, including Nadine Feiler, Rachelle Work, Howard Berkowitz, Kevin Coll, Patricia Porcarelli, Susan McCully, Susan Weintraub, and many more whom I am sure I am missing. Thanks to every Black teacher I had, including Pert Toins-Banks and Craig Ross.

Electra Bynoe. You are missed, you are still loved; thank you for letting me linger in the book stacks with you again in these pages.

Trystan Trazon, you brilliant soul. I will never delete any email or message we exchanged. I miss you.

Obviously, I owe a huge debt of gratitude to my parents, Bob and Judi Thomas, for everything from my molecular structure, to raising me right, to shaping the way I think, and hope, and understand the world, to lending me money, to seeing or reading everything I performed in or wrote that I would let them, even the things that were very not good. They're my parents and I will never have enough words to express how deeply I love them nor how grateful I am for them, even though I wrote a whole book that was basically about that point. I wonder if any one person can ever truly understand what they mean to another person. I don't think it's possible, which is perhaps a sad part about being a human but also a beautiful hope for an understanding after life.

Thank you to my extended family, my extraordinary brothers, Stephen Thomas and Jeffrey Thomas, and to their wives, Kathleen Thomas and Karen Thomas, respectively, who inspire me and delight me and bring me such joy and have agreed not to sue me.

I am lucky to have wonderful, affirming, encouraging in-laws in Rachel Norse and Rick Norse. Thank you.

And finally, if you've read this book, you know how easy it is to fall in love with David Norse. He is the most engaging conversationalist I know, a dedicated and tireless partner, a source of seemingly endless hope, a brilliant leader, and the love of my life. It turns out, he is also the person you most want by your side as you fight with yourself and your words in an attempt to write a book. I love you, David.

Here for It

Or, How to Save Your Soul in America

R. Eric Thomas

A BOOK CLUB GUIDE

One of the most extraordinary and surprising delights about writing a book is that you sometimes get invited to book clubs, which is probably number four or five on my list of life's ambitions. (I could go into the other ambitions I have in life, but I know you're on a tight schedule and I don't want to keep you all day.) Suffice it to say, I have a chronic case of FOMO and I am always looking to be invited to a club. I think about being invited to a book club like Annie thinks about getting adopted by a nice family: in the form of a song. "Maybe someone will realize I am very interested in having an excuse to drink wine and sit on other people's couches while pontificating about plot points," I'll warble just quiet enough that I don't wake Miss Hannigan. And, sure, I could just be up-front with my friends, frenemies, work nemeses, and the assorted exes of friends whom I still follow on Facebook. Sure, I could just post a status that says "Invite me to your book club." Sure, I could even say it directly to someone's face. But I'm shy. Which is why I wrote a book divulging all of the events that have happened in my life and all of my feelings about them. It's my *process*.

The amazing thing, however, about writing a book is

that, like Sandra Bullock in *The Net,* you gain the ability to hack the system. When you write a book, people invite you to their book clubs! And you don't even have to sing a song about it first! If you are looking to make friends or enemies or if you are just looking for quotidian settings in which to drink wine, I highly recommend that you write a book. I suppose there are other ways of accomplishing these goals without going through the rigorous process of publishing, but I simply cannot think of any.

Because this book came out in hardcover a month before the COVID-19 pandemic, all of my book club invitations were over Zoom or some other video-conferencing platform. On the one hand, this was sad because it meant I had to drink my own wine in my own house. I've seen my house! Who cares?! But on the other hand, this meant I got to visit with people in states across the nation and meet with book club members who were dialing in from around the world. At some USA-based book clubs, Europe-based members would stay up till the wee small hours of the morning to chat with me, which was absolutely shocking and has ruined me for all other interactions. If you're not fighting the tyranny of time zones for our relationship, what are we even doing here?

I'm mostly kidding. The fact is, I am pleasantly and deeply surprised any time anyone picks up this book. So to know that a quorum of work friends or college friends or strangers who answered an ad decided to pick up this book, to read about my journey to a place of joy and hope and authenticity, is nothing short of a miracle to me. This book is an invitation to your book club that I am sending to myself, yes, but it's also an invitation I'm sending you. An invitation to climb in an open window in a world full of closed doors, an invitation to dig deep into exuberance in a gray landscape, an invitation to the idea of belonging itself.

Maybe every book is a kind of club, a space where we can meet each other and gather and be seen. I don't know; I haven't read every book. But if you invite me to hang out, I'll get started on it.

Thanks for reading *Here for It;* thanks for having opinions about it on one of your friends' couches; thanks for welcoming me into your life.

Oh, and in answer to your question: I think there was a dog but it was probably hypoallergenic and antisocial.

QUESTIONS AND TOPICS FOR DISCUSSION

1. Which essay in the collection did you like the most, and why?

2. In *Here for It,* R. Eric Thomas writes, "Every story, whether truth or fiction, is an invitation to imagination, but even more so, it's an invitation to empathy." Do you agree? How does reading help people learn to be more empathetic?

3. One of the major themes of *Here for It* is belonging. Thomas writes about living at the intersections of Blackness, queerness, and Christianity in America. Discuss how those parts of a person's identity can be in harmony or in conflict with each other.

4. In the essay "There's Never Any Trouble Here in Bubbleland," Thomas writes about his childhood and the utopia that was his progressive private school. For him, being able to grow up in the bubble of possibilities and opportunities afforded by that school

was invigorating. How did this essay challenge you to think about the various bubbles people live in—and how those are advantageous and how they are not?

5. If you are Black, queer, and/or Christian, how did this book make you feel seen or represented? If you are not, how did this book help you understand some of those experiences?
6. In the essay "Unsubscribe from All That," Thomas writes about how exhausting and toxic the internet and social media can be, especially when he relies on both to do his job. Can you relate? How does your own experience with social media affect how you engage with the rest of the world?
7. In "Historically Black," Thomas writes, "These were the moments when I was reminded that no matter how passively I engaged with my Blackness, it was never not a force at work in my life. And, I found, the knowledge of my Blackness could be used as a weapon against me at any moment. All my life I'd operated under the assumption that there were many kinds of Blackness. . . . But in that passing moment, during the conversation about the SATs, it occurred to me that no matter where I was, perhaps there was only one kind of Black." Discuss what he means and how America tends to homogenize Black people. How have you seen someone's Blackness used as a weapon against them?
8. "Someone Is Wrong on the Internet" is Thomas's story about the first time he went viral, for writing

a satirical piece on Black History Month. How did you react to this essay? How did it make you think about accountability for what we put in a social media space?

9. "When the fact of your being is used as a weapon against you, the process of relearning who you are and what your value is, is a long one. I don't know that I'll ever be finished. I don't know that I'll ever be fully there," Thomas writes at one point in the book. What does he mean? How are people supposed to value themselves when marginalized by the larger society?

10. In an essay about his coming-out experience, Thomas writes, "It was something else altogether. It wasn't a collision, but an expansion. I hadn't expected that. I felt like I was drifting toward an understanding of myself that I couldn't comprehend." If you are queer, how did your own coming-out experience compare? If you aren't, how did Thomas's story help you understand what that might feel like?

11. "And I am doing the thing that I do with things that I love, or am frustrated by, or don't understand, or am infuriated by: I am making jokes," Thomas writes in *Here for It*. How do you use humor as a tool for understanding the world or as a defense mechanism in your own life?

PHOTO: © KATIE SIMBALA

R. ERIC THOMAS is a national bestselling author, playwright, and screenwriter. His books include *Here for It, or How to Save Your Soul in America,* which was featured as a Read with Jenna pick on NBC's *Today,* and *Reclaiming Her Time: The Power of Maxine Waters*, co-authored with Helena Andrews-Dyer. For four years, he wrote "Eric Reads the News," a wildly popular daily humor column covering pop culture and politics on ELLE.com. Thomas is the winner of the 2016 Barrymore Award for Best New Play, the 2018 Dramatist Guild Lanford Wilson Award, and was a finalist for the 2017 Steinberg/ATCA New Play Award. He has written on the Peabody Award–winning series *Dickinson* on AppleTV+ and *Better Things* on FX. Off the page, Thomas is the long-running host of The Moth StorySlams in Philadelphia and Washington, D.C., and has been heard multiple times on The Moth Radio Hour, NPR's *All Things Considered,* and *It's Been A Minute with Sam Sanders*. He lives in Maryland with his extraordinary husband, the Reverend David Norse Thomas.

rericthomas.com
Facebook.com/r.eric.thomas
Twitter: @oureric